T0360971

Routledge Revivals

The Technological Behaviour of Public Enterprises in Developing Countries

First published in 1989, *The Technological Behaviour of Public Enterprises in Developing Countries* presents essays based on original research work conducted for the International Labour Office, to employ a wide variety of approaches and methodologies to analyse the technological choices made by public enterprises in Tanzania, India, Argentina, and Brazil. These empirical studies provide rich and detailed case-study material on key issues such as the choice of technology and the acquisition of advanced technological capabilities. The significance of the research findings in these areas and their policy implications are described in an introductory chapter, and the volume as a whole is accessible and relevant to policy makers and academics who are concerned with industrial development in the developing world.

The Technological Behaviour of Public Enterprises in Developing Countries

Edited by Jeffrey James

First published in 1989
by Routledge

This edition first published in 2022 by Routledge
4 Park Square, Milton Park, Abingdon, Oxon, OX14 4RN

and by Routledge
605 Third Avenue, New York, NY 10017

Routledge is an imprint of the Taylor & Francis Group, an informa business

© 1989 International Labour Organization

Publisher's Note
The publisher has gone to great lengths to ensure the quality of this reprint but points out that some imperfections in the original copies may be apparent.

Disclaimer
The publisher has made every effort to trace copyright holders and welcomes correspondence from those they have been unable to contact.

A Library of Congress record exists under ISBN: 0415026504

ISBN: 978-1-032-32157-8 (hbk)
ISBN: 978-1-003-31312-0 (ebk)
ISBN: 978-1-032-32159-2 (pbk)

Book DOI 10.4324/9781003313120

THE
TECHNOLOGICAL
BEHAVIOUR
OF
PUBLIC
ENTERPRISES
IN
DEVELOPING
COUNTRIES

EDITED BY
JEFFREY JAMES

A study prepared for the International Labour
Office within the framework of the World
Employment Programme

ROUTLEDGE
London and New York

First published 1989
by Routledge
11 New Fetter Lane, London EC4P 4EE
29 West 35th Street, New York, NY 10001

© 1989 International Labour Organisation

Printed and bound in Great Britain by Mackays of Chatham PLC

British Library Cataloguing in Publication Data

The technological behaviour of public
    enterprises in developing countries: a study
    prepared for the International Labour Office
    within the framework of the World Employment
    Programme.
    1. Developing countries. Technology.
    Policies of government. Developing
    countries. Government. Policies on
    technology
    I. James, Jeffrey II. World Employment
    Programme
    609'.172'4

    ISBN 0-415-02650-4

Library of Congress Cataloging in Publication Data

The Technological behaviour of public enterprises in developing
    countries : a study prepared for the International Labour Office
    within the frame work of the World Employment Programme / edited
    by Jeffrey James.
        p.   cm.
    Includes index.
    ISBN 0-415-02650-4
    1. Government business enterprises — Developing countries —
Decision making. 2. Technological innovations — Economic aspects
— Developing countries — Decision making. 3. Technology and
state — Developing countries — Decision making. I. James,
Jeffrey. II. International Labour Office. III. World Employment
Programme.
    HD4420.8.T43 1989
    338'.06–dc19   89–5962
                                                              CIP

Contents

List of figures

List of tables

Preface

This collection of essays, edited by Dr. Jeffrey James of Boston University (and formerly a staff member of the ILO Technology and Employment Branch) is based on two premises: that public enterprises are currently an important phenomenon in many developing countries, and that these enterprises differ significantly from private firms in their behaviour regarding technology choice and development, and therefore possibly in their capacity in employment generation. These considerations led the ILO World Employment Programme (WEP) to undertake studies on the technological behaviour of public enterprises in developing countries. These studies are a logical follow-up of earlier WEP studies on technologies and institutions (see Susumu Watanabe and Jeffrey James (eds.): <u>Technology, institutions and government policies</u>, London, Macmillan, 1985), which underlined the need to examine the role of government and public enterprises in responding to development goals.

The seven essays included in this volume employ a wide variety of approaches and methodologies. For example, some essays are conceptual whereas others relate to a critical examination of the performance of public and private firms in specific countries (e.g. case studies on Argentina, the United Republic of Tanzania and India). One study on the ammonia industry compares public enterprises in India, Mexico, Brazil and the Republic of Korea. The conceptual papers on the other hand identify a number of alternative models of decision-making processes on technology choice. The empirical evidence from the case studies suggests that it is the managerial discretion and political economy models which are generally best able to explain the observed technology choices. However, situations are likely to vary from one country to another. Therefore, no single prescription can be drawn from the empirical results.

The limited number of case studies in this volume provide only a beginning of our understanding of the ways in which technology choice is actually made in public enterprises in developing countries. Many questions still remain: for example, what organisational structures are suitable to promote innovation and learning in different countries? And what circumstances determine the appropriateness of these innovations or the degree of their diffusion within the local economy?

This volume contains the results of a research project, within the ILO Technology and Employment Programme, which was funded by a grant from the Swedish Government (SAREC).

A.S. Bhalla
Chief
Technology and Employment Branch
International Labour Office

Chapter 1

Introduction

Jeffrey James

The past two decades have witnessed rapid growth in both the absolute number and the relative importance of public enterprises in developing countries.[1] Indeed, these enterprises "have come to dominate large segments of many LDC economies".[2] It follows from this observation that an understanding of the technical choices made by these enterprises has now become essential to an explanation of employment, output and other major macroeconomic variables in these economies. The need for an adequate explanation of these choices is made more compelling by the observed "marked capital intensity of state enterprise investment relative to private-sector investment in the same economy. Investment in state enterprise sectors in many LDCs has been focused on projects that involve light use of the more abundant factor of production (labour) and heavy use of the scarcer factor (capital). This pattern has been documented in a series of studies for such countries as [the Republic of] Korea, Ghana, Brazil, India, Bolivia, Algeria, Colombia, Indonesia and numerous others."[3] What is striking about these findings is that they do not conform to what one might expect, namely, that in at least some of the countries mentioned, employment appears to be an important policy goal and this goal should presumably be closely reflected in the technical choices made by the public enterprises (as agents of the state) of those countries. The task of explaining why this expected outcome has not generally occurred is one major concern of this collection of essays.

The choice of technique is not, however, the only aspect of the technical behaviour of public enterprises that bears on the employment problem in developing countries. Although it dominated the literature during the 1960s and 1970s, the static choice of technique relates in fact only to the demand side of the problem. Yet,

1

important implications for employment may arise also on the side of the supply of technologies. These supply-side issues are rooted in the widespread dependence of developing countries on technical change occurring in the advanced countries. In particular, "while there appears to be a certain amount of technological choice today, the continued concentration of technical change on advanced country technology is likely to result in increasingly inappropriate techniques - the choice of technology available in the future will be increasingly circumscribed, and irrelevant to the needs of the world's poorest."[4] If, on the other hand, developing countries successfully acquire their own technical capabilities, they may be in a position to adapt imported technologies or even to develop their own more appropriate alternatives (in the sense, among other things, of being relatively labour using). Such alterations in the available shelf of technologies (especially when they are combined with policies that alter the selection of techniques in the same direction) will tend to have favourable implications for employment and earnings. Indigenous technical capabilities may also lead to exports of technology and of local designs of consumer and capital goods, a possibility which, again, carries direct and powerful implications for employment. There are, finally, a series of potential indirect employment effects of the acquisition of technical capabilities. In the domestic production of capital goods, for example, the skills generated may be diffused to sectors that make use of these goods. "Given the frequent process interruptions attributable to poor maintenance and repair, such a diffusion of skilled workers would permit an increase in the use of plant and unskilled workers."[5]

If there are therefore numerous links between employment and indigenous technical capabilities, there are also reasons to expect public enterprises to play an important role in the process by which these capabilities are acquired. For these enterprises - unlike those that are privately owned - are theoretically in a position to take account of the social (as opposed to the private) costs and benefits that the process often entails. More specifically, "The social benefit of increased technological mastery ... generally exceeds the benefit which an individual firm can expect to capture; there are many avenues by which technological mastery can diffuse to other firms, and not all of these avenues are under the control of the firm that finances the initial acquisition. In addition, the firm may value the benefits that it does capture at less than their true social worth; likewise, the cost of acquiring technological mastery as seen from the firm's perspective may exceed the true social costs. Unless influenced by some form of public intervention, a firm acting alone may therefore not find it in its individual interest to take advantage of opportunities to increase domestic technological mastery as much as social objectives would dictate."[6] In practice, direct intervention through public enterprises has played an important part in the indigenisation efforts of several large countries and it is the analysis of this experience that comprises the second major focus of the volume. Two aspects in particular are emphasised by the case studies dealing with the supply side of the technological behaviour of public enterprises (though the emphasis on each aspect varies from one case to another). The first is the manner in (and the extent to) which technical capabilities have been acquired and the second has to do with the economic consequences - including those for employment - that have followed from these acquisitions.

In analysing the foregoing dimensions of the technological behaviour of public enterprises, the various contributors employ a variety of different research methods. Some of the authors, for example, use cross-sectional comparisons between public- and privately owned enterprises in a given country, another looks in detail at particular public enterprises over time, while yet a further case makes a comparison across countries for a given industry. In part, these methodological differences derive from the choice of particular industries - in some of which, for instance, public enterprises form monopolies and thus have no private competitors with whom structured comparisons can be made. To some degree, however, the differences in method are dictated by the nature of the research questions themselves. In particular, a study of the process by which capabilities are acquired in a particular firm necessarily requires a longitudinal analysis (that is, one encompassing observations over a period of time). In contrast, the choice of technique which is made at a moment of time, can be analysed without such longitudinal data.

I. THE CHOICE OF TECHNIQUES

Alternative models of the decision-making process for technology

Chapter 2, as well as the first part of Chapter 3, are conceptual: they attempt to provide a framework for understanding how decisions for technology are actually made in public enterprises. Together, these discussions suggest the following alternative models of the decision-making process.[7]

Introduction

The neo-classical (cost-minimising) model

The analogue of the traditional theory of the privately owned firm is the public enterprise that minimises costs on the basis of a set of shadow prices that is given to it by the parent government. According to this view, managers of public enterprises behave as "cosmic maximisers". That is, they are "motivated solely by a desire to maximise a clearly defined measure of social welfare, as defined by the parent government, under conditions of perfect information on all shadow prices, externalities and risk".[8] Since in most developing countries labour is abundant relative to capital, shadow pricing on the basis of factor scarcity leads to a general presumption that (the cost-minimising) public enterprise will make relatively labour-intensive technical choices. Underlying this presumption, however, are the assumptions that governments seek to maximise the "common good"[9] and that managers of public enterprises give perfect effect to this goal in their capacity as agents of the state. Relaxing one or both of these assumptions gives rise to alternative models of the decision-making process with very different implications for technological choice.

Political economy models

This model rejects the assumption that government is concerned to maximise the "general welfare" of society. Instead, the government is viewed as responding to political pressures of various kinds and these imperatives require the public enterprise (as an agent of the state) to make inefficient technological choices (i.e., choices that do not minimise costs). For example, in a class-interest model of political economy "decisions will vary according to prevailing class interests; with the bourgeoisie and labour aristocracy dominant, the technologies (and products) chosen will reflect their interests — sophisticated products and recent large-scale techniques may best serve their interests. There may be an alliance of foreign capitalists and local bourgeoisie, leading to decisions which favour foreign technologies".[10] The same outcome is likely under the more general "pressure group" model (in which the groups need not necessarily divide along class lines) since "in general, these pressures tend to favour capital-intensive techniques because pressure groups associated with the production of such technologies tend to be more powerful than producers of older labour-intensive technologies".[11]

Managerial discretion models

Common to both the neo-classical and political economy models is the assumption that the technological choices of public enterprises closely reflect the goals of the state.

4

If, however, this coincidence of interests cannot be secured, it is the goals of managers that will dominate in the choice of technology. A central question, therefore, is whether and to what extent public enterprises are able in reality to pursue goals different from those that have been articulated by government.

Leibenstein has taken up this question in terms of agent-principal theory. He argues that "in standard textbook economics it is implicitly assumed that either all economic actors are principals, or that there are perfect contracts between principals and agents, or that agents act in the principals' interests in the same way as the principal would behave in his or her own interest. In the real world, arrangements between principals and agents are far from perfect. Agents have a strong interest to deviate from the principal's interests at various junctures. To the extent that the owner of a firm is important in its management, he or she can impose considerable pressure from above. Where ownership is largely divorced from management this pressure is considerably less. It is likely to be least (other things being equal) in those instances where it is very difficult to determine who the principal actually is, or where the principal-agent relationship is diffuse. Clearly, in the case of state enterprises the principal-agent relationship is rather tenuous."[12]

The exercise of the managerial autonomy that is often conferred in this way, forms a central part of the analysis in the two chapters by James. He suggests that the behaviour of managers can be analysed according to three different models, each of which represents a fundamental departure from the cost-minimising postulate of traditional neo-classical micro-theory.

X-efficiency theory

According to Leibenstein's X-efficiency theory, the non-minimisation of costs within the firm depends mainly on two factors, namely, the degree to which effort is a variable in the enterprise and the amount of "pressure" that operates on this variable. The variability of effort follows from the incompleteness with which job contracts are normally specified and this variability gives rise to the possibility that without sufficient pressure, lack of effort in the firm will cause X-inefficiency. Leibenstein suggests that this possibility is all too real in the typical public enterprise because of the absence of pressure from either what he calls the "bottom" or the "top". The former refers to the degree of competition faced by the firm. The monopolistic environment in which public enterprises tend to operate "puts much less pressure on the owners of the firm or on the managers" than the perfectly competitive environment, which "puts tremendous

pressure on any individual firm". Equally, "pressure from
the top" (the pressure that is exerted from the firm's
owners or owners' representatives) is likely to be weak,
because of the diffuse nature of the principal-agent
relationship to which we referred above.

In Chapter 2 James examines the implications for
technological choice in the public enterprise, of the low
amount of pressure that is normally exerted from these two
sources. He suggests that the absence of strong pressure
on managers will be manifested in a lack of systematic
search for alternative technologies and in highly
simplified decision procedures (such as "choosing the first
acceptable alternative"). These tendencies, in turn, are
thought to be likely to impart a bias towards relatively
capital intensive (and often inefficient) technologies.
"For it is in the nature of simplifying procedures that
they tend to favour what is known and familiar (because of
the reduction in decision costs that is brought about) and
... it is relatively capital- rather than labour-intensive
techniques that are normally familiar to those responsible
for technology decisions within the public enterprise."[13]

The "engineering-man" hypothesis
The bias towards capital intensity described in the
previous paragraph does not arise out of any active
preference for technology. According to the "engineering-
man" hypothesis, in contrast, managers have distinct
preferences for particular types of technologies. In
particular, the managers' choice of technology appears to
be influenced by two objective functions, which, in
low-wage countries, are generally conflicting. The first
objective, that of the "economic man", is to minimise
costs. This leads to a relatively labour-intensive
production process. On the other hand, the objective of
the "engineering man" tends to lead towards more sophisticated automated technology.[14] The technological
preferences of engineering man derive from a desire to
manage machines rather than labour, a desire to produce
goods of the "highest quality" and from the "aesthetic"
appeal of sophisticated machinery.

As in the case of X-efficiency theory, market
structure is crucial in determining the degree to which
costs rise above minimum levels - in this context, the
extent to which the preferences of engineering man hold
sway over those of economic man. In the monopolistic or
oligopolistic conditions where public enterprises are
normally to be found in developing countries,[15] the
engineering-man hypothesis predicts that technology will be
capital intensive and products sophisticated.

"Bureaucratic man"

Another goal that has been proposed specifically to explain the behaviour of public enterprises in developing countries is expressed in the notion of "bureaucratic man".[16] The main idea here, as explained by James in Chapter 3, is that the incentive system in these enterprises (which, as noted above, are mostly highly sheltered from competitive forces) is such as to reward managers not for cost reductions but rather for rapid growth in output. To achieve this, the manager concentrates on starting as many new projects as possible. Because of the constraint in meeting this goal of a shortage of foreign exchange, the manager is led towards large-scale turnkey projects embodying sophisticated technology, for it is these projects that are usually the most ready source of foreign finance (and they can also be delivered and constructed relatively rapidly). In this process, therefore, the technology in any particular project becomes merely a residual - a "fallout from the chosen source of finance and related project inputs".[17]

A comparison of the technological implications of the alternative models

On the basis of the discussion above, it is possible to represent in summary form the major technological implications of the alternative models that were identified. These implications, with respect to factor intensity, degree of departure from cost minimisation and product choice, are shown in Table 1.1

Case studies of the choice of technique

Chapters 3, 4 and 5 contain case studies of technical choice in public enterprises in the United Republic of Tanzania, India and Argentina, respectively. They help to determine which of the models in Table 1.1 has greater explanatory power in the particular industries under investigation. This is of obvious importance because the policy implications of the various models tend to differ. The cases also reveal how much of each explanation is due to public ownership per se, as opposed to other factors (such as imperfect competition). They are able to achieve this in each case through structured comparisons with privately owned firms in the same industry.

Parastatals in the United Republic of Tanzania

The study by James is concerned to explain previous research findings, that technological choices by public enterprises (or parastatals) in the manufacturing sector in the United Republic of Tanzania seem to be only tenuously

7

Table 1.1

Technological implications of alternative models

Model	Dimension of technology	Factor intensity	Departure from cost minimisation	Products
Neo-classical		Depends on shadow factor prices. Contains a presumption of labour intensity in labour surplus economies.	None	-
Political economy		Depends on the constellation of interest groups allied to decision-makers. Usually implies capital-intensive techniques imported from advanced countries.	Depends on inefficiency of imported techniques at developing country factor prices.	-

Managerial discretion models

a) X-efficiency theory	Limited effort leads to choice of familiar (often capital-intensive) techniques.	Varies directly according to degree of pressure from the "top" and "bottom". In non-competitive environment, choices by public enterprises will be high cost.	–
b) "Engineering man"	"Engineering man" favours capital-intensive techniques and dominates "economic man" in monopolistic conditions.	Varies directly with degree of monopoly. In non-competitive environment, choices by public enterprises will be high cost.	Sophisticated
c) "Bureaucratic man"	Foreign finance is associated with turnkey projects embodying capital-intensive technology.	Varies directly with degree of monopoly and/or government underwriting of activities.	–

related to major development goals in that country.[18] In
particular, the choices were found to be large scale,
capital intensive and often technically inefficient
(relative to other techniques in the same industries). In
his search for an explanation of these findings, the author
begins by noting that they are self-evidently inconsistent
with the neo-classical model (which, it will be recalled,
posits that public enterprises maximise according to an
objective function that is given to them unambiguously by
the government). The author contends that there are two
main components of a valid alternative explanation of this
problem.

The first has to do with the control system over parastatals and, in particular, the extremely limited degree of
control that was apparently able to be exercised over
parastatal investment projects by the various agencies of
government. James attributes this, on the one hand, to the
unwillingness of decision-makers to specify the trade-offs
between conflicting goals of development and, on the other,
to the very limited capacity for control on the part of the
relevant regulatory agencies. The second component lies in
understanding the directions in which the resulting (near
total) discretion of managers was pursued in the choice of
techniques. In this regard much of the behaviour of
managers appears to have been driven by the "bureaucratic-
man" mechanism, as evidenced in part by their stated
intentions of increasing output as rapidly as possible and
also by the general absence of attention that was paid to
the technological choice aspects of projects. In many
cases (for example, in the sugar and textile industries)
the technology (turnkey and capital intensive) appeared to
be merely a derivative of Western sources of finance.

In several other cases, however, factors additional to
the bureaucratic mechanism imparted an independent upward
influence on the capital intensity of technology. The most
important of these factors had to do with product quality
and, in particular, with the bias that was imparted through
the alleged necessity to choose technology capable of
producing to developed country standards of product
quality. This product choice bias was found in the case
studies to originate in three different ways: "the first
is through the alleged need to produce exports to
international standards, the second is through the
historically determined preference of some members of the
society for highly specified, inappropriate products and
the final source of bias originates in the fact that this
same product preference is frequently held by project
consultants".[19]

Having determined the main factors that seem to
account for the systematic bias in the technology chosen by
manufacturing parastatals in the United Republic of

Tanzania, James seeks, finally, to gain an idea of the extent to which these various factors are due to public ownership per se. For this purpose it was necessary to make a set of controlled comparisons (where this was possible) with privately owned firms. What mainly emerged from these comparisons was the finding that the bureaucratic mechanism (so dominant in the case of the parastatals) could not be discerned in the decision-making processes of the private firms (in which technology choice was generally a central aspect of investment projects rather than a mere fall-out from the chosen source of foreign finance).

The overall policy implication of this study is that "improvements in the choice of technology need to be sought in the way decisions are actually made in the public enterprise, rather than in the way the enterprise is assumed to behave according to the tenets of neo-classical micro theory".[20] The author advocates, in particular, policies to reduce the bias that results from the operation of the bureaucratic-man mechanism (such as reform of the price control system and a greater emphasis on profitability), as well as measures to reduce the biases that arise independently of this mechanism (most notably from the choice of inappropriate products).

Public enterprises in India

Deolalikar and Sundaram (in Chapter 4) use primary (interview) and secondary data to compare the technological choices made by public and private firms in three industries in India. On the basis of the secondary data, they show that the former exhibit higher capital/output and labour/output ratios than the latter (though they acknowledge that this evidence of technical inefficiency may be partly due to the effect of price controls that are applied more widely to the state firms). This finding is similar to the description of the choices typically made by public enterprises in the United Republic of Tanzania. But the explanation given by Deolalikar and Sundaram for India is rather different from that which James offered for the Tanzanian case.

For one thing, they describe a decision-making process in Indian public enterprises which is not only very similar to that in comparable private firms, but which is also not at all reminiscent of the "bureaucratic-man" procedure. For, contrary to what is posited in that model, managers (in both types of enterprise) seemed to have well-defined technological preferences (mostly of the "engineering-man" type) and to engage in quite extensive technology search activities. Partly as a result, purchases of machinery were generally not made from technical collaborators. At least in part, these and other indicators of the greater concern with the technological aspects of projects in India than in the United Republic of Tanzania, may reflect the considerable differences in overall technological capabilities between the two countries.

Given the absence of any discernible differences in the decision-making procedures of publicly and privately owned firms, Deolalikar and Sundaram look to other reasons for the technical inefficiency of the choices made by the former. In particular, "if SOE [state-owned enterprise] and POE [privately owned enterprise] managers follow broadly similar methods and criteria of selecting technologies and yet SOEs exhibit larger capital/output and labour/output ratios than POEs, it follows that, i) the incentives (e.g. relative prices) that the two types of firms respond to are systematically different, and/or ii) the final choice (and operation) of technology is determined more by bureaucratic and political interventions than by managerial decisions in SOEs".[21] In relation to the former possibility, they point to soft government loans and tied foreign aid, which, by artificially cheapening the price of capital to Indian public enterprises, encourage inefficient (capital-intensive) technology choices (an outcome, we may note, which is inconsistent with the simple neo-classical model "where all public-enterprise decisions are made in light of the full set of social costs and benefits - including the social-opportunity cost of funds employed").[22] With regard to the second possibility, Deolalikar and Sundaram invoke aspects of what we earlier termed the political economy model, with their reference to the "numerous cases in India where parent ministries have imposed their choice of a particular foreign technology or a particular foreign collaborator on a SOE against the latter's best judgment. SOEs are also frequently subject to political pressures for employment creation, which means they have to hire labour superfluous to the efficient operation of their chosen technologies".[23]

Corresponding to their view of the fundamental causes of the problem, the authors propose a number of policy measures. First, they advocate greater autonomy for public enterprises in respect of both technology choice and operation. Second, they suggest a set of pricing policies that will make imported capital-intensive technologies less attractive (for example, loans to train workers and increase their productivity).

Oil refining in Argentina

Lucángeli's essay (Chapter 5) is different from the studies contained in the two previous chapters in a number of respects. In the first place, unlike the latter, Lucángeli's case is about only one (very large and strategic) public enterprise - Yacimientos Petrolíferos

Fiscales – whose technology choice behaviour is compared to privately owned firms in the oil refining industry. Moreover, the nature of this comparison itself differs from the other studies. This is the case, on the one hand, because the oil refining industry allows a degree of variation in the output (or distillates) mix on the basis of given capital equipment. The "choice of technique" has in this case, therefore, a short-run dimension that is absent from the earlier chapters. On the other hand, the long-run decision (to purchase new refining equipment) is examined from the point of view of the differential speed of adoption of given frontier processes (as opposed to the choice of different methods of production) by the publicly and privately owned firms.

Like the other case studies, however, Lucángeli finds the technological behaviour of the public enterprise to be substantially different from that of the private firms. He attributes this basically to a divergence in goals: in particular, "while the private firms aimed at maximising their profits, the state-owned enterprise's aim was to satisfy excess demand. The dissimilar technological behaviour observed in the refining industry derives precisely from the different objectives established for the private firms and the state-owned enterprise".[24] From this point of view, the behaviour of Yacimientos Petrolíferos Fiscales might seem explicable in terms of "bureaucratic man" (whose goal, as noted above, is to maximise output growth). However, it is important to emphasise that in this case the objective of the public enterprise was imposed on it by an agency of the state (the Energy Secretariat). As such, the explanation would seem to have more to do with political economy than managerial models (though this aspect of the Secretariat's behaviour is not explored).

In his short-run model, Lucángeli uses a set of longitudinal data and regression analysis to show how these disparate goals led to the choice of different distillate mixes (that is, different proportions of petrol, diesel fuel, kerosene, distilled fuel oil and residual fuel oil obtained from a given amount of processed crude oil) by the two categories of firms. In particular, "the private companies acted – on the basis of the restrictions imposed by the regulatory framework – by selecting the vector of distillates that would maximise their profits. But the state company's distillate vector was in line not with the relative prices vector, but with the surplus distillates demand vector. The least 'profitable' distillates were supplied by the state-owned enterprise."[25] In the long run, as well, the goal assigned to the public enterprise of meeting excess demand led it to behave differently from the private firms. In this case, it was led to adopt a new

13

("frontier") technology that was more effective in meeting the prevailing pattern of demand, even though this technology was risky and apparently also, at the time, privately unprofitable (as evidenced by the fact that it was not simultaneously adopted by the private firms).

Taken together, the case studies in Chapters 3, 4 and 5 suggest that technology choice by public enterprises has features that distinguish it from the behaviour of private firms. It was also shown that this distinctiveness could not in general be explained by the neo-classical model of decision-making. For this purpose, an alternative set of (political economy and managerial discretion) models was found to be necessary. But because the explanatory power of these various models appeared to vary from one case to another, no single policy prescription can be based on these findings.

II.   THE DEVELOPMENT OF INDIGENOUS TECHNOLOGICAL CAPABILITIES

As noted above, some of the essays are concerned with the role of public enterprises in promoting indigenous technological capabilities. Two developing countries that have made especially heavy use of these enterprises for this purpose are India and Brazil. The chapters by Deolalikar and Sundaram, Levy and Fleury, are concerned, for the most part, with various aspects of this experience.

Deolalikar and Sundaram (in Chapter 4), for example, address the question of whether public enterprises in India engage in a greater effort to develop indigenous technological capabilities than comparable privately owned firms. They point out that the answer to the question is not self-evidently in the affirmative, in spite of the presumed direct role of publicly owned firms in implementing this goal of the state. One reason is that "development of indigenous technological capacity is not necessarily inconsistent with profit-maximising behaviour. A POE [privately owned enterprise] might be interested in building up its technological capability so as to have greater bargaining strength vis-à-vis the foreign collaborator in future business deals".[26] The secondary data analysed by the authors suggest, nevertheless, "a greater effort at research and development (R & D) and adaptation by SOEs relative to POEs".[27] More specifically, both the absolute and relative size of the R & D and technology adaptation efforts appear to be greater in publicly than in privately owned firms.[28] This differential is reflected, moreover, in greater innovatory activity (measured by patents) on the part of public enterprises, although the relation between public ownership and patenting activity is statistically significant in only one of the three industries examined.

It would be of considerable interest (as well as policy relevance) to determine the direction of the innovations (minor as well as major) generated by public enterprises in India: to know whether, for example, there are any systematic directional differences in relation to: (a) the technology imports that they replace; and (b) the innovations made by comparable private firms. Deolalikar and Sundaram do not directly assess these questions, although their interview data throw indirect light on some of them. For instance, the responses of the sample firms reveal that the focus of the adaptive work on imported technologies (by public and private enterprises) is mostly on "adjustment for different quality of raw materials" and "adapting the product to local demand conditions". Interestingly, however, "increasing labour intensity" was generally viewed as an irrelevant concern of technological adaptation, matching the minimal role that was also attributed to this factor in choice of technique decisions. This pattern of technical change - in which the adaptations to the local environment do not include additional labour use - is similar to recent descriptions of technical developments in the semi-industrial economies of Latin America.[29] And the primary explanation of what has occurred in those economies - that firms producing import substitutes behind high levels of protection need not be overly concerned with effecting cost reductions - seems to apply in good measure also to public enterprise in India.

Levy's chapter (Chapter 6) raises a normative question that is of fundamental relevance to the indigenisation efforts (via public enterprises) of both Brazil and India. It is often merely assumed that these efforts are the appropriate policy response to the condition of technological dependency that plagues most Third World countries. But only very rarely are studies conducted to determine whether the social benefits of this response actually exceed the social costs. Levy's paper is an attempt to answer this question in the context of a comparison of the policies towards technology transfer adopted by four countries (India, the Republic of Korea, Mexico and Brazil) in the ammonia industry. (Of these four countries, Brazil, and especially India, accorded a very high priority to indigenisation, largely through the medium of public enterprise.)

Levy contends, first, that, "the benefits of indigenous development of ammonia technology turn out to be fewer than they might appear at first sight".[30] On the one hand, the industry is characterised by technological rigidities that diminish the possibilities of adaptations to the local environment and, on the other, it is organised

in such a way that "makes foreign investment unlikely even
in the absence of indigenous technological know-how" (thus
diminishing the gains from a reduced dependence on
multinational corporations).[31] Furthermore, the extent
to which indigenisation may have led to beneficial linkage
effects and added to domestic bargaining power in
technology purchases is described as uncertain. The social
costs of this strategy, however (especially in the Indian
case), were all too apparent. Levy shows that the costs of
delays and subsequent losses of capacity were of the order
of one-third of the initial capital requirements. He
concludes that these costs are very likely to have exceeded
any reasonable estimate of the social benefits.

Chapter 6 thus serves as an important caution against
the uncritical acceptance of a policy of building up local
technological capabilities through public enterprises. But
it does not permit one to draw any general conclusions
about the wisdom of this policy. For one thing, only
passing reference is made to technology exports, which, in
some industries in India, including those studied by
Deolalikar and Sundaram, appear to have followed from
indigenisation efforts.[32] In addition, as Levy himself
acknowledges, there are industries where technology is less
complex than that in ammonia and where the scope for local
adaptations is accordingly greater (as evidenced by
Deolalikar and Sundaram's findings noted above). Much
depends, thirdly, on the precise manner in which indigenisation is implemented. In this regard, Levy contrasts the
Indian policy (of going it alone as rapidly and extensively
as possible) with the more gradual process of acquiring
know-how from a foreign technology supplier that was
followed in Brazil. The case of Petrobras (the public
enterprise analysed also by Fleury in Chapter 7) shows how
Brazil was able, partly as a result of competition among
foreign technology suppliers and partly because of the
inducement afforded by a long-term supply relationship with
a developing country, to acquire some of the most specialised technical knowledge. This manner of indigenisation,
though more gradual, is likely to have been effected at
lower social cost than the corresponding Indian method.

The case of Embraer (the state-owned aeronautics
enterprise) analysed in detail by Fleury in Chapter 7,
throws further light on the process by which technological
capabilities were successfully acquired in Brazilian public
enterprises. In this case as well, the firm was able to
secure a substantial transfer of know-how from the advanced
countries (a process which involved three stages of
learning and included the transfer of managerial and
marketing know-how). In part, this favourable outcome was
(as in Petrobras) the result of competition among the major
suppliers of technology, but it seems to have been mostly

due to the incentive provided by the agreement to reserve the Brazilian market (at the time the largest export market of the Unites States) for aircraft made in Brazil. Embraer has subsequently evolved into an enormously successful enterprise, achieving substantial sales of civilian aircraft in the United States as well as exports of technology abroad. Indeed, so rapid has been the growth of this firm, that it is currently "the only non-American company among the top ten general aviation producers in the West".[33] In seeking to account for this exceptional experience, Fleury emphasises the essentiality of the support that was given to the enterprise by the Aeronautics Ministry, especially with respect to the development of military aircraft. He also draws attention to the specific organisational structure of Embraer, which, for example, "greatly favours communication and above all feedback into the groups in charge of basic and detail designs, thus ensuring that learning is efficient".[34]

It bears emphasis that the employment gains achieved in this case were not the result of any specific efforts to produce labour-using innovations. From this point of view, the author stresses instead the very limited flexibility that was imposed by the quality and safety standards in the world market for aircraft. What did lead to substantial employment gains, however, was the international competitiveness of Embraer in this market, to which the acquisition of advanced technical capabilities ultimately gave rise.

III. CONCLUSIONS

Most of the first part of this volume was concerned to throw light on the observed capital intensity of technical choices made by public enterprises in developing countries. The theoretical discussion dealt with alternative models of the decision-making process for technology. It was shown that only in a simple neo-classical decision model is there a presumption in favour of labour-intensive (cost-minimising) choices. Alternative decision-making models carry contrasting implications, that involve capital-intensive and inefficient techniques and sophisticated products. The empirical evidence (especially in Chapters 3 and 4) showed, moreover, that it is these alternative (political economy and managerial discretion) models that generally are able to explain the observed choices in the cases examined. But because the explanatory power of these various models appears to vary from one case to another, no single policy implication can be drawn from the results. Whereas in the United Republic of Tanzania, for example, the decision process is described as one in

which technical choices are mostly excluded from the
selection of investment projects, in India much of the
problem is due instead to an active set of preferences that
bias these technical choices in the same direction. The
policy requirements in the former case tend therefore to be
different from and broader than those in the latter (where
corrective measures can be partly aimed directly at the
technological preferences themselves).

The second main concern of the volume was to analyse
the supply side of the technological behaviour of public
enterprises in selected developing countries where this
aspect of their behaviour has been especially important.
In the case studies (drawn from India and Brazil) the
acquisition of technical capabilities of various kinds was
reflected in adaptations to the local environment, technology exports and filing of patents. Chapters 4, 6 and 7
suggested that these capabilities were built up through:
(a)   an organisational structure of the enterprise that is
      supportive of technological learning (Chapter 7);
(b)   active infrastructural, economic and political support
      to the public enterprise from the agencies of
      government (Chapter 7);
(c)   technology imports that are complementary to local
      innovative efforts (Chapter 4) and where competitive
      conditions exist among technology suppliers who can be
      persuaded to part with their proprietary knowledge by
      the offer of sales possibilities in the developing
      economy (Chapters 6 and 7); and
(d)   a sizable technological effort in the form of R & D
      expenditures (Chapter 4).

As emphasised in Chapter 6, however, the aim of policy
ought not to be indigenisation per se. Rather, the goal
ought to be a mode of building up capabilities that yields
high social benefits in relation to social costs (which, in
turn, depends on the use that is made of these capabilities
in relation to the social opportunity costs of acquiring
them). For example, an important social benefit from the
acquisition of technical capabilities may be increased
employment. But whether this favourable effect actually
occurs seems to depend (among other factors) on whether:
(a)   technology is inherently susceptible of adaptation
      (Chapter 6) and economic conditions are conducive to
      such activity; and
(b)   diffusion of indigenously developed technologies
      occurs within the local economy as well as in the form
      of exports abroad (Chapters 4 and 7).

More generally, as the estimates in Chapter 6 strongly
suggest, policy makers need to be extremely careful in
assessing the net social benefits of indigenisation via
public enterprises and the research reported in this volume
constitutes only a start in this important direction.

NOTES AND REFERENCES

1. See M. Gillis et al.: Economics of development, New York, W. W. Norton, 1983. These authors (p. 566) define public enterprises according to three criteria, namely, "The government is the principal stockholder in the enterprise, or is otherwise able to exercise control over the broad policies followed by the enterprise, and to appoint and remove enterprise management... The enterprise is engaged in the production of goods or services for sale to the public, or to other enterprises, private or public... As a matter of policy the revenues of the enterprise are supposed to bear some relation to its costs".

2. Ibid., p. 567.

3. Ibid., p. 577-8.

4. F. Stewart: "International technology transfer: Issues and policy options", in P. Streeten and R. Jolly (eds.): Recent issues in world development, Oxford, Pergamon Press, 1981, p. 100.

5. H. Pack: "Fostering the capital-goods sector in LDCs", World Development, Vol. 9 (3), Mar. 1981, p. 229.

6. C. Dahlman and L. Westphal: "Technological effort in industrial development - an interpretive survey of recent research", in F. Stewart and J. James (eds.): The economics of new technology in developing countries, London, Frances Pinter, 1982, p. 123.

7. I have adopted here a classification based on that offered by F. Stewart: "Conflicts between employment and output growth objectives of public enterprises in developing countries", Public Enterprise, vol. 4, no. 2, 1983.

8. M. Gillis: "The role of state enterprises in economic development", Harvard Institute for International Development, Discussion paper number 83, Feb. 1980, p. 3. See also the article by James, Chapter 3 of this volume, p. 43.

9. Stewart, 1983, op. cit.

10. Ibid., p. 35.

11. Ibid. The "pressure-group" model is closer to the Buchanan-Tullock view of government behaviour.

12. H. Leibenstein: "X-efficiency theory and the analysis of state enterprises", paper prepared for the Boston Area Public Enterprise Group, 1980, p. 12.

13. Chapter 2 of this volume, p. 35. (The chapter has been reprinted in Public Enterprise, vol. 4, no. 2, 1983, p. 47.

14. L. Wells: "Economic man and engineering man: Choice of technology in a low-wage country" in C.P. Timmer et al.: The Choice of Technology in Developing

Countries, Harvard Studies in International Affairs, no. 32, 1975.

15. See L. Jones (ed.): Public enterprise in less developed countries, Cambridge University Press, 1982.

16. The hypothesis is due to David Williams: "National planning and the choice of technology: The case of textiles in Tanzania", Economic Research Bureau, paper no. 75.12, Dar-es-Salaam, June 1975. Also published in K.S. Kim, R.B. Mabele and M.J. Schultheis (eds.): Papers on the political economy of Tanzania, Nairobi and London, Heinemann, 1979.

17. Ibid., p.8.

18. F. Perkins: "Technology choice, industrialisation and development experiences in Tanzania", Journal of Development Studies, vol. 19, Jan. 1983.

19. Chapter 3 of this volume, p. 60.

20. Ibid., p. 68.

21. Ibid., p. 112.

22. M. Gillis, G. Jenkins and D. Lessard: "Public-enterprise finance: Toward a synthesis", in Jones (ed.) op. cit., p. 257.

23. Chapter 4 of this volume, p. 133.

24. Ibid., p. 152.

25. Ibid., p. 164-5.

26. Ibid., p. 114.

27. Ibid., p. 115.

28. In part, however, this finding is attributed to the fact that the average public enterprise is larger than the average privately owned firm in the same industry and firm size may be positively correlated with the share of R & D in total sales.

29. S. Teitel: "Technology creation in semi-industrial economies", Journal of Development Economics, Vol. 16, 1984.

30. Chapter 6 of this volume, p. 188.

31. Ibid.

32. See, for example, S. Lall: "Technological learning in the Third World: Some implications of technology exports", in F. Stewart and J. James (eds.) op. cit.

33. The New York Times, 3 Nov. 1985, p. F4.

34. Chapter 7 of this volume, p. 220.

Chapter 2

Public Enterprise, Technology and Employment in Developing Countries

Jeffrey James*

I. INTRODUCTION

The past two decades have witnessed a period of rapid growth in both the absolute number and relative importance of public enterprises in developing countries. In fact, state-owned enterprises have come to dominate sizeable segments of the economies of many developing countries. "In countries as diverse as Bangladesh, Bolivia and Mexico, the share of SOEs (state-owned enterprises) in annual gross investment outside of agriculture has been upwards of 75 percent, while it is close to 50 per cent in India and Turkey and has hovered between 25 per cent and 30 per cent in [the Republic of] Korea and Brazil".[1]

Because these enterprises are "creatures of the state" they may frequently be expected to have different goals from firms belonging to the private sector. They may, for example, be concerned to promote employment or to correct imbalances in regional growth. To this extent, public enterprises require a different form of analysis from that which is based entirely on profit maximisation. It follows that the role of technology – analysed so far mainly in relation to private sector enterprises or to firms undifferentiated by the degree of state ownership – needs to be examined, where public enterprises are concerned, within a framework which encompasses the variety of goals (in addition to profit maximisation) according to which many public enterprises operate. The fact that their goal structure may frequently differ from that of private firms suggests that the technological behaviour of the two types of enterprise may also be expected to differ. But the direction of the difference – in terms of overall factor intensity – is somewhat difficult to establish on a priori grounds.

There is some evidence that the overall capital-intensity of public enterprises exceeds that of private firms by quite a substantial margin. For the Republic of Korea, Jones has demonstrated that the public enterprise sector is more than three times as capital-intensive as the economy of the Republic of Korea as a whole.[2] Similar results for India have been reported by Deolalikar.[3]

Findings such as these could, however, be due to either:

i)   the choice of more capital-intensive techniques by public enteprises within given industries;
ii) a concentration of public enterprises within relatively capital-intensive industries; or
iii) a combination of i) and ii).

Whether and to what extent it is i) rather than ii) that explains the sort of results noted above is important for policy purposes, for (as we shall see) it throws a good deal of light on the important question of how far public enterprises are inherently capital-intensive and therefore relatively insensitive to policies designed to secure a more appropriate technology.

The purpose of this paper is to present the evidence that bears on these questions, to consider how the evidence can be explained, and to examine the implications of the resulting analysis for policy. Particular attention is paid to the areas of the subject that are deserving of further research.

In order to examine issue i) above, we shall be concerned with the analysis of public enterprise behaviour at the firm level, whereas ii) requires that the analysis be conducted at the more aggregate level of the industry. We consider first the former.

II. TECHNOLOGICAL BEHAVIOUR WITHIN PUBLIC ENTERPRISES

There is surprisingly little evidence on the question of how the technological behaviour of public enterprises differs from private firms within given industries. What evidence there is, suggests a tendency to greater capital-intensity on the part of the former.

In his comparison between Indonesian public and private firms in the same industries, Wells found a systematically greater capital-intensity for the public enterprises.[4] For India, Deolalikar has concluded that "The capital-output ratio of (foreign) collaborating state-owned enterprises is much greater than that of collaborating private enterprises, even after we have made adjustments for their younger age and the more intensive nature of their investments vis-à-vis private enterprises."[5]

One way to explain this finding - perhaps the most obvious way - is to say that the state has a set of primary goals that are often even less conducive to the adoption of appropriate technology than are the goals of private enterprise (by "the state" we do not have in mind the notion of a single entity, but rather the organisations within the state—ministries, agencies and so on – that are relevant to the particular situation being considered). Employment-creation, on this view, is in actuality (as distinct from what is espoused in plans and other official documents) a relatively minor objective of the state. More important are the goals of modernisation, promotion of foreign interests and those of elites in the industrial sector, all of which are generally better served by (imported) capital-intensive technology (and products) than by a technology which is more consistent with the factor endowments (including skills) of developing countries.[6]

A second possible explanation is that although employment creation may indeed be an important priority of policy, it is nevertheless not promoted through the technology policy of public enterprise (because say, other instruments of employment creation, such as public works schemes, are preferred). The technology policy of public enterprises, therefore, tends to be related instead to other state goals, such as those mentioned above, which are generally inimical to the choice and creation of appropriate technologies.

To the extent that these two explanations accurately describe reality (which is an empirical question that needs to be researched both between and within countries), there is clearly little analysis required to explain the observed propensity of public enterprise to choose highly inappropriate technologies. What is much more difficult to explain, however, and which is on this account deserving of further attention, is the case in which inappropriate technological choices are made, in spite of the fact that employment creation is a relatively important goal of the state, which it tries to realise, among other ways, through the technology behaviour of public enterprise. For in a simple neo-classical model (shown in Figure 2.1), public enterprises could then be thought of as hiring factors according to prices determined by societal goals (i.e. shadow prices) rather than according to the "distorted" prices that actually prevail (as a result of trade unions, overvalued exchange rates etc.) in most LDCs.

The state (through the agency of the public enterprise) is depicted as choosing the technique of production according to the shadow price ratio ($K0/L0$) rather than the actual price ratio ($K1/L1$) according to which private firms operate. In fact, for a variety of reasons the actual prices faced by public enterprises may often be even more distorted than the price ratio $K1/L1$. For one thing, public enterprises tend to pay a lower price

Figure 2.1

The choice of technique by public enterprise in the
simple neo-classical model

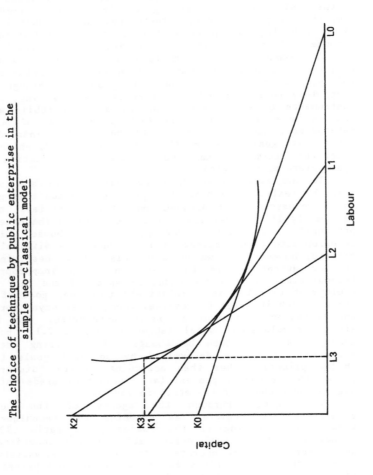

for loan capital than do their counterparts in the private sector because their debt is effectively guaranteed by the state. This tendency is reinforced, secondly, by the fact that on occasion "equity capital provided to state-owned enterprises by the parent is viewed as costless, because governments normally do not place a price upon it as it is transferred to the enterprise".[7] Thirdly, projects of public enterprises are frequently financed by foreign aid, which provides capital on concessionary terms. For these reasons (and providing that wage costs are not correspondingly higher) the actual price ratio confronting the public enterprise may look like say, K2/L2, instead of K1/L1.

In this simple model, the public enterprise chooses a more labour-intensive technique than the private firm which is faced with the same technological alternatives (and the former thus suffers a loss in profits calculated in terms of K1/L1 or K2/L2).

The analysis based on Figure 2.1 is concerned with the choice out of **existing** techniques. To the extent that they generate **new** techniques (in a broad sense) public enterprises - in a dynamic version of the model - may be expected (on the basis of shadow prices) to develop relatively labour-using innovations. That is, just as these enterprises may be expected to reflect social objectives in their choice out of existing techniques, so too may they be expected to pay particular attention to these objectives in the type of new techniques that they are sometimes concerned to develop.

Given the evidence cited above however, and in so far as public enterprises are expected to promote employment objectives to a greater extent than behaviour according to market prices would dictate, it is evident that the simple neo-classical model embodies an oversimplified view of the way in which these enterprises actually behave. In what follows therefore, we shall be concerned to develop a more realistic view of public enterprise behaviour which better accords with the empirical evidence that is available.

To begin with, the assumption implicit in the neo-classical model of a harmony of interests between the state and the public enterprises, as well as within the latter, is criticised. We offer instead a framework in which the technological behaviour of public enterprises is viewed as emerging out of its relationship to the (conflicting) objectives of the state on the one hand, and to the conflicts within the public enterprise itself on the other. Thus, in contrast to the neo-classical view, technology is seen as being embedded in the way that conflicts within, and between institutions are resolved. The advocated approach draws on certain aspects of organisation theory and on Leibenstein's general

X-efficiency theory.[8]

Technology in public enterprise as the outcome of the resolution of competing interests

One of the most crucial assumptions underlying the simple model described in Figure 2.1 is that of a complete identity of interests between the state and the managers of public enterprises and between the latter and those responsible within the public enterprise for making decisions regarding technology. The state, that is to say, encounters no obstacles in implementing its technology decisions because the public enterprises (and those within them) are agents who act merely as extensions of the interests of the state.

This same view of the role of the state, we may note, is contained in Sen's classic work on the choice of technique. As one commentator has described it, "Possibly, the least-noticed assumption in Sen's book is the assumption of a planned economy. There is state ownership; the state represents the collectivity. The state meets no social or political obstacles when it implements its choice of technique decisions."[9] But while this assumption may correspond to the situation in a planned economy (which Sen assumed) it is not likely to be generally true in relation to state-owned enterprises in predominantly mixed economies.

Consider first the relationship between the state and the managers of the public enterprise. In Aharoni's managerial discretion model, managers are not necessarily merely passive recipients of state demands (including those for "social goals" such as employment creation).[10] On the contrary, they will generally seek to increase their discretion; that is, to increase the extent to which they can pursue objectives and strategies that differ from those of the state. Managers desire such autonomy for a variety of reasons. They may, for example, seek to insulate the enterprise from the problems caused by frequently-occurring changes in government. Or they may believe that a greater degree of autonomy is associated with improved bargaining strength. In many cases managers may desire to increase discretion simply in order to be able to run their enterprises without interference from the state.

There are many ways in which discretion may be increased.[11] We shall, however, confine ourselves to only a few illustrative examples.

Firstly, state goals are likely to be articulated to public enterprises through various ministries - most importantly, those of Industry, Labour and Planning - in a highly fragmented and often somewhat vague form. Such fragmentation of the state's influence may often serve to strengthen the autonomy of the public enterprises. Thus, "confronting a series of unreconciled and uncoordinated demands from the ministries, the strong manager stands a chance of being in charge".[12]

Secondly, and relatedly, the more are public enterprises required to meet some kind of market test, the more they are likely to be able successfully to use that fact to fend off "social" demands. And this defence will be especially cogent the more that shadow prices diverge from actual prices (above we suggested reasons why the divergence is in fact likely to be substantial).

Thirdly, "managers who are scarce and hard to replace also gain discretion by that very fact. ... The higher the perceived costs of replacing a manager, the higher his discretion. Very successful and effective managers can get away with ignoring many government demands, since the government may perceive the costs of replacing the manager as higher than the benefits."[13]

Much also depends on the ability and willingness of governments to control the operations of public enterprise. In general, if the enterprise is large or is considered important from a national point of view, it will tend to be more closely monitored, thereby reducing managerial discretion. On the other hand, the capacity for control, especially in poor countries, is limited and this increases the degree of discretion (the problem of control is particularly acute where the enterprise requires a very high degree of technical information and skills for its operation).

That public enterprises are sometimes able to distance themselves in these and other ways from state interference is clearly illustrated from the Latin American experience where, according to Raymond Vernon, "some succeed in dominating the ministries that are supposed to oversee their activities or disregard such ministries altogether".[14] Of course, the nature of the relationship between public enterprises and the ministries representing the state is likely to vary, both between industries and countries. In the French case, for example, a highly co-operative relationship seems to exist. "A common education by top officials both at the state-owned enterprise and at the ministries leads to a process of "acculturation", a process of adaptation to a social group. This consists of the development of shared ethics and values and is portrayed as playing a fundamental role in state-owned enterprise - government relations in France. On this basis it can be said that in sharing government goals and policies the state-owned enterprise is not so much dominated by the French state as a natural extension of it."[15] The nature of the relationship

between the state and public enterprise in countries
differentiated ideologically (and in other ways), as well
as in different industries, is an area where research is
clearly indicated.

Even if the factors described above are ineffective –
if, that is, the objectives of the state and those of the
managers of the public enterprise coincide (i.e. if there
is little managerial discretion) – there is still the
problem that the interests of the latter may diverge from
the interests of those who actually make the technological
choices within the firm, and the two cannot, or only with
great difficulty, be made to coincide. As Sheahan has
expressed it, "public enterprise ... is an instrument which
can be made to respond to the goals toward which the
society wishes to move, but only if the society can bring
these goals to bear directly on the motivations of the
people who make decisions within the enterprise".[16] One
of the major problems in bringing this about is that managers cannot fully control their members and in particular,
those who make technology decisions within the enterprise.

"We normally think of individuals who become members
of firms as being 'employed' by them, and whose efforts are
completely controlled, perfectly agreed upon, and/or
controlled or manipulated by the firm."[17] But it is
surely true, as Leibenstein has pointed out, that all
individuals have some scope for individual
interpretations of their jobs.[18] Contracts are rarely
fully specified with respect to, for example, the amount of
effort that is required. The fact that effort is to some
degree variable, is indeed the basis of the X-efficiency
theory of the firm. Since effort is a variable in this
theory, there is no need to presume that inputs (including
labour) are used as effectively as possible. The
difference between the maximal effectiveness of the
utilisation of inputs and the actual degree of
effectiveness is a measure of the degree of X-inefficiency.

From the point of view of the top management of public
enterprises, "desirable" job interpretations are those that
accord with the objectives of the enterprise, as seen by
management. But the extent to which this coincidence of
interests occurs, depends importantly on incentives and
these may often be such as to prevent the coincidence of
interests between managers and those who make decisions
about technology. (Monetary incentives are by no means the
only way in which firms attempt to influence the behaviour
of employees. There are a host of often subtle ways in
which motivational messages are conveyed to workers - many
firms for example, create "heroes" to be emulated and
"corporate cultures" to indicate "how things are
done".)[19] It may often be the case, for example, that
incentives are structured in such a way that the choice of

risky technological options is discouraged. In particular, there may be little or no reward from the successful outcome of such a choice, but considerable penalties for its failure. This would be true for contractual arrangements that cover penalties for less than minimal performance standards but not rewards for exceeding the minimum.[20] Because it is the relatively labour-intensive techniques that, for a variety of reasons (such as unfamiliarity, bias against local producers etc.), are often (wrongly) perceived to be risky, a built-in bias against the choice of these techniques is the inevitable outcome of this kind of incentive structure.

In a similar way, those concerned with the choice of technology also have a degree of latitude with respect to the degree of search for alternative techniques (which, as we argue below, often requires considerable effort). And to the degree to which search is undertaken without much effort - again, partly a function of incentives - the result (for reasons given below) is likely to be a bias in favour of relatively capital-intensive techniques.

In addition, various "professional" biases may exist that cause a divergence of interests within the public enterprise. Wells, for example, has argued that "engineering man" exhibits biases that derive from his desire to reduce operational problems to those of managing machines rather than people; to produce the highest quality possible, and to use sophisticated machinery that is attractive to the engineer's "aesthetics".[21] He argues that "engineering man" is likely to dominate (profit-maximising) "economic-man" in the monopolistic types of situations that characterise the operations of public enterprises in LDCs (for reasons that we enumerate below). In similar vein, Leibenstein speaks of a "civil-service" atmosphere in public enterprises that is predisposed to risk-averse behaviour and the discouragement of innovations.[22]

Whichever of the above reasons obtains, the point is that those responsible for technology choices will have interests that lead them to a choice that is more capital-intensive than even the technique that is associated with profit maximisation at actual prices (i.e. in Figure 2.1 the choice will be say K3/L3). It may be extremely difficult, if not in some cases virtually impossible, for managers to enforce the choice of the more labour-intensive alternative. For supervision often requires a great deal of detailed, technical knowledge and skills (in addition to the time and effort spent searching for and appraising the alternatives) which few managers are likely to possess. It is likely, therefore, that the supervisor has in mind only some broadly satisfactory range of performance within which no punishments (or rewards) operate. It is the location of this range of performance in relation to the state's goals on the one hand, and the location of actual performance within this range, on the other, that together determine the ultimate divergence of performance from state goals.

Similar kinds of considerations to those described above in relation to the choice of technique, are likely to apply also to R & D decisions within public enterprises and therefore, to the nature of innovations that are generated within these enterprises. In an interesting study of minerals enterprises in Bolivia and Indonesia, Gillis has shown, for example, how incentive structures in these enterprises were obstructive to the generation of socially desirable innovations. Thus, "managers of mine sites almost invariably serve a fixed three-year period at each. The best way to manoeuver oneself into a promotion to a more desirable (in terms of income and prestige) mine site (or the central office) is to generate high profits within the three-year period. ... Short-run maximisation of accounting profits in mining can be easily accomplished by devices inconsistent with both enterprise health and social goals: cream-skimming (picking the eyes) of deposits and failure to move ahead with developmental work."[23]

Equally, professional biases may be as important to determining the direction of R & D as they seem to be in influencing the choice of technique. In addition to seeking scientific satisfaction from problem-solving, scientists and technologists may, for example, be interested in promoting their professional status - a concern which so often seems to be linked to the pursuit of international respectability. Neither of these objectives is likely to favour the development of labour-using innovations.

What we have argued so far then, is that the technological behaviour of public enterprises is likely to be rooted in a complex pattern of relationships, the outcome of which may diverge substantially from that which is sought by the state (as well as from the prediction of the simple model described above). The essential problem that gives rise to the divergence is the classic dichotomy between the agent and his or her principal; that is, neither managers of public enterprises nor their subordinates necessarily have the same interests as those to whom they are accountable. On the contrary, they are likely to have "split motivations" - loyalties to their own objectives as well as loyalties to what they see as the interests of their principal. Schematically, the pattern of relationships envisaged in our approach, as they differ from those envisaged in the neo-classical model, may be represented as in Figure 2.2.

The neo-classical model (as well as Sen's assumption

Figure 2.2

A pattern of goals and objectives

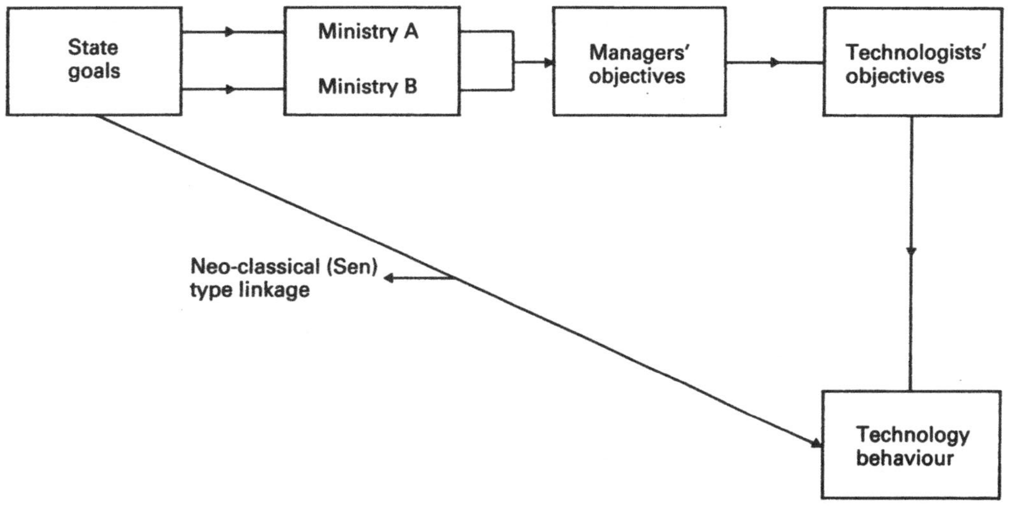

in relation to planned economies) derives technological behaviour directly from the objectives of the state, ignoring all the intermediate relationships shown in the figure. The complexity of the latter could, in fact, be increased even further by including, where relevant, the objectives of foreign aid donors which may coincide with those of some of the agents in the figure (e.g., those concerned with technology choice) but may conflict with others (e.g., the Ministry of Labour).

The second major respect in which the neo-classical model is descriptively unrealistic, and is, therefore, unable to account for the observed technological behaviour of public enterprises, has to do with its assumption of X-efficiency in the choice of techniques.

Differential X-inefficiency in techniques of production

In traditional theory all techniques are assumed to be efficient (that is, inputs are assumed to be used with maximum effectiveness). In Figure 2.3 AB is assumed to represent the boundary of a set of efficient techniques.

In practice, however, for a variety of reasons, including those mentioned above, techniques will usually not be employed with maximum effectiveness and the actual boundary will lie above AB. That is, more of both inputs are required to produce the given level of output. What is more, the actual boundary faced by public enterprises may not be uniformly above AB but may rather show greater X-inefficiency as the degree of capital-intensity increases. That is, it may look like CD.

The reason is that much of the way public enterprises are usually run in LDCs, is geared to capital-intensive rather than labour-intensive techniques (for example, in terms of the skills of engineers/technicians, the co-ordination of activities, work-discipline, the scale of operations and so on). The introduction of labour-intensive techniques would be likely - because they often require major changes in these respects - at least temporarily, to lead to X-inefficiencies greater than those associated with relatively capital-intensive techniques. This reduces the anticipated profitability of the former, and to the extent that the public enterprise is concerned with profitability, also their attractiveness. Put another way, it increases the expected output cost of employment-promotion. The expected profitability of alternative techniques cannot, therefore, (as in neo-classical theory) be thought of as independent from the technique currently in use. Rather, there are good reasons to expect public enterprises to be "locked in" to the particular type of technology that was chosen initially and

Figure 2.3

X-inefficiency and choice of technique
by public enterprise

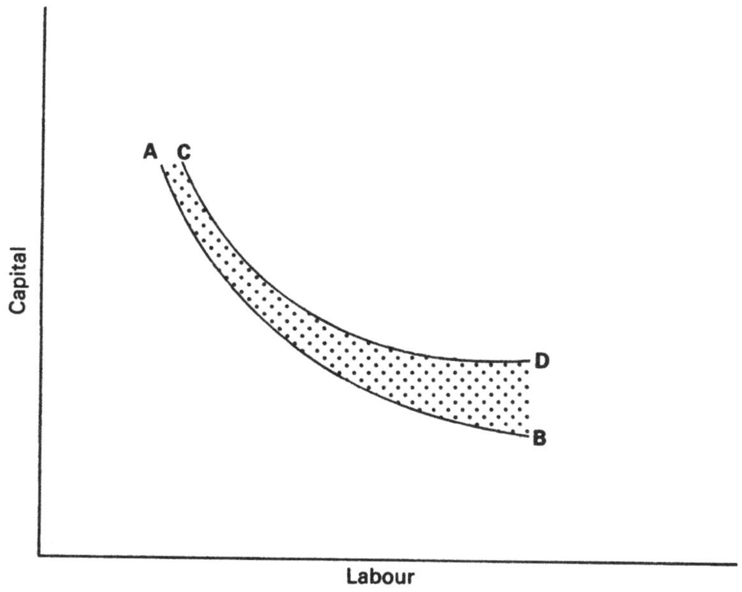

which over time has become familiar.[24] These reasons, we should note, are additional to, and distinct from those described in the following section.

The final major respect in which the neo-classical model is deficient, has to do with the nature of the decision-making process.

The nature of the technology decision-making process

The simple neo-classical model embodies a very simple picture of the decision-making process. In particular, it assumes that all techniques are known and that the public enterprise **optimises** on the basis of shadow (or actual) prices.

A more realistic description of the process however, is likely, here as above, to reveal biases in favour of relatively capital-intensive techniques. The neo-clasical model ignores, in particular, the costs of both search and decision complexity that are associated with an optimising procedure. Firstly, search costs (of acquiring and assimilating information about technology) are frequently lower in the case of modern, relatively capital-intensive techniques. In part this is due to the fact that these techniques tend to be more effectively promoted (through sales staff, advertising etc.) than labour-intensive alternatives. But it is also a question of the nature of the links - cultural, educational and procedural - that exist between those concerned with technology decisions in public enterprises and suppliers of technology in advanced economies. For a variety of reasons - perhaps the most important of which is the training in modern methods (and consequent orientation to modernity) of the former group - these links may often be stronger than those with suppliers of low-cost, more appropriate technologies. This pattern moreover, may tend to become mutually reinforcing - the strengthening of links with suppliers of advanced equipment and the familiarity with (and preference for) modern methods becoming symbiotically related. The appeal of more appropriate technologies is correspondingly reduced.

What this often all means is that though appropriate alternatives may exist outside the public enterprise, they are likely to be known about, at best, in a very vague sort of way. In order to exploit these alternatives there has to be (given the links which exist) a clear-cut effort put forward in completely new directions to discover the details of these techniques, as well as to determine all the changes (in the organisation of the enterprise) that would have to be made in order to be able to accomodate them.[25] This type of effort is only rarely likely to be forthcoming (especially under monopoly/oligopoly, as we shall argue below).

Optimisation requires, in addition to the search for information about relevant alternatives, an often complex (and hence costly) set of calculations (such as those for determining shadow prices) in order to select the "best" available. As in the case of search, however, the extent to which the effort required for optimisation is actually forthcoming in the public enterprise depends partly on the conflicts of interest that exist and the way in which they are resolved. It is useful here to think of a type of continuum. At the one end, the degree of effort is such that calculations are performed in a rather sloppy fashion; at the other end, a high degree of effort produces calculations that are very careful and tight (the latter approximating traditional optimising behaviour).[26]

It seems plausible to argue that pressures within the public enterprise for optimisation – through careful search and a high degree of "calculatedness" – will tend to be less pronounced in monopoly or oligopoly situations (which, as we shall see in the following section, are precisely the types of industries in which public enterprises are normally concentrated). In these cases, where enterprises can make non-optimal decisions and survive, it is more likely that the decision process adopted corresponds more closely to the end of the continuum representing a loose degree of calculation. One version of this loose type of decision-making behaviour is Simon's notion of "satisficing" – i.e. the public enterprise seeks to make satisfactory rather than optimal choices. "Satisficing" would be consistent for example with a choice rule such as "choose the first acceptable alternative". To the extent that technological choices within the public enterprise are based upon simplifying rules such as this, a bias against appropriate technologies is likely to be created. For it is in the nature of simplifying procedures that they tend to favour what is known and familiar (because of the reduction in decision costs that is brought about) and we have already argued that it is relatively capital-intensive rather than labour-intensive techniques that are normally familiar to those responsible for technology decisions within the public enterprise.

We know little about the details of the technological decision-making process within public enterprises but what is known suggests that this process differs substantially from optimisation according to shadow prices (as posited by the neo-classical model) and appears to be closer to the class of procedure outlined above. Sheahan for example, has observed that "it is not possible to identify any case of a developing country which has systematically taken advantage of the possibility of using accounting prices to improve resource allocation and generate productive new employment opportunities".[27] In his study of public enterprise in Indonesia, Wells noted that "few of the Indonesian firms did any calculations to investigate the appropriate technology to employ".[28]

We also know that decisions in many countries are often liable to be influenced by corruption.[29] This fact in itself, of course, does not bias choice in the direction of capital intensity; illicit payments can be associated with labour as well as with capital (managers are known for example to be able to extract payments from labour for securing well-paid jobs). However, because the risk of discovery increases with the number of transactions and because capital is purchased less frequently than labour, the former is a less risky basis for corruption. Moreover, because the risk of discovery decreases with the degree of technical sophistication of the technology, there is some expectation for corruption and capital-intensity to go together.[30]

Having offered some broad explanations as to why public enterprises appear to choose more inappropriate technology than private firms in the same industry, we turn now to the second issue raised in the introduction, namely, the factor-intensity of the types of industries in which public enterprises in the Third World are predominantly located.

III. TECHNOLOGY AND THE INDUSTRIAL LOCATION OF PUBLIC ENTERPRISES

The industrial concentration of public enterprises is closely related to the reasons for their formation. Jones and Mason argue persuasively that it is predominantly market failures – that is, the failure of private producers to undertake investments that are socially desirable – that lead to the formation of public enterprises in developing countries. In particular, "information is absent, impacted or costly. There is a shortage of capable entrepreneurs and managers. Externalities abound. Markets are small so natural monopolies and oligopolies (which are a function of scale relative to market size) are much more common than in developed countries".[31]

These market failures, they argue, are likely to be especially pronounced in the most modern, large-scale, capital-intensive industries. The benefits of establishing public enterprises – in the form of the removal of the market failures – will accordingly be highest in these industries, where, on this view, they should tend to be most highly concentrated. Data cited by the authors for the Republic of Korea strongly support the hypothesis. Thus, of the eleven most capital-intensive sectors in the economy of the Republic of Korea, public enterprises produce virtually the entire output in four and enjoy a 10-50 per cent market share in six. In the only relatively capital-intensive sector where public enterprises are not found (that of cement), "high capital-labour ratios are combined with relatively small scale and a relatively simple technology, so that entrepreneurial failures are likely to be absent".[32] Less detailed data from a variety of other developing countries tend to support this evidence.

These findings carry powerful implications for the employment-generating capacity of public enterprises as this capacity is affected by technological behaviour. For at least some of the industries in which public enterprises are concentrated (for example, fertilisers and petrochemicals) are also those in which "technical rigidities" are most marked (technical rigidities are physical barriers to the substitution of labour for capital).[33] On the one hand this means that there is limited scope (at least in the core process) for choice out of the existing range of techniques, and on the other hand it means that there is a restricted range of innovations that are biased in a labour-using direction.

It is true that some of the industries in which public enterprises are found (such as textiles) are far less subject to the problem of technical rigidities, and in which the scope for choice of appropriate techniques and innovations is correspondingly greater. But the main point is that to some extent the high overall capital-intensity of public enterprises is inherent in the very reasons for their formation.

IV. CONCLUSIONS

The finding that public enterprises are (overall) significantly more capital-intensive than firms in the private sector appears (on the basis of the very limited available evidence) to be due to a combination of, on the one hand, selection of more capital-intensive techniques within given industries, and on the other to the concentration of public enterprises within industries that are generically capital-intensive. Only in part, therefore, can it be said that public enterprise is by its very nature capital-intensive, and there is corresponding scope for policies designed to secure more appropriate technological behaviour on the part of these enterprises.

But if technology policies are to be at all successful in achieving this objective, much more information about the actual functioning of public enterprises is required. Throughout the paper we took pains to stress that the technological behaviour of these enterprises is far more complex than is posited in traditional economic theory. Indeed, we think it plausible to argue that at least part of the reason for the notable failure to secure a more widespread application of appropriate technologies, is that policies have operated on the basis of assumptions that correspond more closely to simple neo-classical theory than to the more complex framework described above. We also showed that it is partly a question of certain state goals that are better served by inappropriate technologies.

Two main relationships in particular were stressed in our framework. The first is between the state and managers of public enterprises and the second between the latter and their subordinates. Depending on circumstances, a wide variety of outcomes is possible in each case. What is required for an understanding of the technological dimension of public enterprise behaviour is, therefore, research that throws light on these and other key aspects of their functioning in circumstances that differ across industries and countries.[34] Only then, when a more realistic description begins to emerge, is policy to secure the choice and creation of appropriate technologies by public enterprises at all likely to be effective.

NOTES AND REFERENCES

*   I am grateful to Ajit Bhalla, Armand Pereira, Frances Stewart and Susumu Watanabe for many helpful comments on an earlier draft of this paper, which was published in Public Enterprise, Vol. 4, No. 2, 1983.

1. M. Gillis (1980): "The role of state enterprises in economic development", Harvard Institute for International Development, Development Discussion Paper, No. 83.

2. Leroy P. Jones (1976): Public enterprise and economic development, Republic of Korea Development Institute.

3. A. Deolalikar (1978): "Transfer of Western technology to India through State-Owned Enterprises: A Study of Foreign Collaboration Agreements in the State Sector", A Study for the State-Owned Enterprise Project at the Graduate School of Business Administration, Harvard University.

4. Louis T. Wells (1975): "Economic man and engineering man: Choice of technology in a low-wage country", in C.P. Timmer et al., The choice of technology in developing countries, Harvard Studies in International Affairs, No. 32.

5. Deolalikar, op. cit., p. 82.

6. Killick has drawn attention to the role of some of these factors in Ghana. See Tony Killick: Development economics in action, London, Heinemann, 1978, p. 229. For the Nigerian case see G.C. Winston: "The appeal of inappropriate technologies: Self-inflicted wages, ethnic pride and corruption", Williams College, Center for Development Economics, Research Memorandum Series, No. 68, Jan. 1978.

7. Gillis, op. cit. p. 34.

8. The main theoretical statement of X-efficiency theory is contained in H. Leibenstein: Beyond economic man, Cambridge, Massachusetts, Harvard University Press, 1976. A useful application of organisation theory to public enterprise is by R. Mazzolini: Government controlled enterprises, New York, Wiley-Interscience, 1979.

9. C. Cooper (1973): "Technological Choice and Technological Change as Problems in Political Economy", in International Social Science Journal, No. 3, p. 293, emphasis added.

10. Yair Aharoni (1981): "Managerial Discretion", in R. Vernon and Y. Aharoni (eds.): State-owned enterprise in the Western economies, New York, St. Martin's Press.

11. For a full discussion see ibid.

12. R. Vernon (1980): "State-owned enterprises in Latin America and Western Europe: A comparative analysis", Harvard Institute for International Development,

Discussion Paper No. 111, Dec.

13. Aharoni, op. cit., p. 191.

14. Vernon, op. cit., p. 31.

15. F. Sercovich (1980): "State-owned enterprises and dynamic comparative advantages in the world petrochemical industry: The case of commodity olefins in Brazil", Harvard Institute for International Development, Discussion Paper No. 96, May, pp. 55-6, emphasis in original.

16. John B. Sheahan (1976): "Public enterprise in developing countries", in W.G. Shepherd (ed.): Public enterprise: Economic analysis of theory and practice, Lexington, Massachusetts, Lexington Books, p. 229, emphasis added.

17. H. Leibenstein, 1976, op. cit., p. 5.

18. Ibid.

19. See T.E. Deal and A.A. Kennedy (1982): The rites and rituals of corporate life, Reading, Massachusetts, Addison-Wesley. It is also important to note that workers have "internal" pressures that derive from their "consciences" or "superegos". Even in the absence of external pressure therefore, motivation and effort can be high. For a full discussion, see H. Leibenstein (1980): "X-Efficiency theory and the analysis of state-enterprises", paper prepared for the Second Boston Area Public Enterprise Group Conference.

20. Gillis has shown how this type of incentive structure resulted in a built-in bias against innovation in public enterprise in Bolivia and Indonesia. In these enterprises government agencies had imposed fairly rigid limits on compensation. In 1975 and 1976 the incentive structure facing these enterprises was changed in the direction of greater freedom of compensation. Gillis suggests that the result has been "a palpable shift away from highly risk-averse attitudes characteristic under the previous incentive structure". See M. Gillis (1977): "Efficiency in state enterprises: Selected cases in mining from Asia and Latin America", Harvard Institute for International Development, Discussion Paper No. 27.

21. Wells, op. cit.

22. H. Leibenstein (1978): General X-efficiency theory and economic development, New York, Oxford University Press.

23. Gillis, 1977, op. cit., p. 56.

24. See the discussion in Leibenstein, 1978, op. cit.

25. Ibid.

26. Leibenstein, 1976, op. cit.

27. Sheahan, op. cit., p. 216.

28. Wells, op. cit., p. 84.

29. See Winston, op. cit. and Killick, op. cit.

30. Winston, op. cit.
31. L.P. Jones and E.S. Mason (1980): "The role of economic factors in determining the size and structure of the public enterprise sector in mixed economy LDCs", Boston University, Department of Economics, Discussion Paper, p. 33.
32. Ibid.
33. D. Forsyth, N. McBain and R. Solomon (1982): "Technical rigidity and appropriate technology in less developed countries", in F. Stewart and J. James (eds.): The economics of new technology in developing countries, London, Frances Pinter, 1982.
34. As Mazzolini has put it "The analyst must understand the interplays between GCEs (government-controlled enterprises) and the government and he must understand the workings of the government and of GCEs: how state agencies, departments and ministries and how company divisions, departments, subsidiaries, work and interact. Depending on the aim of the analysis, one may need to go quite far in the degree of disaggregation of an organisation". See Mazzolini, op. cit., p. 367.

Chapter 3

Bureaucratic, Engineering and Economic Men: Decision-Making for Technology in the United Republic of Tanzania's State-Owned Enterprises Jeffrey James*

I. INTRODUCTION

In 1982, Julius Nyerere, former President of the United Republic of Tanzania, observed that "Working towards the goal of 'people-oriented development' means ... allowing our national objectives to determine what type of technology we adopt or adapt from the North."[1] Because the United Republic of Tanzania has, following the Arusha Declaration of 1967, relied extensively upon public enterprise, and since the Government has had the chance to directly influence the technology chosen by these enterprises, one might reasonably expect to find in the latter a fairly close reflection of national objectives. Yet, what evidence is available suggests that this has not occurred - on the contrary, the degree of coincidence in manufacturing parastatals appears to be remarkably slight.

Clark's study of socialist development and public investment in the United Republic of Tanzania between 1964 and 1973, for example, found that "The failure of the post-Arusha companies to distinguish themselves significantly and favourably from the pre-Arusha companies points to one of the most important conclusions which can be made about the performance of the manufacturing parastatals, indeed about all parastatals. There has been as yet no developmental innovation on the part of parastatals to make themselves more consistent with the Tanzanian ideology".[2]

Perkins has also studied technology choice by Tanzanian parastatals in ten manufacturing industries. She concludes that "In general the observed pattern of technological choice ... only reflects to a limited degree [the United Republic of] Tanzania's articulated development goals".[3] In particular, the technology choices of parastatals were found to be large-scale and capital-intensive, often technically inefficient compared to other techniques in the same industries. These choices have therefore "failed to promote the achievement of major national development objectives,

42

such as employment creation, economic self-reliance, decentralisation of development, rapid growth of output, conservation of scarce development capital and efficient allocation of resources".[4]

Both Clark and Perkins observed, moreover, a distinct tendency for parastatals, when faced with a choice between products, to opt for the much more sophisticated alternative.

Though there is no shortage of attempts to explain these findings, most existing explanations offer only a limited degree of insight into the problem because they fail to adequately analyse the process by which technology decisions are actually made in public enterprises. In this paper, it is contended that these decisions can only be properly understood when they are viewed as the outcome of a clearly defined sequence of behaviours in the firm. More specifically, it is argued that the choice of technology in the United Republic of Tanzania's public enterprises is a very highly-staged, or sequential process, and that at each stage there are systematic biases that operate to impede the selection of technologies that accord with the country's development goals. Evidence for this view is drawn from a series of case-studies of parastatal decisions in a range of manufacturing industries. The specifically public aspects of these decisions are highlighted through comparisons with a sample of comparable privately owned firms.

The first part of the paper sets out the conceptual framework of analysis. Then, following a description of the research method, the results of the field-work are presented.

II. A CONCEPTUAL FRAMEWORK

According to Gillis, the traditional view in economics is that managers of public enterprises are "cosmic maximisers". That is, they are "motivated solely by a desire to maximise a clearly defined measure of social welfare, as defined by the parent government, under conditions of perfect information on all shadow prices, externalities and risk".[5] This idealised model, we should note, embodies not only the basic behavioural assumptions of traditional neo-classical micro-theory, but it also contains a particular, and extreme view of the political/economic relationship between the public enterprise and the agencies of its parent government.

It is apparent, even from the brief description of the Tanzanian problem presented above, that this idealised model will not do. For in that country, what has to be explained is precisely why the technological behaviour of public enterprises diverges so sharply from what appear to be many of the most important objectives of the government. Consequently, an alternative theoretical framework is required, which, on the one hand, posits alternative behavioural assumptions at the level of the firm and which, on the other, contains an alternative, and more realistic model of the relationship between the firm and the agencies of government. It needs to be stressed that both of these modifications are necessary for an alternative framework, for even if public enterprises do seek to pursue goals different from those that have been articulated by government, it becomes necessary to explain the relationship between the two that enables them to do so. We shall begin with the behavioural alternatives to the simple neo-classical model.

Behavioural alternatives to the neo-classical model

In the context of firms in developing countries, three main alternatives to the neo-classical model have been proposed, namely, Leibenstein's X-efficiency theory, Williams' "bureaucratic man" hypothesis and the notion of "engineering man" associated with Wells and Pickett.

X-efficiency theory

The central focus of X-efficiency theory is the possibility of the non-minimisation of costs (i.e. X-inefficiency) within the firm (a possibility that does not arise in the neo-classical theory).[6] Whether X-inefficiency occurs and the extent to which it occurs depends principally upon two factors, namely, the degree to which effort is a variable in the firm and the amount of "pressure" that operates on this variable.

That effort is to some degree variable, follows from the fact that job contracts in the firm are rarely fully specified. In consequence, all individuals have some scope for individual interpretations of their jobs. Further, with the notion that there is some degree of discretion available with respect to effort in the firm, comes the possibility that without sufficient pressure, the effort will not be used most effectively. What is it then, that determines the degree of pressure and, hence, the extent of X-inefficiency?

Leibenstein distinguishes between pressure from the "bottom" and pressure from the "top".[7] The former refers essentially to the degree of competition faced by the firm. At the one extreme, the perfectly competitive environment "puts tremendous pressure on any individual firm". At the opposite extreme is the monopolistic environment which "puts much less pressure on the owners of the firm or on the managers". By pressure from the top is meant the pressure for performance from the firm's owners' or owners' representatives. Total pressure will be equal to whichever is the higher of these two sources.

One further aspect of X-inefficiency theory should be

noted. It is the question of the extent to which an effective "cybernetic entity" operates within the firm. Is there, that is, any kind of feedback mechanism between costs per unit and effort which operates to increase effort when costs are judged to be too high? In general, "How well such a feedback mechanism works will depend on three aspects of the system: (1) the appropriateness of the observed results, (2) the effectiveness of the transmission to the effort source, and (3) the responsiveness of the effort source."[8] The important point is that we should consider not only the impact of pressure, through effort, on the choice and use of technology, but also any reverse causality between them.

The "engineering-man" hypothesis

In seeking to explain data collected from a sample of private and publicly owned firms in Indonesia, Wells formulated the hypothesis that "the managers'choice of technology appears to be influenced by two objective functions, which, in low-wage countries, are generally conflicting. The first objective, that of the "economic man", is to minimise costs. This leads to a relatively labour-intensive production process. On the other hand, the objective of the "engineering man" tends to lead toward more sophisticated, automated technology."[9]

"Engineering man" has among his main objectives (i) a desire to manage machines rather than workers, (ii) a desire to produce the highest possible product quality and (iii) a preference for using sophisticated machinery that appeals to his sense of "aesthetics".

As in the case of X-efficiency theory (where the degree of competition is a fundamental determinant of effort and hence costs), the degree of competition is crucial in determining the degree to which costs are allowed to rise beyond minimum levels, i.e. the degree to which the preferences of "engineering man" dominate those of "economic man". In competitive conditions one may expect a greater degree of attention to cost minimisation and a smaller role for "engineering man" than under monopoly or oligopoly where the converse is more likely to be true.

While, as noted above, the influence of product quality does form part of the "engineering-man" hypothesis, the relationship between product choice and technology is not dealt with in any detail by Wells. In Stewart's approach, in contrast, this issue finds its most elaborate and sophisticated expression.[10] Using a Lancasterian product characteristics approach to conceptualise product quality, she shows that the relationship between products and techniques has to be understood in the dynamic/historical context of the industrialised countries. Since almost all new products and techniques are developed in and for these societies, it follows that they are likely to be closely associated with average incomes and other socio-economic features of these societies. In this dynamic scheme, products acquire an increasingly high proportion of "high-income" characteristics over time, and, partly as a result, the techniques required to produce them become increasingly capital-intensive and large-scale. What evolves, consequently, is a very close inter-temporal relationship between products (defined as bundles of characteristics) and the nature of production technology. The closeness of this relationship, which derives, as we have said, mainly from historical factors, means that once the product is chosen by the firm and is closely specified in terms of its characteristics, the range of alternative technologies is frequently very narrow. However, to the extent that the same human needs can be met by products embodying characteristics in different proportions, the range of available technologies can be substantially widened. For example, "detergents possess various advantages over soap – they are labour saving and produce a 'whiter' wash. But they also involve a far more capital-intensive technology than some methods of producing soap, and their additional qualities may not be a sensible way for a poor society to spend its income. Such a society might well be better off with a poor quality soap that everyone could afford than sophisticated detergents whose consumption must be confined to a rich minority.

Developing countries are thus just as much in need of appropriate products, as of appropriate techniques. Inappropriate products are products with excessive characteristics and standards in relation to needs and income levels of the country in question."[11]

The "bureaucratic-man" hypothesis

Among the behavioural alternatives to the simple neo-classical model that we have so far considered, only the "bureaucratic-man" hypothesis was specifically formulated to explain the choice of technology in Tanzanian public enterprises. It is also the least well-known of the three alternatives (and we shall therefore elaborate the model somewhat more fully).

The point of departure of this approach, which has been proposed by Williams, is the connection between the economic environment and managerial goals.[12] In the environment in which parastatals for the most part operate in the United Republic of Tanzania, market forces have been substantially replaced by government controls. "The price-control system, for example, is in many cases based on a cost-plus formulation which both shelters the inefficient and gives only a weak incentive to become more efficient. ... The incentive-structure to which the parastatal manager responds offers little in the way of personal financial rewards and, in any case, may focus on surpluses which are more related to windfall gains from the pricing system than to productive efficiency."[13]

Thus deprived of any incentive to minimise costs, the manager turns to other goals that appear to offer greater scope for advancement in the eyes of superiors in the planning hierarchy. In particular, managers shift their attention to initiating as many projects as possible. But managers are constrained in pursuing this goal by the need to acquire finance (especially foreign exchange) and they are well aware that this can usually be much more easily accomplished by searching for aid-related projects than by seeking funds from the planners. "The project which can be secured, presented, moved past the planners, delivered and staffed fastest and at the least effort to the parastatal is the one that is chosen."[14]

The key element of this hypothesis is thus that, given the goals of the Tanzanian manager, it is the securing of a source of finance that becomes critical to the achievement of his or her objective. And since the technology for projects is usually very closely associated with the financial source (e.g. aid donors or export credits), it follows that "the 'choice of technique' in any particular project is often merely a fallout from the chosen source of finance and related project inputs".[15] The bureaucratic-man hypothesis may indeed be expressed in the even stronger form that "the bureaucratic decison-maker attempts to achieve objectives which eliminate the choice of technology from the decision process".[16]

In addition to its principal implication – that technology (in the form of alternative combinations of factor inputs) is not a decisive factor in investment projects in the United Republic of Tanzania – bureaucratic man embodies a number of subsidiary hypotheses. First, actual investment decisions are made by individuals "who are not, by experience and training, in possession of special competence in the technological aspects of the industry in question".[17] Second, "Investment decision-makers are sometimes ignorant of the possibility of alternative technologies."[18] Third, "Investment decision-makers do not seek or use advice on the technological choice aspects of investments."[19]

What can be said about the characteristics of the technological choices that emerge from this process? According to Williams, it is large-scale, turnkey projects that tend best to meet the requirements of rapidly raising finance for projects and ensuring their rapid delivery and construction. Such projects, moreover, also have the advantage of providing economies of scale in terms of scarce managerial resources at headquarters.

But while the bureaucratic process has, therefore, a systematic bias associated with large-scale production, it does not, according to Williams, also have a systematic factor-intensity bias. Rather, the factor-intensity of the technology that results from the "bureaucratic-man" process is thought to be random.

A comparison of the technological implications of the behavioural alternatives to the neo-classical model

So far, we have merely provided a sketch of the main behavioural alternatives to the simple neo-classical model in the hope that the former may have technological implications that accord more closely with the observed facts than the latter. Let us therefore, derive, and compare in summary form, these technological implications with respect to scale, factor-intensity, degree of departure from cost-minimisation, and product choice. (The neo-classical model is included in Table 3.1 for comparative purposes.)

It appears from the table that each model seems to be capable of explaining at least some element of the actual choices made by Tanzanian parastatals as these were characterised in the introduction (namely, large-scale, capital-intensive and inefficient processes producing overly-sophisticated products). But because the policy implications of the various approaches differ, we need to have some means of identifying which of them has greater explanatory power in particular situations. And since we view technology choice as the outcome of a process, the explanatory test will consist of the ability of each model to explain the way in which these processes actually take place.

We turn now to the second component of the conceptual framework, which, as noted above, concerns the relationship between the enterprise and the agencies of government.

The limits of government control of public enterprise

Apart from specific problems that vary from one country to another, there is a set of intrinsic difficulties in seeking to ensure that public enterprises are effectively used for implementing government policies. Much of this inherent difficulty can be explained in terms of agent-principal theory.

Raymond Vernon has expressed the basic problem in this branch of theory as follows. "How does the principal ensure that the agent acting for him responds to the same information and the same congeries of objectives as the principal would do if acting on his own behalf?"[20] While this problem pervades, by definition, all organisations in which agents act on behalf of principals, its severity depends largely on the degree to which the behaviour of the former

Table 3.1

Technology implications of alternative models

Model	Scale	Factor intensity	Departure from cost-minimisation	Products
Bureaucratic man	Large	Random	Varies directly with degree of monopoly and/or government underwriting of activities	--
Engineering man	--	Capital-intensive	Varies directly with degree of monopoly	Embody a high proportion of 'high-income' characteristics

Table 3.1 (continued)

X-efficiency theory	--	--	Varies directly according to degree of pressure
Neo-classical	--	Depends on relative factor prices	None

Note: Dashes indicate no specific prediction with respect to the dimension concerned.

can be made accountable to the latter. For without an adequate system of accountability, control of the agent by his or her principal becomes extremely difficult.

Howard Raiffa has correctly observed that the problems of accountability and control are likely to be much less acute in private than publicly owned firms. For in the former, "Managers usually have a bottom-line figure that holds them accountable to some extent. In private enterprise, the profit motive is strong and serves as a sieve through which gross incompetents are weeded out and others rewarded."[21] In public enterprises, however, as is well-known, the objectives are usually far more diffuse, since these firms are formed to fulfill a variety of different functions.

In itself, however, the diversity of objectives of the public enterprise creates no particular problem for the accountability and control system. If, as is assumed in the 'cosmic maximisation' model described above, the numerous objectives of the enterprise are combined into an unambiguous objective function, managers could be judged, and held accountable, according to this function in the same way that the private enterprise manager is held accountable in terms of profits. In practice, however an unambiguous objective function is rarely, if ever, presented to the managers of the public enterprise and the multiplicity of goals consequently creates severe problems of enterprise accountability and control.

The difficulties involved in aggregating multiple objectives into an operational composite index have been lucidly described by Raiffa, in relation to the chief executive officer (the principal) of a public enterprise, whose problem it is to communicate the multiple conflicting objectives of the firm to his or her agents in such a way that those agents act as the principal would in the same situation. The dilemma is as follows: on the one hand, if the chief executive is to be able effectively to control the agents, he or she will need to formalise the trade-offs between the conflicting objectives of the firm (for only with such formalisation can an unambiguous objective function be derived).

On the other hand, because there is unlikely to be any kind of consensus among the board members about the various trade-offs, whatever formalisation of these that the chief executive enunciates, will cause "political trouble" with at least some members of the board. "Thus, the chief executive officer is in an uncomfortable squeeze: he is damned if he formalises his trade-offs and damned if he does not".[22]

Raiffa's example can be readily extended to the case in which "the government" is the principal and the public enterprise its agent, because the problem of distilling from the various agencies of government a comprehensive set of trade-offs among conflicting goals is likely to be no less serious than it is for the board of directors in the firm. Indeed, Vernon points to "the disconcerting fact that, where conflicting and mutually inconsistent goals seem to exist, politicians may find it undesirable -- even dangerous -- to try to clarify the ambiguity".[23]

The political difficulties of formalising trade-offs (and consequently of controlling public enterprises effectively) may perhaps be especially severe in open, participatory democracies in which there is a diffuse set of opposing interest groups. Certainly, there have been marked difficulties in the control of many types of public enterprise in the mixed West European economies. For example, "State-owned oil companies serve multiple interests... governments have particular difficulty providing clearly defined goals for state-owned enterprises".[24]

Somewhat fewer difficulties may be predicted in less participatory regimes where political power is more highly concentrated among a small group of decision-makers. But even in such cases, a quite considerable amount of disagreement about fundamental trade-offs among development goals can still exist.

Managerial discretion

What we have shown so far in this section is that there are some inherent (and seemingly often intractable) difficulties of making public enterprise conform to national goals. These difficulties often confer substantial autonomy on the enterprises. Thus, "In Italy the lack of government consensus on goals for state-owned enterprises allows ENI a high degree of independence. In France, conflicts between the Ministry of Finance and the Ministry of Industry... have empowered SNEA to act with relative autonomy".[25]

But there are also measures that may be actively pursued by managers to further this goal. The degree to which managers are successful in these endeavours is a further determinant of the likelihood that the outcomes of the behaviour of public enterprises will be at variance with what is intended by government.

According to Aharoni, a variety of variables bear on the ability of the manager to increase his autonomy.[26] Among the most important of these are finance, the legal organisation of the firm and the efficacy of the control functions exercised by government.

III. THE SAMPLE ENTERPRISES

The aim of the research conducted in the United Republic of Tanzania was to apply the above conceptual framework to the analysis of decision-making for technology in a sample of public enterprises selected from the following industries: sugar, textiles, footwear, detergents, printing ink, grain and oil milling.

Many of the industries were selected with the intention of utilising, and building upon, the considerable data that Perkins had already collected for them (the remainder – detergents and printing ink – were chosen largely because of data availability). More specifically, we wished to draw upon the finding that in most of the ten industries she examined, there appeared to be labour-intensive alternatives which were more efficient than the large-scale, capital-intensive technologies (typically) chosen by public enterprises. As a result, the industry-composition of our study bears a close similarity to the sample chosen by Perkins. However, the firms we selected within each of the sample industries, overlap to only a fairly slight degree with those which Perkins analysed. There are two main reasons for this.

The first has to do with the two different ways in which public enterprises have been created in the United Republic of Tanzania, namely, by nationalisation and by the formation of entirely new institutions. The majority of the public enterprises studied by Perkins came into existence by means of the former method. But because the technologies in these firms were invariably chosen by their former, private owners, Perkins' findings, in relation to her overall sample of public enterprises, appear to have implications for questions of firm size rather than ownership. To avoid this problem, our sample is confined to newly created public enterprises. Interestingly, Clark has shown that in these enterprises much the same pattern of investment seems to have continued. Indeed, "in the immediate post-Arusha period parastatal firms tended to be larger, more capital intensive, less efficient and more import oriented."[27]

The second reason for the limited degree of overlap with the sample of firms chosen by Perkins, is that a large number of new public enterprises were created after 1975 – the year on which most of her data are based – and it is these, more recent firms which seemed better suited to an attempt to reconstruct details of the decision process that led to technology choice.

For these two reasons, most of the case-studies form part of the Third Five-Year Plan period i.e. from July 1976 to June 1981.

IV. METHODOLOGY

In each of the sample enterprises an attempt was made to reconstruct the investment decision-making process in order to discover how technological choices had really been made. For this purpose two main sources of information were relied upon. The first was information provided by managers in the parastatal holding companies (such as the Sugar Development Corporation) where investment decisions are normally made. The managers were asked a series of questions about the initiation of projects during the Third Five-Year Plan period, the evolution of these projects through various stages (such as the feasibility study, the tender and so on), the role of technology at each stage of the projects and the determinants of technological choice (including the role played by government objectives such as employment creation). The second main source of information was documentary. A search was made of all available documents – such as feasibility studies, board minutes and annual reports – that were relevant to a particular project or projects. In some cases, the combination of oral and documentary sources enabled a quite complete reconstruction of the technology decision process, but in others, the unavailability or lack of access to data permitted only a rather sketchy account to be drawn. For this reason, as well as the small size of the sample, the findings that follow should be interpreted with a corresponding degree of caution.

V. RESULTS AND ANALYSIS

In the conceptual part of this paper it was argued that there are likely to be two main components of a valid explanation of technological choice in Tanzanian public enterprises, namely, an understanding of the nature of the decision-making process on the one hand, and of the limits to government control on the other. This empirical section of the paper begins with the analysis of the latter issue.

The investment planning system and managerial discretion in the United Republic of Tanzania

In spite of the admirable procedure for the initiation and control of investment projects that has been developed, it is widely agreed that in practice this system has been an almost total failure. Even a fairly recent government evaluation of the operation of parastatals, for example, concludes that "The elaborate internal and external control system over parastatal activities, which exist on paper are in reality, very weak."[28] In a similar vein, the World Bank Report of 1977 described the outcome of parastatal investment decision-making as "unplanned socialism".[29] What then, has gone so badly wrong with the practice of the control system?

The major difficulties appear to be directly related to agent/principal theory and in particular, to those aspects of the theory that form part of the models of Raiffa and Aharoni that were described above.

It will be recalled from our discussion of these models that among the most important problems for the government (as principal) with respect to controlling its agents (the parastatals) effectively, are, its ability to provide them with an unambiguous objective function and its capacity (legal, managerial and administrative) for such a degree of control. We shall investigate the situation in the United Republic of Tanzania from each of these standpoints.

Difficulties in the formulation of a national objective function

Formulation of a national objective function requires, as we have seen, that decision-makers are able and willing to specify the trade-offs between multiple and conflicting goals of development. In the United Republic of Tanzania, however, this requirement appears to be entirely unmet. For what one finds repeatedly in official documents as well as in interviews is that the willingness to specify national goals is matched by a reluctance to formalise the extent of the trade-offs between them. Consider, for example, the Report of the Parliamentary Working Party on the Long-term Industrial Strategy which specifies three national goals to be met in the selection of technology (namely, regional balance, growth and employment). However, "these 3 objectives are not ordered and there is no discussion ... of which should receive priority if conflicts arise between them".[30] Another manifestation of the problem is to be found in the nebulousness of the guidelines that are presented to the holding companies. The order establishing the Sugar Development Corporation, for example, offers merely the injunction that it function so as "to develop and promote the sugar industry".[31] Because of the pervasiveness of this feature of Tanzanian planning one finds that "both the proposing parastatals and the central planning authorities appear to lack clear criteria on which to assess the alternative projects which they develop and evaluate".[32]

According to Saul and Loxley, the vagueness with which development goals are articulated in the United Republic of Tanzania is far more than a mere technical problem.[33] Rather, it is symptomatic of a lack of fundamental political consensus, and in particular, one which centres around basic ideological questions, such as "the nature and causes of underdevelopment and on the type of society that [the United Republic of] Tanzania wishes to create".[34] Saul and Loxley believe that, "Until the development policies and goals of government itself are defined more clearly there will always be ambiguity over what parastatals are supposed to be doing and therefore doubts as to what the control mechanism is designed to achieve."[35]

The limited capacity for control

Even if there was no problem of formulating a reasonably unambiguous national objective function, it is still extremely doubtful that the degree of managerial discretion in Tanzanian parastatals would be low. For as Aharoni's model indicates, discretion is also an important function of the government's capacity to control. This capacity has a number of dimensions.

Most obviously, the capacity for control depends on the resources available, and in this latter respect, the United Republic of Tanzania, in common with most other African countries, is severely deficient. The consequences of this state of affairs were forthrightly described to me by a senior official in the Planning Ministry, where projects ought theoretically to be evaluated (after being passed from the parastatal holding company and its parent Ministry). What happens instead, according to the official, is that this Ministry is inclined to simply assume that projects have been adequately screened by the parent ministry concerned. Unfortunately, the very same assumption is made by the latter with respect to the holding company from which the project originated. The outcome of this procedure is, not surprisingly, that the technological aspects of projects conform only as a coincidence to overall development goals.

With respect to the legal environment within which parastatals operate, Mihyo has argued that the widely used company form (which vests control in the board of directors, subject to any regulations and law to the contrary) "excludes the chances of government, party, parliamentary and public operational control".[36] In his view, the Government's position as a shareholder in this type of parastatal invests it with limited control, relative to the directors who are typically authorised by the articles of association to decide on the scope and form of investments. Since the shareholders can only object if an investment is not authorised by the memorandum, it is clear that the influence of Government may be quite narrowly circumscribed.

The case studies

The discussion above suggested that managerial discretion is often considerable, and sometimes nearly total in Tanzanian parastatals. In the case-studies, we sought to examine the directions in which this discretion is pursued in the choice of technology.

An overview of the findings is presented schematically in Table 3.2, which shows, for each case, the form in which the various models described above contribute to an explanation of the technology choice made by the sample of public enterprises (which, typically, is one that is based on a turnkey contract, is large-scale and capital-intensive and inefficient relative to available small-scale alternatives). Of course, such an abbreviated form of presentation represents an oversimplified view of a much more complex reality that was revealed by the attempted reconstruction of the decision processes, but it does nevertheless enable us to highlight at least some of the most important conclusions from the research.

First, in most of the seven cases shown in the table, the "bureaucratic-man" mechanism played an important role. What mainly seems to have produced this motivation during the Third Five-Year Plan period was the emphasis on achieving self-reliance in "basic goods" (such as textiles and sugar) in as short a time as possible. This emphasis in turn had both an ideological basis - that formed part of the so-called basic industry strategy[37] - and an economic rationale that was shaped by the foreign exchange crisis that plagued the country over the Plan period.

The concern with rapid output maximisation that is suggested by the quotations in the first row of Table 3.2, led managers in these enterprises to search for foreign sources of finance, which under the circumstances offered the most effective means of attaining this goal. In many cases these financial sources originated in the developed market economies, as did the technology, with which the finance was often closely associated. In the case of the Musoma textile mill, for example, a French contracting company was responsible for the financing and construction of the plant on a "semi-turnkey" basis. This enterprise identified not only the consortium of financing institutions in Europe (whose loans were effectively tied to procurement in each particular country) but also the machinery suppliers. Similarly, in the expansion of capacity of the sugar mills at Kilombero, Kagera and Mtibwa, turnkey tenders were floated in the countries to which the external finance was tied.

The second main conclusion that emerges from Table 3.2 is that in most of the cases shown in the table, no single approach appears to be capable of accounting entirely for the pronounced bias in the choice of technology; in general, elements of several approaches are required for a satisfactory explanation. There are several reasons for this complexity. One is that the operation of the bureaucratic-man mechanism imparts a (large) scale bias to the choice and though this in itself tends to raise the

Table 3.2   An overview of the survey findings

Model	Industry (firms in parentheses)	Textiles (Musoma & Mwatex)	Sugar (Kilombero, Kagera & Mtibwa)	Oil-milling (Moproco)
Biases arising from operation of bureaucratic-man mechanism		Major goal of rapid output growth ('to clothe the nation as fast as possible').	Major goal of rapid output growth ('to achieve self-sufficiency at the earliest opportunity'); managerial diseconomies of small-scale production.	Major goal of rapid output growth.
Biases arising from product-choice		--	Choice of refined sugar (at Kilombero) which is 'a higher grade than is found in many under-developed countries'.	Preference for product of 'uniform colour'.
Engineering-man biases		--	--	Bias against second-hand equipment; preference for well-known suppliers; British standards for plant construction.
Elements of X-efficiency theory		Cybernetic mechanism (i.e. pressure to reduce costs by more effective use of chosen inputs within loss-making enterprises).	Cybernetic mechanism (i.e. pressure to reduce costs by more effective use of chosen inputs within loss-making enterprises).	--

Detergents (Sabuni Industries Ltd.)	Maize-milling (Korogwe)	Printing Inks (Printpak)	Footwear (Morogoro)
?	?	?	Ease of raising finance for large (vs. small-scale) projects; managerial economies of scale in large (vs. small-scale) production.
Desire to replicate previously imported detergent ('to produce a detergent of the same standard or even better').	Desire for 'quality products' (i.e. 'free from foreign matter' and 'more consistently uniform').	Preference for 'more sophis- ticated inks than the ones already in use'.	Requirement to meet 'inter- national standards' for exports.
--	Exaggerated view of the efficiency of modern roller milling.	Simplification of managerial problems through use of modern machinery.	--
--	--	--	--

degree of capital intensity (insofar as there is a positive correlation between the two variables), there is still plenty of scope for other factors to impart an independent upward bias to the capital-intensity at the scale that is determined in this way. From the table it can be seen that the most important of these factors is related to choice of products (though other engineering-man type influences also play a role).[38]

The product-choice bias in the case-studies is imparted in three ways: the first is through the alleged need to produce exports to "international standards", the second is through the historically determined preference of some members of the society for highly specified, inappropriate products and the final source of bias originates in the fact that this same product preference is frequently held by project consultants.

The recently established Morogoro Shoe Company may be cited as an instance of the predominance of the first factor. The choice of product for this project – which was financed by the World Bank – was dictated almost entirely by its orientation to exports, as is made quite clear in the Bank's Appraisal Report. Thus, "One fairly modern shoe factory presently produces leather and canvas shoes for the internal market. The output is of acceptable quality within [the United Republic of] Tanzania, but does not meet international standards. The new shoe factory... would produce about 4 million pairs of shoes to international standards, primarily for export, but it is expected that a small part of the production will be sold internally".[39] The same Report also makes explicit the link between production for export and the nature of the technology that is required. To quote again from this document, "During the detailed engineering design phase, efforts will be made to substitute labour for capital without compromising product style, quality and cost competitiveness but the extent to which this can be done is limited in export-oriented industries".[40]

The case of Sabuni Industries Limited – the only parastatal in the United Republic of Tanzania which produces powdered laundry detergent – is perhaps the clearest example of the second main influence on product choice which emerged from the case-studies, namely, that which originates in historically determined tastes. When the Sabuni project was conceived in the 1960s, it seemed to the National Development Corporation (at the time the holding company responsible for the detergent industry) that local production of a substitute for the previously imported brand was required. In the decision merely to replicate or even improve this brand ("OMO"), what appears to have been crucial was the consideration that "since most of the people in the country had used the Kenyan brand of detergent ("OMO"), which is of very high quality, it was envisaged to produce a detergent of the same standard or even better, in order to capture the market previously supplied by the Unilever Company in Kenya. The intention was also to produce a product which could be exported to neighbouring countries by competing effectively with other high quality brands."[41]

That the influence of consultants serves to impart the same type of bias to the characteristics of products can be illustrated with reference to the proposed maize mill at Korogwe in the Tanga region. In the report of the feasibility study that was conducted for this project by the Tanzanian Industrial Studies and Consulting Organisation (TISCO), one is confronted at the very outset with a revealing non-sequitur. Thus, "the demand for maize flour whether in a household or in a restaurant or in the other industrial uses is ever present and increasing due to the increase in population. To produce quality products, it is necessary to have quality maize flour manufactured under scientific and hygienic conditions. ... There is no modern roller flour mill in Tanga region producing quality maize flour".[42] In other words, the consultants simply take it as axiomatic that any increase in demand has to be met by "quality products". There is no discussion of whether different types of flour, of varying qualities, may be more appropriate to the incomes and needs of different groups in the population. (The failure to even raise this issue takes on particular significance in relation to the finding by Perkins[43] that hammer-milled flour appears to be just as acceptable to Tanzanian consumers as roller-mill flour.) Nor is there any allusion to the possibility that alternative varieties might be better suited to the different purposes for which they are used (e.g. industrial versus household uses).

Another reason why a multi-faceted explanation of technological choice is required, has to do with the nature of the decision process on which these choices are based. Much of the existing literature implicitly assumes that technology choice is a single "one-shot" transaction, or, to the extent that it recognises the staged nature of the choice, tends to focus on only a single stage. In either case, the result is a predisposition to search for a single-factor explanation of the problem. Our research, in contrast, points to the fact that there are numerous stages in the decision, among the most important of which are the feasibility study, the search for finance, the choice of consultants, the floating of the tender and the evaluation of the tender bids, and that at each such stage, more or less subtle biases in the choice of technology can and often do arise.

The case of Moproco, the multi-purpose oil-mill at Morogoro (see Table 3.2) is a particularly good illustration of this important point. Though the scale of this operation, as well as its highly packaged form, appear to derive largely from the workings of the bureaucratic-man mechanism, a further set of factors, operating at different stages of the decision process, exacerbated the capital-intensive bias of the technology that was chosen.

Firstly, the tender document specifies that all the equipment should be new.[44] This prohibition against second-hand equipment is not unique to the process of acquisition of oil-milling equipment; on the contrary, it is a practice which is endorsed in the bidding rules of the World Bank and by the government of the United Republic of Tanzania itself.

In a second respect as well - which concerns the link between products and techniques - the specification of the tender document appears to have imparted a bias against the use of more appropriate techniques. Specifically, the document embodies requirements for buildings which have necessarily to be met by relatively sophisticated products and techniques. Thus, to quote from the document, "Building and construction work must meet local building and hygienic requirements and standards, which to a great extent are of British origin".[45] Or, to take another example, the use of locally produced roofing tiles is precluded by "the minimum requirements for roofing materials - corrugated aluminium sheets or corrugated asbestos sheets".[46]

If there were therefore biases in the manner in which the tender document was specified, it was also true that in the next stage - the evaluation of the tenders received - engineering-man type factors further reduced the pressures for cost-minimisation in the choice of technology. At the very outset of the evaluation procedure, for example, we find that most of the many quotations were rejected on the grounds that they had not come "from potentially competent and internationally known companies".[47] Further, in the selection from among the five contractors that did conform to this description, "considerable emphasis" was laid on the following factors (in addition, of course, to costs) - "goodwill of the bidder in his country and abroad", "competence and capability of the bidder to successfully complete the project", "quality of the end products", and "experience in export and establishment of plants in foreign countries".[48]

One of the major technological issues that confronted the sub-committee formed by Moproco to evaluate the bids, was the choice between a batch and a continuous refining process. Despite the relatively high cost of the latter this was nevertheless the method selected. With respect to the bleaching component of the refining process, the sub-committee motivated its choice with what amounts to a nearly complete statement of the "engineering-man" hypothesis. Thus, "Continuous bleaching plants have gained wide acceptance as they are now feasible, but they are relatively costly owing to their expensive control instruments... Continuous bleaching units are favoured by processors because of their independence of human operation, because they permit savings in bleaching earth and oil loss in it, finally because they render a finished product of uniform colour."[49] In the opinion of the General Manager of Moproco, who was a member of the sub-committee for evaluating the tenders, the last reason - the uniformity of product quality associated with continous refining - was perhaps most influential in the choice of this process. But in this, as in most of the foregoing examples, the question arises as to whether the product improvements were attained at the cost of allowing only a minority of the population to share in the benefits. It is unfortunately a question that was not addressed by those involved in the decision-making process.

Comparisons with privately owned firms

From the case studies in the previous section, we have gained some important insights into the factors that bias, in a systematic fashion, the technology chosen by manufacturing parastatals in the United Republic of Tanzania. But in order to try to gain an idea of the extent to which these various factors are due to public ownership per se, it is necessary to make some controlled comparisons with privately owned firms. Among the seven industries from which the case-studies were drawn, such comparisons were possible only in oil processing, textiles and detergents. Only in these industries, that is, were there privately owned firms of a size comparable to the public enterprises.

Oil processing

Established in 1975, Rajani Industries Ltd. is an entirely privately owned oil processing mill which has recently expanded its capacity to 35,000 tons per annum. In terms of both its size and the period of acquisition of its technology, this firm is thus comparable to the Morogoro Oil Processing plant (Moproco), which was analysed in the previous section.

The comparison between the decision process in these two firms reveals some degree of similarity but also a wide array of rather fundamental differences.

The point of similarity concerns the crucial influence of external finance on the choice of technology. At Rajani Industries, I was informed of the often considerable difficulties of obtaining foreign exchange for technology in recent years. These difficulties have, on occasion, led the

63

firm to sources of finance with which were associated relatively high-cost technologies (the solvent extraction unit at Rajani's, for example, was financed with Indian suppliers' credit). This is, of course, a phenomenon that we observed repeatedly in the case-studies above (including Moproco). But to ascribe this similarity to the same bureaucratic-man type procedures that characterise the parastatals, would be to greatly misrepresent the process of technology choice in the privately owned firm.

For this procedure implies that technology is a mere residual (which in no way features in the preference function of the manager) and this is not at all the case at Rajani Industries. On the contrary, decision-makers appeared to have quite distinct preferences for technology (of an economic and engineering-man variety) and frequently external finance was sought with a very clear view of the desired type of plant and machinery. In some cases, however, external finance is available only for less-preferred technologies and it is in this sense that finance can be said to determine the technology that is adopted. (Rajani are, for example, currently trying to raise finance for a decorticator that is made in the United States, but they are not at all sure that they will be successful). But this is clearly quite different from, and is indeed the reverse of, what is implied by the bureaucratic-man procedure.

The foreign exchange constraint that has confronted the United Republic of Tanzania with increasing severity in recent years, means that even relatively cost-conscious firms may be forced to purchase technology at a substantially higher cost than would be attainable in the absence of such a constraint. (Though Rajani's could scarcely be described as a profit maximising firm, the managers did stress that profitability is an important criterion in the choice of technology.) There are, however, numerous areas in which the firm that is oriented to profitability can compensate for the high costs of imported technology. It is precisely in the vigour with which these attempts at compensation are pursued that one finds a second major difference between the private and state-owned oil processing mills.

Firstly, whereas the construction at Moproco was undertaken as part of the turnkey contract, Rajani Industries, with a view to cost savings, undertook this operation itself (the latter also manufactures all its own containers). Secondly, at the privately owned mill, a vigorous effort was being made to utilise capital and labour inputs to the fullest extent possible. No equivalent effort was apparent at Moproco.

The textile industry

As noted in Table 3.2, the process by which technology was acquired in the textile industry seemed to be best explained by the model of "bureaucratic man". We attempt now to assess how this process differs from that adopted at Commercial and Industrial Combine Ltd. (CIC), a large-scale, privately owned integrated textile mill located in Tanga.

The production of textiles in the privately owned firm is closely integrated into its garments manufacturing operations (which began some 20 years ago). Because the garments are produced for the "top-end" of the local market and for export to Western Europe, they demand, as an input, textile fabrics of a fine variety. Since this quality of fabric was unavailable from local textile mills, Commercial and Industrial Combine (CIC) decided to manufacture the product itself.

The export orientation of CIC (with its clear implications for the choice of products) had – as in the case of the Morogoro Shoe Company – a distinct bearing on the choice of textile technology. On the one hand, the rapidly changing nature of the export market required the machinery to be versatile, capable of adapting rapidly to changes in demand. On the other hand, the high degree of specification required of products for the European markets forced the firm to substitute capital for labour in some aspects of the production process. For example, even in a process as simple as the tying-of-knots, I was informed that manual operation might have jeopardised the quality of the product even though it would have permitted a reduction in costs. In general, relatively labour-intensive technology (conventional technology) was chosen in preference to the latest machines for only those aspects of the production process in which its use did not compromise product quality.

Even from what we have described so far, it is clear that the process of technology choice in CIC was a very far cry from one in which technology and products are a mere "fall-out" from the source of finance that happened to be available (a description which, as we noted above, approximately describes what seemed to occur in the publicly owned firms). This is not to say that CIC experienced no problems of raising external finance for its new textile technology. On the contrary, the firm encountered difficulties on several occasions. But as in the case of Rajani Industries (examined in the section immediately above), these financial difficulties were the consequence of prior technological decisions (which resulted in attempts to secure foreign funds for specific types of technology).

In the extensive search that was undertaken by CIC in order to reach these decisions, one finds another feature of the process that distinguishes this case from the procedure that appeared to take place at Moproco (as well as in many of the other parastatals that we have examined). The search was conducted in Asia, Europe and America and included visits to manufacturers and exhibitions. Thereafter, the firm was able to prepare a short-list of the three most preferred technologies, on the basis of which external finance could be sought (a process that was described as "working down the list"). The point is that technology appeared to play a more central role in the project in this case than in the public enterprise (although this finding could also reflect the previous technological experience of the managers of the privately owned firm in the related garment industry).

The detergent industry

Highland Soap and Allied Products Ltd., which commenced production in 1980, is a large-scale, mainly privately owned producer of laundry cleaning products for the Southern Highland Regions of the United Republic of Tanzania. Although its capacity (8,000 tons of laundry soap and 1,000 tons of detergent per annum) is similar to Sabuni Industries (the parastatal examined above), the two firms are not directly comparable insofar as the latter produces only detergents. Even if cost-differences between the respective technologies are not, therefore, very meaningful, a comparison of the decision procedures adopted may nevertheless still be instructive in isolating the distinguishing features of the decision process in the publicly owned firm.

It will be recalled that the decision-makers at Sabuni had a distinct and unusually specific preference for the type of product that they wished to manufacture. In particular, they sought to replicate the characteristics of the product that previously had been imported. Precise specification of product characteristics was important, too, for the senior management at Highland Soap and for some of the same reasons.

Although the market served by the privately owned firm comprises, for the most part, rural and relatively low-income consumers, the Managing Director expressed a desire to produce goods whose quality is "as good as anywhere in the world".

In part, this seemed like an expression of what may be called "national pride" (although in this case applied to products rather than processes). But it was also associated with the image of his firm being part of a "quality group". To produce less than world standards of quality, would, presumably, be inconsistent with this image. The Director had little difficulty in squaring the firm's emphasis on highly specified, "high-income" products with the poverty of the individuals that comprise most of the market for its products, for in his opinion, even the poorest households are prepared to pay the premium associated with high quality. In any case, this question was less relevant to that component of the firm's output that it proposed to export to neighbouring African countries.

If, with respect to the product choice variable, there

seems to be some degree of similarity between the two firms, there are also important differences in other aspects of the decision process. Most of these can be expressed in terms of a differential degree of involvement of managers in the technological aspects of their respective projects.

Although both firms had to confront the same basic stages of the process of preparing a feasibility study, raising external finance, floating tenders and commissioning and erecting the plant - the managers of the private firm took a far more active role in this process than their counterparts in the parastatal and, as a result, the entire process was completed within a much shorter period of time at Highland Soap than at Sabuni. For example, in the case of the former, the Managing Director and the General Manager (who is an engineer) acquired, through apparently quite extensive research, and in the preparation of the feasibility study, a clear idea of their technology requirements (the Managing Director for example, was adamant that his firm and not the financier "should dictate the destiny of the project"). In particular, they had formed an opinion of the superiority of the technology supplied by Mazzoni mainly on the grounds of its comparative reliability (and this was the machinery that ultimately was chosen).

VI. CONCLUSIONS

The point of departure of this study was earlier research findings that the technology choices made by public enterprises in the United Republic of Tanzania appear to be only tenuously related to the major development goals of this country. In an effort to throw more light on these seemingly puzzling findings, we began by relaxing both major assumptions of the traditional economic model, namely, that public enterprises maximise according to an objective function that is given to them unambiguously by the government. In place of these assumptions, two different sets of models were presented. The first set deals with a more complex relationship between the government and the public enterprise than is posited in the traditional model. The second set of models offer behavioural alternatives to the simple neo-classical theory of the enterprise. Taken together, the two sets of models allow for the possibility that the public enterprise is able to pursue goals other than those of the government.

In the empirical section of the paper it was shown that this framework is able to provide considerable insight into some of the most recent technological choices made by public enterprises in the United Republic of Tanzania. What emerged from the case-studies of these enterprises, was, among other things, the finding that the pronounced tendency towards the

selection of large-scale, capital-intensive and highly
packaged technologies is the result of biases arising at
different stages of the decision-process.

Comparison with the decision-making processes in several
comparable privately owned firms suggested, moreover, that to
some extent these biases derive from the fact of public
ownership per se.

In general, the main policy implication of the study is
that improvements in the choice of technology need to be
sought in the way decisions are actually made in the public
enterprise, rather than in the way the enterprise is assumed
to behave according to the tenets of neo-classical
microeconomic theory. In particular, measures will be
required, on the one hand, to reduce the large-scale bias
that results from the operation of the bureaucratic-man
mechanism and on the other, to eliminate the biases that
arise independently of this mechanism, most notably, from the
choice of inappropriate products. Success in the pursuit of
the former objective will demand reform of the price-control
system (in the direction of specifying the extent to which
any cost reductions are allowed to accrue to the enterprise
as profits), a greater emphasis on profitability, and
institutional change wich provides a focus for the
technological choice aspects of projects (e.g. a technology
unit that offers guidance to public enterprise managers in
the various stages of the selection of technology).

All of these reforms will work in the direction of
making it more difficult for managers to ignore the
technological aspects of projects. In addition (and
especially to the extent that this change in direction is
difficult to achieve for political and other reasons), it
would be useful to implement a set of policies to correct the
finance bias that is often associated with developed-country
sources of finance. In particular, there is a need to
promote a more active search for developing country (e.g.
Indian and Chinese) sources of finance because appropriate
techniques are more likely to be associated with these
sources. A somewhat wider range of technological options may
also be promoted by the search for multilateral rather than
bilateral sources of finance.

Policies to correct the product-choice bias should seek,
firstly, to counter historically conditioned consumer tastes
for advanced-country imports (through, for example,
promotional campaigns for local goods based on appeals to
nationalism), and secondly, to draw the attention of
consulting groups (especially the Tanzania Industrial Studies
and Consulting Organisation) to the economic advantages that
are afforded by the choice of more appropriate products. As
Clark has correctly observed, "Part of the challenge of
socialist development is the need to develop an ideology
which frees the country from imitation of the standards of

developed countries, standards which the country cannot afford if it is to meet the needs of all the people."[50] Finally, while product policies may be the major means of combating "engineering-man" type biases, attention also needs to be paid to other areas of this problem - for example, to lifting the effective prohibition of used equipment (which, even if not always the most suitable alternative, is often at least deserving of consideration).

NOTES AND REFERENCES

*   This is an expanded and revised version of a paper with
      the same title in S. Lall and F. Stewart (1986) (eds.):
      Theory and reality in development, London, Macmillan.
1.   J.K. Nyerere (1982): South-South option, London, Third
      World Lecture, Third World Foundation, Monograph 10.
2.   W.E. Clark (1978): Socialist development and public
      investment in Tanzania: 1964-73, Toronto, University of
      Toronto Press, p. 140.
3.   F. Perkins (1980): "Technological choice, industrialis-
      ation and development: The case of Tanzania", D. Phil.
      thesis, University of Sussex, July, p. 408.
4.   F. Perkins (1983): "Technology choice, industrialis-
      ation and development experiences in Tanzania", in
      Journal of Development Studies, Vol. 19, Jan., p. 211.
      As we show below, however, the significance of these
      results is weakened by the inclusion of public
      enterprises whose technologies were chosen by their
      former, private owners.
5.   M. Gillis (1980): "The role of state enterprises in
      economic development", Harvard Institute for
      International Development, Discussion Paper No. 83,
      Feb., p. 3.
6.   The most complete exposition of the theory is to be
      found in H. Leibenstein (1976): Beyond Economic Man,
      Cambridge, Massachusetts, Harvard University Press. The
      theory is applied to development problems in H.
      Leibenstein (1978): General X-efficiency theory and
      economic development, New York, Oxford University Press.
7.   H. Leibenstein (1980): "X-efficiency theory and the
      analysis of state enterprise", paper prepared for the
      Boston Area Public Enterprise Group.
8.   Ibid.
9.   Louis T. Wells (1975): "Economic man and engineering
      man: choice of technology in a low-wage country", in
      C.P. Timmer et al.: The choice of technology in
      developing countries, Cambridge, Massachusetts, Harvard
      Studies in International Affairs, No. 32, p. 85.
10.   F. Stewart (1977): Technology and underdevelopment,
      London, Macmillan.
11.   F. Stewart (1974): "Technology and employment in LDCs",
      in World Development, Vol. 2 (3), Mar. p. 23.
12.   D. Williams (1975): "National planning and the choice
      of technology: The case of textiles in Tanzania",
      Economic Research Bureau Paper No. 75.12, Dar es Salaam,
      June. Also published in K.S. Kim, R.B. Mabele and M.J.
      Schultheis (1979) (eds.): Papers on the political
      economy of Tanzania, Nairobi and London, Heinemann.
13.   Ibid., p. 7.
14.   Ibid., p. 7-8.

15. Ibid., p. 8 (emphasis added).
16. Ibid. (emphasis added).
17. Ibid., p. 9.
18. Ibid.
19. Ibid.
20. R. Vernon (1981): "Introduction" in R. Vernon and Y. Aharoni (eds.): State-owned enterprise in the Western economies, New York, St. Martin's Press, p. 10–11.
21. H. Raiffa: "Decision making in the state-owned enterprise" in Vernon and Aharoni, op. cit., p. 57.
22. Ibid., p. 62.
23. Vernon, op. cit., p. 12 (emphasis added).
24. O. Noreng: "State-owned oil companies: Western Europe", in Vernon and Aharoni, op. cit., p. 142.
25. Ibid., p. 142.
26. Y. Aharoni: "Managerial discretion", in Vernon and Aharoni, op. cit.
27. Clark, op. cit., p. 134.
28. The United Republic of Tanzania (1982): Structural adjustment programme for Tanzania, Ministry of Planning and Economic Affairs, Dar es Salaam, June, p. 42. The nominal control system is based on a hierarchical structure, at the base of which producing parastatals are located. They are, in effect, subsidiaries of parastatal holding companies, which, in turn are responsible to a parent ministry. In theory, the relations between the different layers of the structure are such as to ensure that national objectives are closely incorporated in all decisions regarding technology.
29. IBRD (1977): Tanzania: Basic industry Report, Annex V, Dec., p. 121.
30. Perkins (1980), op. cit., p. 133.
31. Sugar Development Corporation, Annual Report and Accounts, 1976–77.
32. Perkins (1983), op. cit., p. 236.
33. John Loxley and John S. Saul (1975): "Multinationals, workers and the parastatals in Tanzania", Review of African political economy, No. 2.
34. Ibid., p. 65.
35. Ibid., p. 71.
36. P. Mihyo: "The legal environment and the performance of public enterprises in Tanzania", mimeo, University of Dar es Salaam, undated, p. 13.
37. United Republic of Tanzania (1978): Third Five Year Plan for Economic and Social Development, Dar es Salaam.
38. The operation of Leibenstein's cybernetic mechanism in the loss-making enterprises of the textile and sugar industries (see Table 3.2), is a further indication that the "bureaucratic-man" hypothesis is not a sufficient explanation of the Tanzanian problem. For in this

formulation, X-inefficient technology choices are tolerated (even encouraged) by the price-control system, which operates on a cost-plus basis. Yet, in the case of the Musoma textile mill, for example, whose costs of production were well above those of the established textile mills, the system did <u>not</u> protect its inefficiency. The Price Controller allowed a selling price that was based not upon costs of production at Musoma, but rather upon the average costs of other established mills. A similar story appears to be true of the sugar mill at Mtibwa.

39. IBRD (1977): <u>Tanzania: Appraisal of the Morogoro Industrial Complex</u>, Industrial Projects Department, Mar. p. ii.
40. Ibid., p. 29 (emphasis added).
41. From a document prepared by the present Holding Company of Sabuni, namely, the National Chemical Industries, at the request of the author (emphasis added).
42. Tanzania Industrial Studies and Consulting Organisation (1978): <u>Maize mill at Korogwe: A feasibility study for the German Agency for Technical Cooperation Ltd.</u>, Dar-es-Salaam, p. 1-8, (emphasis added).
43. Perkins (1980), op. cit.
44. Industrial Studies and Development Centre (1975): <u>Tender document for a Turnkey project for a multipurpose oil mill company</u>, Dar es Salaam, 25 Apr., p. 14.
45. Ibid., p. 13 (emphasis added).
46. Ibid.
47. Industrial Studies and Development Centre (1975): <u>Evaluation of tender bids for multi-purpose oilseed processing plant for Morogoro</u>, Dar-es-Salaam, Oct., p. 2.
48. Ibid., p. 3.
49. Ibid., p. 14.
50. Clark, op. cit., p. 142.

Chapter 4

Technology Choice, Adaptation and Diffusion in Private- and State-Owned Enterprises in India

Anil B. Deolalikar and Anant K. Sundaram*

I. INTRODUCTION

State-owned enterprises (SOEs) from less-developed countries (LDCs) have emerged as relatively new actors in the international technology transfer arena, challenging the monopoly of multinational corporations (MNCs) and privately owned enterprises (POEs) in LDCs in channelling foreign technology to these countries. Evans, for example, attributes much of the extremely rapid growth of the Brazilian petrochemicals industry during the 1960s and 1970s to the large-scale collaboration between SOEs and MNCs that took place in this industry.[1] He concludes that the state in the LDC can succeed in modifying the behaviour of MNCs substantially by directly collaborating with them.

However, with the exception of Evans' case study, there has been hardly any research into the question of whether SOEs are any more or less efficient at the task of importing technology than similarly placed POEs. The general view may be that SOEs, like any other government-run operation in LDCs, are likely to be grossly inefficient and that their emergence in this area is merely one more instance of bureaucrats in LDCs attempting to reassert their power over private enterprise.

The objectives of this paper are to study the technological dimension of SOE behaviour in India and to compare it to that of POE behaviour; to account for these differences in terms of the organisational, managerial, or environmental factors facing SOEs and POEs; and to analyse the implications of these behavioural differences between SOEs and POEs for social goals like employment, growth, and the development of indigenous technological capacity in an LDC. These issues are studied using primary survey data as well as some secondary data available from official publications. Within POEs, a distinction is made between foreign-owned enterprises and indigenously owned private companies. India is one of the few LDCs where all three types of enterprises can be found in most industries. As such, it was a logical choice for this study.

We address a whole range of technology-related decisions in this paper. It includes the choice of technology; the terms and sources of purchase; the assimilation, modification, and eventual local production of technology; and, finally, its diffusion to other enterprises within the country. For each of these sets of decisions, we compare the performance of the three ownership categories.

The paper is organised as follows: in the next section, we describe our methodology, including the selection procedure and characteristics of the sample firms. The process of technology choice is discussed in its theoretical and empirical dimensions in Section 3, while SOE-POE comparisons with respect to the assimilation and adaptation of technology are described in Section 4. In Section 5 we address the issue of diffusion of technology that has been imported and assimilated to other, smaller firms in India. Finally, in Section 6 we discuss the implications of our results for policy.

II. METHODOLOGY AND SAMPLE

Choice of industries

In choosing industries for this study, we were confronted with a wide choice, since India has a fairly well-diversified industrial structure. The choice, however, was constrained by the need to have an adequate representation of the three ownership categories of interest and by the need to have industries that had a significant input of imported technology. Further, we desired that the firms in our sample represent varying levels of technological sophistication. We therefore narrowed the choice down to the following industries: pumps and compressors, pharmaceuticals, and heavy electricals, representing various levels of technological sophistication. Further, the three industries also represent a reasonable degree of breadth in terms of the stage in the inter-industry transactions in which they lie. Pharmaceuticals are largely a consumer product; pumps and compressors, an intermediate product; and heavy electricals, a more basic product.

Of the Rs. 341,000 million (Rs. 12 = $1 in 1985) of output in the large-scale manufacturing sector in India in 1976-77, 8.2 per cent was from these three industry categories, the share of pumps and compressors being 0.3

per cent, of pharmaceuticals being 2.3 per cent, and of heavy electricals being 5.5 per cent. Thus, in crude terms, the industries covered in the current sample account for about one-twelfth of large-scale corporate sector activity in India, which, in turn, accounts for approximately two-thirds of all manufacturing activity in India (the rest being accounted for by the small-scale unorganised sector).[2]

The share of the three ownership categories has changed over the years. In general, the SOEs and indigenously owned private companies have steadily expanded their share of corporate activity, while the role of foreign-owned subsidiaries has decreased over the years. For example, the public sector accounted for 46.8 per cent of the assets of all companies in India in 1969-70. By 1978-79, this share had increased to 75.7 per cent.[3] In other words, the assets of SOEs grew by approximately 350 per cent during this period. Assets of the multinational sector grew slower, by 86 per cent, from Rs. 12,900 million in 1969-70 to Rs. 23,900 million in 1977-78 (all figures in nominal terms).[4] Although exact data on the assets of the indigenous private sector are not available for the corresponding years, casual evidence suggests that this sector has grown much more rapidly than the foreign sector.

All three industries surveyed have grown steadily over the last three decades in India. The pumps and compressors industry increased its production at an annual compounded rate of 8.8 per cent (in nominal terms) between 1950-51 and 1977-78, while the heavy electricals industry grew only slightly slower, at a rate of 6.7 per cent over the same period.[5] During the period 1948 to 1974, the pharmaceuticals industry saw its output increase at an annual compounded rate of 14.7 per cent.[6]

Description of sample firms

Our sample consists of 16 firms in the large-scale corporate sector, with 5 firms in the pharmaceuticals industry, 4 firms in the pumps and compressors industry, and 7 firms in the heavy electricals industry. Of the 16 firms, 5 are SOEs, 7 are indigenously owned private companies, and 4 are foreign-owned companies.

The sample represents a broad range of firm sizes. The sales turnover of the sample SOEs varies from Rs. 146 million to Rs. 9,431 million, with an average of Rs. 2,294 million; in the case of indigenously owned private companies, the range is Rs. 377 million to Rs. 955 million, with an average sales turnover of Rs. 576 million; the average sales turnover of the sample multinational subsidiaries is Rs. 792 million, with a range of Rs. 110

million to Rs. 1,598 million. (All sales figures are for 1982.) Thus, on average, SOEs tend to be the largest firms and indigenously owned private companies, the smallest firms in our sample -- a situation that is typical of Indian industry.

All the firms in the sample are publicly held companies. All four foreign-owned companies are subsidiaries of large multinational firms which hold over 40 per cent of the equity in the subsidiary. In most cases, the share of foreign equity among the sample firms is 49 per cent.

In terms of number of employees, the SOEs in the sample are largest, having anywhere from 2,500 to 70,000 employees, while the subsidiaries are the smallest, having between 400 and 9,000 employees. The indigenously owned private companies have anywhere from 5,000 to 12,000 employees.

Methodology and presentation

The instrument used in this study was a detailed questionnaire (not attached). Some data, particularly of a quantitative nature, were collected or verified from the annual reports of the sample firms. The questionnaire, which covered a broad range of issues relating to technology imports, adaptation, R & D activity, and technology diffusion, was administered to senior executives in charge of production and/or R & D. In some cases, chief executives of the firms were also interviewed to obtain a broader, company-wide perspective on issues that went beyond the purview of functional heads. In addition, manufacturers' associations in all three industries were also contacted to obtain a broader industry-wide perspective on related topics.

Since it was uniformly desired by most respondents that their identities not be revealed, we have avoided naming companies and persons throughout this report (unless permission was explicitly given).

In analysing and presenting the data, we are painfully aware of the fact that our sample consists of only 16 firms. Besides, these firms have not been chosen in a scientific manner so as to be representative of all of Indian industry. The figures presented in this report are not to be construed, therefore, as industry estimates with any degree of statistical validity. In fact, the primary survey data cannot even strictly be used to test hypotheses about behavioural differences between SOEs and POEs, since we cannot hold other factors such as size constant in our comparisons. (There are marked size differences across the three ownership categories.)

Our approach in this paper is to use industry-wide (representative) data from secondary sources to test hypotheses and draw comparisons, and to use the primary survey data to add a qualitative dimension to the comparison. The primary data provide rich qualitative details which are rarely available from secondary data sources.

III. TECHNOLOGY CHOICE

Introduction

There are several dimensions of comparison of the technology choice processes of SOEs and POEs. First, there is the comparison of the types of technology chosen by the two firm types, e.g. whether indigenous or foreign, whether capital intensive or labour intensive, whether efficient or inefficient, whether the latest or the not-so-latest, and whether from large or small firms abroad. Second, one can distinguish between the ways in which SOEs and POEs make their technology choice decisions. It is possible that the criteria or personnel used in making technology choice decisions differ between the two firm types. Third, the terms on which SOEs and POEs obtain their technology are also important. For instance, the two firm types may differ in terms of what they pay for the same type of technology or in terms of the number of restrictive clauses that are imposed on them by the seller (because of possible differences in bargaining positions).

All of these differences are important from both policy and social perspectives. Given the relative scarcity of capital and abundance of labour in most LDCs, it may be socially appropriate, at least in an allocative efficiency sense, for LDC firms to use labour-intensive and capital-saving technologies. Similarly, since foreign exchange is a scarce resource and has a high shadow price for many LDCs, it may be socially efficient for LDC firms to use indigenous technology, provided it is available at a cost not greater than that of foreign technology. From a dynamic efficiency perspective, use of indigenous technology by firms may be socially desirable even if it is somewhat more expensive than foreign technology, because it may promote development of indigenous technological capability and allow local firms to build international comparative advantage in technology production.

For the same reasons as above, the manner in which technology decisions are made in a firm and the terms on which foreign technology is purchased are also important from a social point of view. Managers who make technology choice decisions on the basis of an economic calculus -- and not on the basis of arbitrary or ad hoc rules -- are likely to make allocatively efficient decisions not only for their companies but also for the economy (assuming no price distortions). Similarly, export restrictions or restrictions on the transfer of foreign technology to other local companies could be suboptimal from the point of view of the buyer country.

There are some a priori reasons to expect SOEs and POEs to differ in the types of technologies they use and the manner in which they utilise these technologies. First, SOEs may use technology requiring more capital per unit of output and having a greater foreign content than POEs, since they are likely to have a relatively easier access to capital (particularly, foreign capital). The latter arises out of the fact that "... state-owned installations, especially heavy industry, frequently are financed under circumstances in which capital used is seen as having little or no opportunity cost to the nation; for instance, from foreign sources, such as foreign governments or international agencies, whose offer of capital is tied to a very few particular projects and is not available for alternative uses".[7] Another source of cheap capital for SOEs would be the special exemptions from tariffs or import restrictions that they often enjoy.

Second, the different target markets chosen by SOEs and POEs may have an important bearing on their choice of technology. SOEs producing military goods will require more sophisticated technology than POEs catering to civilian markets. Similarly, export-oriented firms are likely to choose technology that is different from that chosen by POEs.

Third, even if SOEs and POEs choose the same production techniques, it is likely that the former will operate it less efficiently than the latter due to inherent motivational (X-efficiency) differences of the kind described by Leibenstein between the two types of firms.[8] According to Leibenstein, not only is there much less pressure on costs but also less pressure to operate on an "outer-bound production possibility surface consistent with the availability of resources" in manager-operated than in owner-operated units.

It is often difficult, if not impossible, for the economist to separate inefficiencies in the choice of technology from inefficiencies in the operation of technology, since the true potential or maximum technical efficiency of a given technology is rarely observed. The X-inefficiencies of SOEs are likely to be manifested in higher capital/output ratios as operation below an "outer-bound production possibility surface consistent with the availability of resources" would result in lower capacity utilisation.

It is also likely that SOEs will employ labour that is superfluous to the efficient operation of a technique, since they are often guided by government concerns for employment creation and worker welfare. For instance, a study of industrial labour disputes in India found that POEs lost almost six times as many work days per 1,000 workers as SOEs due to industrial disputes between 1961 and 1977.[9] Along with other evidence that SOEs pay higher wages than POEs, this suggests that workers are treated well in SOEs. SOEs in India often offer lifetime employment contracts to workers and have strict rules that make worker lay-offs virtually impossible. Such labour-management practices can result in an excess labour force and larger labour/output ratios for SOEs.

If SOEs indeed use both more capital and more labour per unit of output, it could suggest that they are inefficient in the use of both factors. A factor that promotes such inefficiency in technology choice/operation is the fact, cited by Jones and Mason that "... it is seldom possible to distinguish 'good' from 'bad' performance. If there are both legitimate and illegitimate reasons for losing money and no techniques for distinguishing between the two, managerial performance cannot be judged. A public manager under pressure to hire unproductive workers has little reason to resist, as any effect on profit can be hidden by attribution to government pricing policies on inputs or outputs".[10] We should note, however, that it is easy to exaggerate the extent of "inefficiency" of SOEs because these enterprises may be subject to official price controls (on both inputs as well as outputs) to a much greater extent than POEs.

Within POEs, there are likely to be differences in the technology decisions of subsidiaries and indigenously owned private companies. In much the same way that SOEs may be restricted, MNC subsidiaries may be restricted too, to the technologies developed by their parent firms. As a result, both SOEs and subsidiaries are likely to have a narrower choice than indigenously owned private companies in their search for technology. Of course, the fact that the latter have fewer constraints does not imply that they will necessarily choose the "best" technology. It merely means that indigenously owned private companies are not as likely as SOEs and subsidiaries to be "forced" into inefficient technology choices.

The terms on which SOEs and POEs obtain their foreign technology — which would include the price for a given type and quality of technology and the number of restrictive clauses in the technical collaboration agreement (TCA) (on such things as sublicensing of know-how, export of products manufactured under the TCA, tied equipment purchase, etc.)

- will depend on the relative bargaining positions of these enterprises vis-à-vis the foreign seller. The buyer who has more information about the know-how is obviously better placed than one who is ignorant. Similarly, the buyer who is aware of other sources of supply of know-how has greater bargaining strength than one who is less aware. Proximity to the government, access to local factors of production, knowledge of the local market, and reputation in local and export markets are some other factors that improve the negotiating position of comparable buyers.

It is unlikely that the importance of most factors mentioned above varies much between SOEs and POEs. For instance, there is no reason to expect a SOE to have a greater knowledge of the local market than a POE, or vice versa. The only factor that could be important in this respect would be the access to governmental authority. If governmental authority is itself considered a factor of production in the Indian context, SOEs would be better placed against foreign collaborators than POEs.[11]

Another factor that could affect the quality of technology transferred under a TCA is the almost total absence of foreign financial participation in SOEs. Balasubramanyam has hypothesized that "... the foreign firm would be inclined to charge a higher price for the technology transmitted under a technical collaboration agreement where it has been denied an opportunity to engage in the more permanent and closer association with foreign markets that a direct investment venture would have made possible".[12] In so far as TCAs with SOEs involve less association with local markets (because of the absence of any financial participation) for the foreign firm, either the price charged for the technology will be higher or the extent and quality of knowledge transmitted to SOEs will be more limited than in the case of TCAs with POEs.

Further, since most SOEs are required (by government regulations) to make lump-sum payments, as opposed to royalty payments linked to the value of production, the foreign firm will have an even weaker motivation to help the local firm expand production. Also, under a TCA involving payment via royalty, know-how tends to be supplied to the recipient enterprise on a continuous basis. Under a TCA involving payment in technical fees, on the other hand, the foreign firm has a strong incentive to disassociate itself from the project once the technical documentation has been supplied and the technical fees received.

Thus, the foreign collaborator is likely to have a greater stake in the success or failure of a private-sector collaboration project than in that of a state-sector collaboration project, and is hence likely to have a greater propensity to transfer better quality know-how at a fair price to the collaborating POE than to the collaborating SOE.

It is impossible to say a priori whether the favourable effects of proximity to governmental authority on the SOEs ability to bargain with the foreign collaborator dominate the likely unfavourable effects of equity non-participation by the foreign collaborator. We, therefore, cannot predict which of the two firm types -- SOE or POE -- will obtain better terms for its technology from abroad.

Secondary data

Some secondary data exist to test some of the hypotheses mentioned in the earlier section. For instance, the Reserve Bank of India (RBI) surveys on foreign collaboration in Indian industry, undertaken in 1964-65 and in 1969-70, report data on capital employed, total production, value added by manufacture, and extent of collaborations by enterprises having foreign technical or financial collaborations, by ownership category (subsidiaries of foreign companies, indigenously owned private companies, and SOEs) and industry. Analysis of these data, however crude, may provide some idea of the differences in propensity to use foreign technology and differences in types of technologies imported by the different enterprise types. Since there are wide variations in capital/output ratios and foreign technology needs across industries, it is important to control for industry differences when comparing SOEs and POEs. We accomplish this by comparing the performance of SOEs and POEs for each two-digit manufacturing industry, wherever possible. Since the two-digit industry categories are quite broad and aggregated, the control for industry effects is not perfect, but it is the best that can be done with the available data.

RBI surveys suggest that, not controlling for industry effects, SOEs have a greater propensity to enter into technology transfer agreements than POEs (Table 4.1). During the period 1964-65 to 1969-70, each collaborating SOE had an average of over 4 TCAs, compared to under 2 TCAs for every collaborating POE. This could, however, merely reflect the fact that SOEs tend to be concentrated in industries that are basic and technology-intensive. Unfortunately, industry-specific data on the number of TCAs are not available for SOEs from the RBI surveys, but an industry-specific comparison of TCAs across subsidiaries and indigenously owned private companies reveals that, in textiles, transport equipment, machinery and machine tools, medicines and pharmaceuticals, and rubber goods,

Table 4.1

Number of foreign technical collaboration agreements
entered into by collaborating companies, 1964-65 to 1969-70

Enterprise type	Number of firms with TCAs	No. of foreign TCAs	Number of TCAs per firm
Subsidiaries	86	167	1.94
Indigenously owned private companies	247	442	1.79
State-owned enterprises	39	163	4.18

Source: Reserve Bank of India: Foreign Collaboration in Indian Industry –
Survey Report, Bombay, 1974, p. 3.

indigenously owned private companies tend to have, on
average, a somewhat larger number of TCAs than subsidiaries
(Table 4.2). The reverse is the case in industries like
metals and metal products, electrical goods and machinery,
and chemicals and allied products. However, the
differences in the average number of TCAs per firm are not
large across the two enterprise types.

Data on capital/output and capital/value added ratios
by industry, which are shown in Table 4.3, indicate that
collaborating SOEs in virtually all industries either use
technologies that are more capital-intensive (i.e. with
higher capital/output and capital/value added ratios) or
operate given technologies more capital-intensively than
POEs, both indigenously and foreign-owned. The differences
are largest in the case of machinery and machine tools,
medicines and pharmaceuticals, and other chemicals. Among
POEs, indigenously owned private companies are more
capital-intensive than multinational subsidiaries, although
the difference is much smaller than the difference between
SOEs and indigenously owned private companies.

The RBI data on the incidence of restrictive clauses
in TCAs (Table 4.4) indicate that the average number of
restrictive clauses per TCA in the public sector was much
lower than in the private sector during the period
1964-70. Furthermore, this trend was valid across all
industries. In fact, in four out of five industries,
collaborating SOEs had a smaller number of restrictive
clauses per TCA than even subsidiaries. This is rather
impressive, since TCAs between subsidiaries and their
parent firms generally include very few, if any, explicit
restrictions. However, we cannot surmise, on the basis of
these data, that SOEs obtain their foreign know-how on
unambiguously better terms than POEs, since we have not
held constant the price and quality of know-how obtained by
the enterprises. Data on these variables are extremely
difficult, if not impossible, to obtain.

The other data we use for testing some of the
hypotheses mentioned in the previous section are also
industry-specific data for India, but these are available
in considerably greater detail and for a larger number of
industries and years, so as to make multivariate regression
analysis possible. The entire sample consists of
observations on fifty 3- and 4-digit manufacturing
industries for each of the years between 1960 and 1970.
The data have been largely derived from various issues of
the Annual Survey of Industries (ASI). (See Appendix A for
the sources of the data used in the regression analysis.)
We have divided the entire sample of industries into three
industrial groups: light industries, comprising food
processing, beverages and tobacco, textile spinning and

Table 4.2

Average number of foreign technical collaborations per
firm, by industry and ownership category, 1964-65 to 1969-70

| | Average no. of TCAs per firm | |
Industry	Subsidiaries	Indigenously owned private companies
Food, beverage, tobacco	1.00	1.00
Textile products	1.00	1.75
Transport equipment	1.17	1.83
Machinery and machine tools	1.53	2.33
Metals and metal products	3.38	1.69
Electrical goods and machinery	2.83	1.78
Chemicals and allied products	2.05	1.65
-- Basic industrial chemicals	4.75	1.33
-- Medicines and pharmaceuticals	1.62	2.86
-- Others	1.00	1.27
Rubber goods	1.00	1.75
Miscellaneous	1.67	1.16
Total manufacturing	1.98	1.80

Source: Reserve Bank of India: Foreign Collaboration in Indian Industry -
Survey Report, Bombay, 1974, pp. 31 and 71.

Table 4.3

Capital/output and capital/value added ratios among
collaborating enterprises, by industry and ownership category, 1969-70

Industry	State-owned enterprises	Indigenous private enterprises	Subsidiaries
Manufacturing	2.89 / 7.05	1.24 / 3.65	0.94 / 2.44
- Transport equipment	1.94 / 3.51	1.16 / 3.57	0.90 / 2.69
- Machinery and machine tools	7.31 / 23.48	1.28 / 3.82	1.50 / 3.44
- Metal and metal products	2.89 / 7.01	1.68 / 4.64	1.15 / 2.67
- Electrical goods and machinery	2.50 / 5.52	1.65 / 5.00	1.30 / 3.20
- Chemicals and allied products	2.78 / 8.97	1.02 / 3.10	0.88 / 2.56
-- Basic industrial chemicals	2.27 / 7.01	1.54 / 3.41	1.92 / 6.41
-- Medicines and pharmaceuticals	6.84 / 30.66	0.77 / 2.29	0.83 / 1.91
-- Others	5.77 / 23.82	1.19 / 7.62	0.56 / 1.91
All industries (including those not shown above)	1.87 / 5.59	1.25 / 3.69	0.88 / 2.63

Source: Reserve Bank of India: Foreign Collaboration in Indian Industry –
Survey Report, Bombay, 1974, pp. 35, 37, 43, 72, 77.

Table 4.4

Average number of restrictive clauses per foreign TCA,
by ownership category and industry, 1964-65 to 1969-70

Industry	SOEs	Indigenous private enterprises	Subsidiaries
Transport equipment	0.57	1.38	1.29
Machinery and machine tools	0.92	1.77	0.48
Metals and metal products	0.25	1.08	1.04
Electrical goods and machinery	1.04	1.40	1.09
Chemicals and allied products	0.10	0.84	0.27
All industries (including those not shown above)	0.71	1.27	0.62

Source: Reserve Bank of India: Foreign Collaboration in Indian Industry -
Survey Report, Bombay, 1974, pp. 110-15 and 131.

weaving, and knitting; chemical industries, comprising basic industrial chemicals (including fertiliser), miscellaneous chemical products, petroleum and coal products, and cement; and engineering industries, comprising metal products, machinery, electrical machinery and equipment, transport equipment, and automobiles and cycles.

The ASI data are used to estimate a system of input demand equations for each of the three industry groups. The inputs that are considered are production labour, nonproduction labour, fuel, foreign technology, and local innovation. The last two are somewhat unconventional inputs, and are proxied by the amount of royalty and technical fee payments made by firms in an industry and by the number of patents granted to India-based firms within the industry, respectively. The latter particularly is an unsatisfactory proxy, but, since industry-specific data on R & D expenditures or personnel are not available for the period 1960–70, it is the best measure of local innovation and adaptation available to us.

Only the demand equations for labour and for foreign technology are of interest in this section. All the demand equations have, however, been estimated jointly as part of a system of factor demand equations arising out of cost minimisation by firms. The independent variables, which are common to all the demand equations, include three prices – the wage rate for production labour, the wage rate for nonproduction labour, and the price of fuel (which varies only over time, not across industries) – and output, and several fixed factors, including the level of international inventive activity (proxied by the cumulative number of patents granted in the United States in a particular industry during the previous five years), the average stock of fixed capital in the industry, the share of output produced by SOEs in the industry, and the average share of foreign equity in the industry. For estimation purposes, cross-sectional and time-series data have been pooled within each of the three industry groups, which implies that the parameters of the demand equations are identical within each industry group. A full set of three-digit industry dummies has been included in each system to isolate industry shift effects.

Since the industry-level variables are totals over a varying number of firms in each industry, all dependent and independent variables, with the exception of the output share of the public sector, the equity share of the foreign sector, and prices, have been divided by the number of firms in the industry before estimation. This procedure removes a potential source of heteroskedasticity in the residuals of the demand equations.

The factor demand systems have been estimated jointly

by the iterative Zellner method, taking account of error
interdependence and symmetry restrictions across
equations. This assures us of efficient estimates for the
systems.

The variables used in the analysis, and their means
and standard deviations, are listed in Table 4.5. The
elasticity estimates from the systems estimation are
presented in Tables 4.6 and 4.7. These seem to suggest
that, in the light industries sector, SOEs tend to have
greater (production) labour intensity or inefficiency of
labour use than POEs (since they use more production labour
holding output and input prices constant -- see Table 4.7),
while foreign-owned firms tend to have significantly lower
(production) labour intensity (or greater efficiency of
labour use) than indigenously owned private companies. In
the case of the engineering sector, however, the reverse is
true: SOEs tend to show lower (production) labour
intensity, and foreign-owned firms have higher (production)
labour intensity. Neither foreign nor state ownership
seems to have an appreciable impact on the intensity of use
of nonproduction labour, except in the case of the
engineering sector in which state ownership tends to be
associated with slightly lower nonproduction labour
intensity.

The results also suggest no significant differences
between SOEs and POEs and between foreign-owned firms and
indigenously owned private companies in their propensities
to use foreign technology when we control for the effects
of prices, output, and other factors. Thus, the greater
apparent use of foreign technology by SOEs observed in
Table 4.1 is not borne out by the more rigorous regression
analysis.

The factor that emerges as perhaps the strongest
determinant of foreign technology use from the regression
analysis is the level of international inventive activity.
In the case of all three industry groups, this variable has
a very strong and significant positive effect on technology
imports, perhaps reflecting the fact that, as the
international supply of technology expands (because of
increased patenting in the United States), its world
'price' falls, thereby stimulating the demand for foreign
technology by firms in India.

Primary data

The secondary data in the previous section provide
tests, albeit somewhat crude, of the hypotheses in Section
A. In this section, we interpret the data we collected
from the primary survey to highlight qualitative
differences in the manner in which SOEs and POEs make their

Table 4.5

Variable means: Indian industries 1960-1970

	Light industries[d]	Chemical industries[e]	Engineering industries[f]	All Industries
Production labour[a] (in work hours)	687,635	1,092,343	864,790	836,425
Number of non-production workers[a]	32.70	112.50	252.88	122.92
Fuel consumption (= expenditure on fuel - fuel price index)[a]	1,143	12,955	3,341	4,509
Technology imports (royalty and technical fee payments for foreign know-how)[a]	33,510	57,451	948,175	339,492
Domestic patenting (number of patents X 1000 granted to nationals in India)[a]	432	183	215	305
W_P (Hourly wage rate for production labour)	0.52	1.00	0.83	0.73
W_N (Annual wage rate for non-production workers)	3,948	8,073	5,119	5,256
P_F (Price index for fuel)[b]	120.02	120.16	117.35	119.17
USPATNTS (Cum. no. of patents granted in USA over previous 5 years)[a]	126.80	326.77	1,389.33	586.51

Table 4.5 (continued)

FORSHARE (Share of equity held by foreigners over the period 1965-1970)[c]	26.81	13.63	23.22	22.68
PUBSHARE (Share of production in public-sector enterprises over period 1970-1973)[c]	3.70	15.75	18.17	11.15
FIXEDCAP (Fixed capital stock in rupees)[a]	1,008,852	19,517,808	4,217,698	6,241,176
OUTPUT (Gross output in rupees)[a]	5,150,564	25,268,988	6,244,962	10,005,713
Number of observations	192	96	141	429

Notes:
a   Variable has been divided by the total number of firms in the industry. The means, therefore, reflect the situation of the average firm in the industry.

b   Variable varies only with time.

c   Time-invariant variable.

d   Include all food manufacturing, beverage, tobacco, textile spinning and weaving, and knitting industries.

e   Include basic industrial chemicals (including fertilisers), miscellaneous chemical products, petroleum and coal products, and cement industries.

f   Include metal products, machinery, electrical machinery and equipment, transport equipment, railroad equipment, and automobile and cycle industries.

Table 4.6

Own- and cross-price elasticities of demand: Indian industries, 1960–1970[a, b]

(t-statistics in parentheses)

Industry group	With respect to:	Production labour	Non-production labour	Fuel	Technology imports	Domestic patenting
			Elasticity of:			
Light	W_P	−2.652* (−10.3)	−0.277* (−6.7)	1.536* (2.3)	1.396* (2.0)	−0.003* (−5.1)
	W_N	−0.727* (−6.7)	−0.390* (−5.7)	1.562* (5.5)	−0.443 (−1.5)	−0.001* (−4.4)
	P_F	−0.512* (−1.6)	0.039 (0.2)	−2.449* (−3.1)	2.919* (3.5)	0.002* (2.9)
Chemicals	W_P	−0.893* (−5.7)	0.093 (0.9)	0.803* (3.8)	−0.004* (−1.6)	0.001 (0.6)

Table 4.6 (continued)

(t-statistics in parentheses)

W_N	0.110	-0.344*	0.237	-0.004	0.001
	(0.9)	(-2.3)	(1.0)	(-1.2)	(0.9)
P_F	-0.330	0.486*	-0.155	-0.000	-0.001
	(-1.1)	(2.5)	(-0.4)	(-0.0)	(-0.4)
Engineering W_P	-0.196	-0.250*	0.057	0.389*	-0.001
	(-1.2)	(-2.6)	(0.4)	(4.1)	(-0.8)
W_N	-0.143*	-3.887*	3.914*	0.115	0.001
	(-2.6)	(-10.6)	(7.4)	(0.3)	(0.2)
P_F	-0.948*	0.064	0.509	0.375*	0.001
	(-2.5)	(0.3)	(1.4)	(1.7)	(0.4)

Notes:

a   Elasticities have been evaluated at the sample means of each industry group.

b   Since all prices have been normalised by the fuel price in the estimated equation, no symmetry has been imposed between the fuel price effects on labour demand and the wage effects on fuel demand. As such, the signs of these effects may not be the same.

*   Significant at the 0.10 level of significance.

Table 4.7

Output and fixed factor elasticities of demand:
Indian industries, 1960-1970[a]

Industry group	With respect to:	Elasticity of:				
		Production labour	Non-production labour	Fuel	Technology imports	Domestic patenting
Light	USPATNTS	-0.327*	-0.119*	0.218*	1.308*	1.128*
	FORSHARE[b]	-0.751*	0.205	-1.404*	0.578	0.159
	PUBSHARE[b]	0.330*	0.010	0.317*	-0.258	0.011
	FIXEDCAP	0.658*	0.617*	0.830*	-0.248	-0.013
	OUTPUT	0.297*	0.242*	0.453*	0.114	-0.108*
	YEAR[b]	-0.092*	-0.015*	-0.056*	0.181*	0.101
Chemicals	USPATNTS	-0.012	0.099	-0.065	1.107*	2.120*
	FORSHARE[b]	-0.014*	-0.013	0.006	-0.011	-0.120*
	PUBSHARE[b]	0.007	0.007	0.050	0.026	0.216*
	FIXEDCAP	0.947*	1.075*	0.664*	-0.157	0.464
	OUTPUT	0.260*	0.021	0.622*	0.025	-0.809*
	YEAR[b]	-0.105*	-0.073*	-0.068*	0.167	0.111*

Table 4.7 (continued)

Engineering	USPATNTS	-0.059	0.055	0.051	0.557*	0.196
	FORSHARE[b]	0.105*	0.111	0.101	0.095	0.027
	PUBSHARE[b]	-0.030*	-0.039*	-0.020*	0.001	0.030
	FIXEDCAP	0.785*	0.123	0.360	-0.356	-0.655*
	OUTPUT	0.169*	0.553	0.827*	0.391*	0.499
	YEAR[b]	-0.040*	-0.338*	-0.046	-0.038	-0.114*

Notes:

a   Elasticities have been evaluated at the sample means of each industry group.

b   The figures in these rows are partial elasticities. That is, they show the percentage change in the dependent variable due to a 1 unit increase in the independent variable.

*   Significant at the 0.10 level of significance.

technology choices. As in the previous section, we control for industry differences in the analysis that follows.

Use and source of foreign technology

Of the 16 firms in the sample, 13 had foreign TCAs of some kind -- the three that had no foreign TCAs were, significantly, all indigenously owned private companies, one in each industry category. The earliest year in which a foreign TCA was entered into was 1937. The year of establishment of firms in our sample considerably predates this. This prima facie implies that some firms were established without recourse to foreign technology. A slightly closer examination reveals that this is indeed true, but only for the indigenous private sector.

The number of foreign TCAs per firm varies widely, from 1 to 36, with an average of a little over 7 foreign TCAs per firm (Table 4.8). There is a difference between the industry categories. Heavy electricals has the largest number of TCAs, followed by pumps and compressors and pharmaceuticals. This is probably to be expected. Across ownership categories, we find that SOEs generally tend to have a larger number of TCAs on average than indigenously owned private companies and subsidiaries, although this could be due to their much larger size (which we do not hold constant in our comparisons).

Out of the three firms that do not have any foreign TCAs, two started out with a limited range of products, and hence did not initially perceive the need for foreign TCAs. However, as these firms and the technological sophistication of their products grew (both these firms are market and technology leaders in their respective product categories today), they kept constant pace with developments abroad on their own and updated the technological content of their products through search and adaptation. Neither of them felt the need at any stage for foreign TCAs. Equally important to note is the fact that these firms did not cite factors such as limited foreign exchange availability or lack of information as being reasons why they did not go for foreign collaborations.

The third firm (without any foreign TCAs) began to diversify its product base around the time when strict controls were imposed on the growth of the multinational sector by the Government of India (GOI). This was also the time when formulations technology was fairly widely known and adequate research had been done into the use of indigenously available raw materials as substitutes for imported raw materials. The firm took advantage of these events to initiate manufacture of pharmaceuticals products on its own. This firm, however, is currently pursuing the possibility of a foreign TCA for a new range of drugs that it plans to manufacture in the near future.

Table 4.8

Year of first foreign technical collaboration and average number
of foreign collaborations per firm as of 1982,
by industry and ownership category

Industry	SOEs	Indigenous private firms	Subsidiaries
Pharmaceuticals	1954 (4.5)	? (2.5)	1961 (1.0)
Pumps & compressors	1971 (8.0)	1962 (2.0)	1962 (5.0)
Heavy electricals	1956 (19.5)	1937 (9.0)	1958 (8.5)

Notes: Figures in parentheses are average number of agreements per firms as
of 1982. They include expired agreements.

Source: Interview data.

Table 4.9, which shows the range of countries represented in the TCAs by industry and ownership category, suggests that the range is widest in the case of SOEs, followed by the indigenously owned private companies. It is most limited in the case of subsidiaries. In the case of SOEs, the addition to the range is primarily due to countries in the Eastern bloc. None of the firms in the private sector had foreign TCAs with the Eastern bloc. Of the four subsidiaries in the sample, three had dealings with only their parent companies.

The table, however, does not reveal some information. For example, although Japan is seen as being a collaborator country of significance in our sample, this has largely been a post-1970s trend. Prior to this, almost all collaborations were with firms in Europe and the United States (and the Eastern bloc, in the case of SOEs).

Almost all firms report a trend toward diversifying their sources of technology purchase. In most cases, this trend has been a shift toward Japan. The reasons cited for this trend were: the technological superiority of Japan; the better terms that Japan offers on both price and restrictive clauses; the perception that the Japanese treat buyers more as "equals" (for instance, at least two of the respondents mentioned that American firms did not treat them with the same degree of respect for their technological capabilities as Japanese business executives did); and the decreasing importance of factors like "language compatibility" and "past associations".

The four countries that account for a predominant share of TCAs are the United States, the Federal Republic of Germany, Japan, and the United Kingdom. Despite being a late starter, Japan had already become one of the leading three collaborator countries among the sample firms.

Technology choice process

In most of the firms, the technology choice process is quite complex and involves various stages of decision-making as well as various groups of decision-makers. At least three firms in the sample -- one in each ownership category -- have formalised systems. Such systems include detailed market appraisals (usually, information about initially perceived demand for products is passed on from the bottom up), followed by appraisals of various technologies and sellers and their prices and terms, in turn followed by cost-benefit analyses. At the final stage, typically two to three firms are short-listed (see Table 4.12), and the R & D division plays a major role in deciding which technology to obtain.

However, some differences emerge when we examine the importance of various groups in the decision-making process across the three ownership categories (Table 4.10). In the

97

Table 4.9

Range of countries represented in foreign collaboration agreements of firms, by industry and ownership category as of 1982

Industry	SOEs	Indigenous private firms	Subsidiaries
Pharmaceuticals	United States, Hungary, Netherlands, USSR, Sweden, Italy	United States, Federal Republic of Germany, Japan	United States
Pumps and compressors	France, Italy, Japan, Federal Republic of Germany, United States, Romania	United States, United Kingdom	Sweden

| Heavy electricals | United States, United Kingdom, USSR, Federal Republic of Germany | United States, United Kingdom, Italy, Federal Republic of Germany | United States, Japan, Federal Republic of Germany |

Notes: The total number of foreign TCAs by the sample firms were 18 with the United States, 12 with the Federal Republic of Germany, 9 with Japan, 8 with the United Kingdom, 5 with the Eastern Bloc, and 2 with Sweden.

Source: Interview data.

Table 4.10

Number of times agents cited as being major decision-makers in technology choice decisions by respondent firms, by ownership category

State-owned enterprise	Indigenous private enterprises	Subsidiaries
Chief Executive (2)	Chief Executive (5)	Chief Executive (4)
Parent Ministry (2)	R & D Division (4)	Prodn. Chief (1)
Production Chief (2)	Production Chief (3)	Other Functional
R & D Division (1)		Heads (1)
Special Group (1)		

Source: Interview data.

case of SOEs, the parent ministry is as important as the chief executive in making decisions. Equally important are the production chiefs, followed by the R & D group. In the case of indigenously owned private companies, the chief executive is again the major decision-maker, closely followed by the R & D group and then the production chiefs. In subsidiaries, a major part of the decision authority seems to be with the chief executive, and the role played by others seems quite low by comparison. In particular, the R & D group does not seem to figure at all.

Thus, if one were to think in terms of a crude dimension of engineering orientation of technology decisions, the indigenously owned private companies appear to come out on top, followed by the SOEs and then the subsidiaries.

Table 4.11 shows the importance of various means of obtaining information on technologies. For the SOEs, the ranking of sources is: professional trade journals, industrial exhibitions and private consultants, and frequent trips abroad by the chief executive. For the indigenously owned private companies, professional trade journals and foreign trips by both the chief executive and the R & D group are the most important sources of ideas on technology. For the subsidiaries, the ranking is: the parent company and frequent foreign trips by the R & D personnel, followed by frequent trips abroad by the chief executive and industrial exhibitions. Overall, it appears that the indigenously owned private companies use the largest variety of information sources in their technology choice.

In conjunction with the earlier findings on who makes technology decisions, it would appear that only in the case of indigenously owned private companies are R & D personnel responsible for both searching for new technologies and making decisions about which technologies to purchase. In the case of SOEs, while the R & D personnel seem to have some authority in decision-making, they do not seem to play a role in scouting for the technology. In the case of subsidiaries, the reverse is true. Overall, in the case of SOEs and subsidiaries, the integration of R & D personnel into the technology decision-making process appears to be limited.

It is interesting to note that none of the sample firms listed prospective sellers or their marketing representatives as being important in providing information on technologies.

Finally, we look at the number of seller firms that buyers short-list before making the final decision on a collaboration (Table 4.12). In general, most firms appear to short-list anywhere from 2 to 6 firms before they make their final decision. Two out of the three subsidiaries (for whom information was available) indicated that the

Table 4.11

Average ranking of importance of various sources of information on technology, by ownership category

Source of information	SOEs	Indigenous private firms	Subsidiaries
Frequent trips abroad by Chief Executive	3	1	2
Frequent trips abroad by R & D people	-	1	1
Frequent trips abroad by others	-	3	-
Industrial exhibitions	2	2	2
Private consultants	2	4	-
Professional trade journals	1	1	-
Parent Company	-	-	1

Notes: A rank of 1 indicates most important and 4, least important.

Source: Interview data.

parent company was the only collaborator considered. The subsidiary that had a fairly well-diversified set of suppliers, however, short-listed anywhere from 6 to 10 firms before deciding on a technology purchase. Two of the firms -- both in the pharmaceuticals industry and both of which largely manufacture antibiotics -- indicated that their choice was limited in the antibiotics market because of the limited number of sellers in the industry.

In general, therefore, it would appear that Indian firms are not constrained by having to deal with few technology suppliers willing to sell. Most appear to have a fairly clear idea of where to look for their technology needs and how many sellers to shortlist before making their final decision.

Table 4.12

Average number of potential vendors (of technology)
shortlisted by firms, by industry and ownership category

Industry	SOEs	Indigenous private firms	Subsidiaries
Pharmaceuticals	2.5	1.5	?
Pumps & compressors	3.5	2.5	1
Heavy electricals	5.0	5.0	4.5

Source: Interview data.

Technology choice criteria

Here we analyse information on the importance of
various factors in the technology choice decision. The
results from this analysis are summarised in Table 4.13.
Overall, the most important criterion in choosing a
technology is that "the know-how should represent the
latest breakthrough and state-of-the-art" -- this criterion
had an average ranking, across all ownership categories,
that is more than half-way between "very important" and
'important'. This is followed by two criteria that are
close to each other and listed as "important". These are
that "the know-how should be appropriate to local
conditions" and that "the seller of the know-how should be
world-famous and well-established".

Surprisingly, the criterion that "the know-how should
be inexpensive" -- one that would presumably be important
in a capital-scarce country like India -- turns out to be
less than "somewhat important" in the ranking of
respondents. And yet another criterion whose satisfaction
presumably would be important in a labour-surplus country
like India, viz., that the "know-how should be
labour-intensive", was cited as largely irrelevant in the
technology choice decisions of most firms.

Disaggregation by ownership category largely preserves
the ordering, except for some minor differences. It is
interesting to note that the scores for the different
criteria seem to be a little more closely bunched together
in the case of indigenously owned private companies,

Table 4.13

Considerations in technology choice -- average scores
received by each criterion, by ownership category

Criterion	SOEs	Indigenous private firms	Subsidiaries	All firms
Latest breakthrough	3.0	2.5	2.5	2.7
Inexpensive	0.8	1.3	0.5	0.8
Appropriate to local conditions	1.6	1.8	3.0	2.0
Seller's reputation	2.0	1.8	2.3	2.0
Labour intensity	0.	0.5	0.	0.2

Notes: Scores are: 3=very important, 2=important, 1=somewhat important,
0=not important.

Source: Interview data.

suggesting that these firms give somewhat more equal importance to the various criteria than do SOEs or subsidiaries.

The opinions expressed by some respondents provide some additional insights. For example, in relation to the technology having to be the latest, most respondents saw this as being necessary to retain their competitiveness in the market-place. In relation to "appropriateness", the most critical issue was generally seen to be that of compatibility with local raw-material availability. In relation to cost, none of the respondents cited limited availability of foreign exchange for technology purchase as a problem. Finally, in relation to the labour intensity of technology, the responses for the most part stopped short of amazement: it was mostly seen as a totally irrelevant factor in technology choice. Arguments against labour intensity typically offered by respondents included: the necessity for maintenance of quality control, the need to maintain production at as large a scale as demand would permit (which, by developed country standards, is already small to begin with), and the difficulties of managing labour.

One of the respondents blamed government policies for capital intensity. For instance, there are no financial advantages in employing more labour per unit of capital -- instead, all income tax benefits are geared toward higher capital investment. Also, labour laws are seen as being anti-employer rather than pro-employee; it is often difficult to lay-off labour. Finally, soft loans are available for capital imports quite easily; however, no financial institution will give a loan for training workers and enhacing their productivity.

Finally, we note that all but one of the firms in the sample use detailed cost-benefit calculations in analysing various technologies for purchase. They also have clearly defined internal rates of return criteria. The one firm that does not perform such calculations is a subsidiary, whose technology choice decisions are made by its parent company.

Technical collaboration agreements

In this section, we study the types of collaboration (viz., technical or financial) that firms undertake, their methods of payments, the size of collaborators they generally deal with, the duration of their TCAs, and the number of restrictive clauses in their TCAs.

If a firm had a choice in its mode of collaboration, it would be free to choose anywhere along the spectrum of purely technical collaborations to purely equity-based collaborations. The former may be preferred if the firm wants to retain its management control without any outside interference, while the latter may be preferred in situations where the firm is willing to trade-off a certain degree of loss of independence against increased technological access provided by the collaborator.

Of the 12 firms that responded to this question, 7 said that they preferred purely technical agreements without any equity participation. All of these were either SOEs or indigenously owned private companies. The reason given by the SOEs for going in for purely technical collaborations was that government restrictions do not permit them to do otherwise. All four of the indigenously owned private companies that preferred purely technical collaborations liked them for the independence they offered them. One of these, in addition, suggested that there would be no advantage in equity participation, because foreign collaborators rarely passed on improvements in the technology that they sold to buyers.

The one indigenously owned private company that preferred both options, viz., technical as well as financial collaboration, did so for the reason that the collaborator would have a stake in the indigenous company's growth and would, therefore, pass on any modifications and improvements to it.

The duration of TCAs are more-or-less standard across categories: they largely follow the stipulations laid down by the GOI. Most firms in the sample tended to take advantage of the maximum length of time that government rules allow: usually this is a maximum of 8 years, which includes 3 years from the date of signing the agreement and 5 years from commencement of production. The rules also permit an extension of up to 5 years in addition to the 8 years. In the present sample, only two firms took recourse to this.

There were three exceptions to the rule above: by two subsidiaries and one SOE. In the case of the subsidiaries, one had agreements that ran to an average of 20 years and the other had agreements that were described as being "indefinite". In the case of the SOE, agreements with an Eastern bloc country were not covered by any duration restrictions.

Methods of payment to collaborators are again constrained by the GOI regulations, which restrict payments to a one-shot lump-sum technical fee and/or a short-term royalty (usually for no more than 5 years). Long-term royalty agreements are no longer entered into now, and those that exist are carry-overs from agreements drawn up in the past.

Table 4.14 summarises the methods of payment to foreign collaborators by ownership category of the sample firms. We observe that all the firms use lump-sum

Table 4.14

Methods of payment in foreign technical collaboration
agreements, by ownership category
(number of firms using each method)

Method	SOEs	Indigenous private firms	Subsidiaries
Lump-sum	5	4	4
Short-term royalty	3	3	1
Long-term royalty	–	1	1

Source: Interview data.

technical fees as the main method of payment. In the case
of SOEs and indigenously owned private companies, however,
short-term royalty agreements are not uncommon, while in
the case of subsidiaries, lump-sum technical fees are the
primary method of payment.

Table 4.15 indicates the type of firms abroad that the
sample firms tend to collaborate with. Firms in all three
ownership categories tend to collaborate with large-sized
foreign firms. However, while private sector firms in
India appear to collaborate only with private-sector firms
abroad, about 10 per cent of the SOE collaborations are
with foreign SOEs (generally in the Eastern bloc
countries). In the case of subsidiaries, almost all of
their collaborations are with large private-sector
companies abroad.

The Indian preference for large private sector
companies abroad appears to be consistent with the high
ranking that the sample firms gave to the criterion of
"well-established and world famous" collaborators and with
the low ranking they gave to the price criterion.

Looking at the extent of restrictive clauses in TCAs,
we find that all (100 per cent of the) SOEs had
restrictions, compared to 95 per cent of indigenously owned
private companies and a surprisingly low 25 per cent of the
subsidiaries. The only possible explanation for the low
prevalence of restrictive clauses in the case of TCAs of
subsidiaries is that formal imposition of such restrictions
on a subsidiary is usually not required, since the

Table 4.15

Number of foreign technical collaboration agreements,
by size and ownership of firm abroad and
by ownership category of Indian firm

Size/ownership of firm abroad	SOEs	Indigenous private firms	Subsidiaries
Small - private	13.6%	8.0%	2.0%
Large - private*	76.6%	92.0%	98.0%
Large - state-owned	9.8%	0. %	0. %
TOTAL	100.0%	100.0%	100.0%

Notes: * Includes parent companies of foreign subsidiaries.

Source: Interview data.

objectives of the subsidiary and its parent company are generally congruent.

Export restrictions were the most important for SOEs, followed by those on resale of technology to other firms (Table 4.16). In the case of the indigenously owned private companies, both were equally important. Tied machinery purchases do not turn out to be a significant restrictive clause in the case of any ownership category. Most firms were vehement about this -- the opinion usually expressed was that they would make sure that they had complete freedom in looking anywhere they wanted to for their machinery purchases.

This is consistent with the responses to the question on what proportion of TCAs **actually** involved machinery purchases from the collaborator. Of 14 firms that responded, 10 had negligible amounts of purchase from the collaborator, 2 had 10-25 per cent of their machinery purchases, and 2 had 100 per cent of their purchases from the collaborator. Of the last two, one was a subsidiary and the other, an SOE. But, in both cases, the explanation offered was that the machinery was purchased from the collaborator out of choice rather than necessity.

Table 4.16

Frequency of types of restrictions in foreign technical
collaboration agreements, by ownership category

Type of restrictions	SOEs	Indigenous private firms	Subsidiaries
Export	5	5	1
Resale of technology	4	5	1
Tied machinery and equipment purchases	1	0	0

Notes: Figures are the number of times restrictions were
cited as occurring by respondents.

Source: Interview data.

Use of Indigenous Technology

Of the 16 firms in our sample, only 3 had ever
acquired know-how from an Indian supplier. There was one
such firm in each ownership category. While the indigenous
private company had bought know-how from a local inventor,
the SOE had bought it from one of the national government
laboratories. The subsidiary had bought pharmaceuticals
know-how from a quasi-private sector research firm. Given
the size and number of research establishments in India,
this would appear to be a somewhat low number.

However, the firms in our sample purchased a
predominant share of their capital equipment from Indian
suppliers (Table 4.17). The percentage varies from 55 per
cent to 95 per cent across various industry and ownership
categories. In general, subsidiaries appear to purchase a
larger share of their capital equipment from domestic
suppliers -- across the three industry categories, the
number varies from 75 to 95 per cent. Indigenously owned
private companies buy between 65 and 90 per cent of their
capital equipment from domestic suppliers, while the share
for SOEs is between 55 and 85 per cent. Across industries,
the share of domestic capital purchases for heavy
electricals is low in general. While the share for
pharmaceuticals varies between 85 and 90 per cent and for
pumps and compressors between 80 and 95 per cent, the share

109

Table 4.17

Percentage of capital equipment bought from
Indian suppliers, by ownership category and industry

Industry	SOEs	Indigenous private firms	Subsidiaries
Pharmaceuticals	85	90	90
Pumps and compressors	85	80	95
Heavy electricals	65	55	75

Source: Interview data.

Table 4.18

Performance of Indian capital equipment suppliers
vis-à-vis their foreign counterparts,
by ownership category

Indigenous criterion	SOEs	Private firms	Subsidiaries
Quality	2.0	1.8	1.5
Timeliness of delivery	1.2	1.0	1.8
Price	3.0	2.3	2.5
Service and maintenance	1.6	2.0	1.8
Passing on improvements	1.3	1.7	1.7

Notes: A score of 2.0 implies "as good as", above 2.0 implies "better than", and below 2.0 implies "worse than".

Source: Interview data.

for heavy electricals is between 55 and 75 per cent. This is probably due to the greater technological sophistication of firms in this sector.

How do Indian suppliers of capital equipment compare with those from abroad in terms of factors like price and quality? Table 4.18 provides sample responses in terms of a single rank score. On the quality front, SOEs and indigenously owned private companies viewed local suppliers of capital equipment as being as good as foreign suppliers. Subsidiaries, however, perceived them as being slightly inferior on this count.

Indian suppliers perform quite poorly on "timeliness of delivery". All three ownership categories rated them worse than foreign suppliers on this count. However, Indian suppliers were seen to be superior to foreign suppliers as far as price was concerned. This may, however, be due to the stiff import tariffs on most imported machinery in India which provides domestic suppliers with a comfortable degree of price protection.

On service and maintenance, Indian suppliers were rated the same as foreign suppliers. However, on the attribute of "passing on improvements after purchase of equipment", they fared poorly.

Summary

Although the primary survey data cannot be used to make any rigorous comparisons between SOEs and POEs, one is nevertheless struck by the apparent similarities in the process and determinants of technology choice by the two types of firms. For instance, managers in both POEs and SOEs considered factors like newness and sophistication of the technology and the reputation of the technology supplier to be important in choosing foreign technology; on the other hand, considerations of cost and labour-absorbing capacity of the technology were treated as close to irrelevant by both sets of managers. Both SOEs and POEs seemed to follow extensive search procedures to locate foreign technology suppliers and to perform detailed cost-benefit calculations in choosing collaboration projects.

The similarities between SOE and POE managers in the motives and methods of technology choice apparent from the interview data are, however, in striking contrast to the differences in technology choice outcomes that are observed from the secondary data. The latter reveal greater inefficiency in capital and labour use (in the sense of larger capital/output and labour/output ratios) by SOEs relative to POEs. There is a problem here, of course, of distinguishing between the choice of inefficient techniques and inefficient operation of given techniques. The larger capital/output and labour/output ratios could imply either. In a very careful plant-level study of firms in the textile and pulp-paper industries in Colombia, Brazil, Indonesia, and the Philippines, Amsalem did not uncover any significant differences in the choice of technology made by foreign and local firms.[13] He observed a tendency, however, for government-owned firms in these countries to select capital-intensive technologies. It is not clear whether this is the case with our firm sample.

If SOE and POE managers follow broadly similar methods and criteria of selecting technologies, and yet SOEs exhibit larger capital/output and labour/output ratios than POEs, it follows that (i) the incentives (e.g. relative prices) that the two types of firms respond to are systematically different, and/or (ii) the final choice (and operation) of technology is determined more by bureaucratic and political interventions than by managerial decisions in SOEs. The latter possibility is not unknown in India. There have been numerous cases, some of which have turned into major press scandals, of SOEs being forced by government ministries to import a particular technology or select a specific collaborator after having gone through an elaborate search procedure. It is also not uncommon to find personnel managers in SOEs succumbing to political pressures for employment creation by hiring labour that is superfluous to the efficient operation of technology (thereby raising the labour/output ratio of SOEs relative to POEs). The former possibility, viz., of different prices of capital, is also very real. Many SOEs in India have in the past obtained capital from foreign donors which is tied to particular projects and is not available for alternative uses. Such capital has little, if any, cost to the firm.

It should, however, be realised that the inefficiency of SOEs may be exaggerated because they are subject to official price controls to a much greater extent than POEs. A controlled (and low) price of output would serve to reduce the value of production and artificially inflate the capital/output and labour/output ratios. The only way around this problem would be to calculate capital/output and labour/output ratios for SOEs and POEs at border (or world) prices. What our results basically suggest is that factors like inherent motivation-related inefficiency normally associated with SOE management are not likely to be very important in explaining the greater inefficiency of these enterprises. All of these findings have important implications for policy which we discuss in Section VI.

IV. TECHNOLOGY ASSIMILATION AND ADAPTATION

Introduction

Once the choice of a technology is finalised, there is
still the question of what a firm does with it. Does it
assimilate and absorb the technology? Does it constantly
improve upon the technology and adapt it to the local
environment to make it workable? Does it try to develop
the technology internally? Or does it keep the imported
technology as an expensive showpiece, left to become
obsolete?

These are important questions because technology is a
product that tends to become obsolete very soon, unless it
is constantly improved upon. Also, since most technology
is developed in the West, it needs to be adapted to the
factor proportions within the LDCs and to be scaled down
for their smaller, often less sophisticated markets.

Development of indigenous technological capacity
(sometimes, it would seem at any cost) is perceived by most
LDCs as a highly desirable goal. Technological
self-reliance and independence has been a paramount goal of
Indian industrial policy ever since the Industrial Policy
Resolution of 1956, the basic policy document guiding the
development of Indian industry. Technological self-
reliance does not mean autarky; it only means that the
recipient firm should have technological expertise which
allows it to exchange know-how with foreign firms on the
basis of equality rather than on the basis of dependency.
Furthermore, in a country like India, which has an abundant
supply of scientists and technologists, R & D work, besides
building up long-term indigenous technological capacity,
costs very little in terms of labour costs.

The problems of assimilation, absorption, and
adaptation of imported technology require considerable
attention, not all of which is available from the supplier
of the know-how and which, therefore, must also be provided
by the buyer. It is for this reason that the latter must
carry on some training and R & D work of its own to
supplement the input of the seller.

The buyer can speed up the processes of technological
assimilation by hiring the services of a large number of
foreign technicians from the foreign collaborator's plant,
sending engineers and technicians for training at the
collaborator's plant, establishing an R & D department to
deal specifically with product/process adaptation and
import substitution, and by generally expanding the R & D
budget. These requirements are, of course, bound to vary
with the particular technology and industry in question.
The more complex a technology, the greater will be the need

to hire the services of foreign technicians. Similarly, a technology being introduced for the first time in the country will necessitate sending a larger number of local technicians abroad for training.

It might be argued that Indian SOEs will devote greater effort to the assimilation and adaptation of foreign technology than POEs in the same industry. They are expected to help attain the state's objective of achieving complete self-reliance in the area of technology and know-how. It may also be argued that POEs have no such policy directive to follow, and they would, therefore, not go in for a similar intensive learning process. They would be motivated by immediate profit-maximising considerations which could (although not necessarily) work against the adoption of such long-term policy measures as technological self-reliance.

This argument is essentially a static argument. Development of indigenous technological capacity is not necessarily inconsistent with profit-maximising behaviour. A POE might be interested in building up its technological capability so as to have greater bargaining strength vis-à-vis the foreign collaborator in future business deals. Vaitsos' thesis that the payment for receiving know-how is an increasing function of the recipient's technological ignorance is pertinent to this issue.[14] The greater the degree of technological ignorance of a buyer vis-à-vis another, the higher will be the price charged to the buyer for the technology by the seller, the lesser would be the knowledge transmitted under the TCA, and the larger would be the number of restrictive clauses introduced into the TCA by the seller. In general, the enterprise's relative bargaining position vis-à-vis the seller would be weaker than that of the technologically more-capable and informed buyer negotiating against the same seller. It would, therefore, be in the buyer's interest to improve the enterprise's technological capabilities by means of personnel training and R & D.

Another latent benefit of research and adaptation, which is available to both SOEs and POEs, is reduction in plant and capital costs. Firms with research capabilities and experience in adaptation can buy second-hand machinery and be confident of making it work. Thus, on a priori grounds, it is not possible to say definitively that SOEs will fare better than POEs in assimilating and adapting foreign technology.

Secondary data

The RBI survey data used in the previous chapter can be used to compare the R & D and technology adaptation efforts of SOEs and similarly placed POEs, both indigenous and foreign-owned. Table 4.19 lists the industry-specific R & D expenditures of the two enterprise types as a percentage of value added over the period 1964-65 to 1969-70. The data indicate that, in six out of eight manufacturing industries, SOEs had a larger (much larger in several cases) ratio of R & D expenditure to value added than indigenously owned private companies or multinational subsidiaries. Comparing the latter two types of firms, subsidiaries had a larger ratio of R & D expenditure to value added than the indigenously owned private companies in seven manufacturing industries. In the remaining five industries, the reverse was true. On average, for the entire manufacturing sector, subsidiaries spent twice as much on R & D as a proportion of their value added as indigenously owned private companies.

RBI data are also available on the exchange of R & D personnel under foreign TCAs. Unfortunately, these are not available by industry. These data (Table 4.20) again indicate a high level of personnel exchange, both in absolute terms as well as per TCA, among SOEs relative to POEs. On average, each TCA in a SOE involved the exchange of 7.1 persons, as compared to 4.1 persons in the case of POEs. Among POEs, subsidiaries had the largest exchange of R & D personnel.

Thus, the data on R & D expenditures and personnel both suggest a greater effort at R & D and adaptation by SOEs relative to POEs. Does this effort result in more innovation being "produced" in these enterprises? We can answer this question by merging industry-specific ASI data used in the previous section with data on patents. While not all inventions are patented, especially in a country like India which does not have a system of utility models or "petty patents" (minor adaptive inventions), there is a large literature that treats patents as an intermediate output of inventive effort.[15] Besides, R & D expenditure data are simply not available at the 3-digit industry level for the period 1960-70 to match the ASI data.

The results in Table 4.7 suggest that only in the chemicals industry group is patenting significantly related to ownership. Interestingly, it is related negatively with foreign ownership and positively with state ownership in this industry group. The results are thus at least somewhat consistent with the data presented in Table 4.19 which suggest that SOEs spend a larger share of their value added on R & D than POEs. However, it was observed in Table 4.19 that, among POEs, subsidiaries spent more on R & D than indigenously owned private companies. Putting the results of Tables 4.7 and 4.19 together, then, it appears that, while subsidiaries may spend a larger share of their value added on R & D than indigenously owned private

Table 4.19

R&D expenditure on current account as percentage of value added of
collaborating enterprises, by ownership category and industry,
1964-65 to 1969-70

Industry	SOEs	Indigenous private firms	Subsidiaries
Manufacturing	7.9	3.6	7.7
- Foods, beverages, tobacco	-	0.	3.3
- Textile products	-	0.2	21.1
- Transport equipment	18.8	8.2	4.6
- Machinery and machine tools	6.4	1.6	5.9
- Metals and metal products	0	1.4	2.8
- Electrical goods and			
- Machinery	13.9	5.3	10.4

- Chemicals and allied products	24.5	15.9	15.4
- Basic industrial	21.9	0.1	11.8
- Pharmaceuticals	59.9	24.6	23.9
- Other allied	0.0	11.0	7.7
- Rubber goods	-	20.0	0.6
- Miscellaneous products	-	2.2	2.6
All industries (including not shown above)	7.6	3.6	7.3

Notes: - Indicates no presence in particular industry.

Source: Reserve Bank of India: Foreign Collaboration in Indian Industry - Survey Report, Bombay, 1974, pp. 43, 63, 77, 89 and 139.

companies, they tend to 'produce' fewer patentable inventions or they simply tend to underpatent their inventions.

Table 4.20

Number of personnel transferred under foreign technical collaboration agreements, by ownership category, 1969-1970

Personnel transfer	SOEs	Indigenous private firms	Subsidiaries
Total no. of personnel transferred	1,150	149	691
No. of personnel transferred per TCA	7.1	0.3	4.1

Notes: Number of personnel transferred includes number of foreign advisers received by firms and the number of Indian trainees sent abroad to the collaborator's plant.

Source: Reserve Bank of India: Foreign Collaboration in Indian Industry – Survey Report, Bombay, 1974, pp. 25-7, 50, 69, 84, and 93-4.

The strong finding that emerges from Table 4.7 is that indigenous inventive output is positively and significantly associated with the level of international inventive output, proxied by the cumulative number of patents granted in an industry in the United States during the previous five years. Earlier, we had noted the positive impact of international patenting on foreign technology imports of enterprises in India. The results for the patent equation thus suggest that local innovation (patenting) and foreign technology use are complements, not substitutes, of each other. In other words, before being applied successfully to production activities, foreign technology needs to be extensively worked on and adapted to local conditions. Thus, firms which import more foreign technology are also those that perform more R & D and patenting.

Patenting in the United States can have two opposite effects on patenting by firms in India. If United States patents are primarily used by multinational companies for blocking purposes in India, they will have an adverse effect on Indian patenting and innovation. However, United States patenting can also have a disclosure effect whereby Indian companies can learn of an invention which they would otherwise not have known about, modify it, and patent an adapted invention in India. (Disclosure, while required in patent documents, is often provided by the exposure of the product to the market.) By increasing the pool of knowledge from which to learn, imitate, and adapt, international inventions can have a positive effect on Indian inventive activity. The net effect of international inventive activity on Indian innovation will depend on the relative magnitudes of the blocking and disclosure effects. The positive association we have found between patenting in India and patenting in the United States indicates that the disclosure effect of United States patenting dominates the blocking effect.

Primary data

In this section, we examine the evidence from our primary survey on the following issues: presence of R & D departments, R & D objectives, R & D personnel, patenting behaviour, objectives of adaptive work, and the use of outside technologists and service support. We compare the performance of SOEs and POEs on these activities.

Presence and size of R & D divisions

Of the 16 firms interviewed, 15 have separate R & D divisions. The only firm that did not have one was a subsidiary in the pumps and compressors industry. In all of the 15 firms that had R & D divisions, respondents spoke about a fair degree of "developmental" work that also went on outside of their formalised R & D departments. While most of the firms had a single firm-wide R & D department, three firms in the sample had decentralised R & D units within each major company division.

We can get an idea of the sizes of the R & D divisions in the sample firms from Table 4.21 which shows the average number of full-time R & D personnel per firm by ownership and industry categories. Since the numbers from which the averages have been calculated have a very large variance (from a low of 0 in the case of some small private-sector firms to a high of 1,015 in the case of a large SOE in the heavy electricals industry), the averages presented should be interpreted with a great deal of caution. The data indicate that, in all three industries, SOEs have the largest number of R & D personnel, followed by indigenously owned private companies. Subsidiaries have the smallest average number of R & D employees. (These figures, however, exclude those persons whose work may be of an R & D nature but who do not belong to a formal R & D department. They also exclude part-time R & D workers.)

Table 4.21

Average number of full-time R&D personnel per firm, by industry and ownership category

Industry	SOEs	Indigenous private firms	Subsidiaries
Pharmaceuticals	170	153	26
Pumps & compressors	650	12	0
Heavy electricals	608	80	74

Source: Interview data.

The large number of R & D employees in the SOEs may simply reflect the larger size of these enterprises relative to POEs. To control for size differences, we have calculated the number of full-time R & D personnel as a percentage of the total number of employees in an enterprise. Even according to this indicator of relative size of the R & D division, SOEs come out on top, with 2.2 per cent of their employees in R & D divisions. The indigenously owned private companies and subsidiaries have equal percentages of R & D personnel of 0.8 per cent each. In terms of R & D expenditure per R & D employee, however, subsidiaries rank highest, spending Rs. 328,000 on average for each R & D employee, followed by the indigenously owned private companies, which spend an average of Rs. 211,840 per R & D employee. SOEs perform quite poorly, spending only Rs. 128,000 per R & D employee.

Almost all R & D personnel in all ownership categories and industries had at least a bachelor's degree. In three companies, all personnel had postgraduate or doctoral degrees. These companies were not confined to any particular industry. Two other firms had 70 postgraduate or doctoral degree holders on their R & D staff. In general, the level of education of R & D personnel is not related to either ownership category or industry.

R & D objectives

One way of knowing how firms view R & D would be to see how clearly and precisely their R & D objectives are formulated. Most of the firms in our sample had clear-cut R & D goals. We attempted to rank the importance given by our respondents to each of the following four R & D goals: import substitution, new product development, process improvements, and innovations, recognising the fact that these goals are not mutually exclusive and often go together. The summary of rankings and scores received for each of the goals is shown in Table 4.22. For the corporate sector as a whole, process improvement emerges as the most important R & D goal, followed closely by import substitution, and new product development; producing innovations ranks the lowest.

The rankings differ across the three ownership categories as well as industries. Import substitution is the top priority in the case of SOEs and (surprisingly) subsidiaries, while the indigenously owned private companies rank process improvement as the highest goal of their R & D effort. Innovations are uniformly low in the rankings of all three enterprise types. Finally, in the pharmaceuticals and heavy electricals industries, process improvement ranks as the most important goal, while, in the pumps and compressors industry, import substitution is seen as being most important.

The overall ranking of R & D goals also indicates the nature of R & D investments and skills that are required by firms. For instance, process improvements and import substitution require the least amount of R & D investments and skills, since they involve adaptive research and developmental work. On the other hand, producing innovations requires basic R & D and therefore greater levels of R & D investments and skills.

The typical R & D decision-making process as practiced in firms runs as follows: initial inputs into R & D are primarily determined on the basis of market conditions and financial viability ("market research" and "feasibility study"); from then on, R & D follows various stages, the important ones being design and assembly of working prototypes, specification verifications, assembly of prototypes, testing and field trials, documentation for production, and, finally, commercial production.

Patenting behaviour

Patenting on any appreciable scale has been a recent phenomenon in all the firms for whom data were available. However, most firms have developed several products and processes over the years that they considered patentable. The number of patentable products or processes was the highest in the case of indigenously owned private companies

Table 4.22

Importance of various R&D objectives -- scores received by different objectives, by ownership category and industry

Industry	SOEs	Indigenous private firms	Subsidiaries	All firms
Pharmaceuticals	PRI (3)	PRI (3)	PRI (3)	PRI (3)
	ISU (2)	ISU (3)	ISU (3)	ISU (2.8)
	NPD (2)	NPD (2)	NPD (3)	NPD (2.3)
	PIN (2)	PIN (0)	PIN (2)	PIN (1)
Pumps & compressors	ISU (3)	ISU (3)		ISU (3)
	NPD (3)	NPD (3)		NPD (3)
	PRI (3)	PIN (3)		PRI (2.7)
	PIN (0)	PRI (2.5)		PIN (2)

Heavy electricals	ISU (3)	PRI (2.7)	PRI (3)	PRI (2.7)
	NPD (3)	NPD (2.3)	ISU (3)	ISU (2.4)
	PRI (2.5)	PIN (2)	PIN (1.5)	NPD (2.1)
	PIN (2.5)	ISU (1.7)	NPD (1)	PIN (2)
All Three Industries	ISU (2.8)	PRI (2.7)	ISU (3)	PRI (2.6)
	NPD (2.8)	ISU (2.4)	PRI (3)	ISU (2.5)
	PRI (2.8)	NPD (2.4)	NPD (1.7)	NPD (2.2)
	PIN (1.8)	PIN (1.8)	PIN (1.7)	PIN (1.6)

Notes: PRI=Process Improvement, ISU=Import Substitution, NPD=New Product Development, PIN=Producing Innovations. Higher scores indicate greater importance of an objective. Scores are: 3=Very Important, 2=Important, 1=Somewhat Important, 0=Not Important.

Source: Interview data.

-- it ranged from 5 to 150. It was much lower (from 2 to 15 patentable products or processes) for SOEs. The subsidiaries had the lowest number of patentable developments, ranging from merely 2 to 5.

Of course, since there is likely to be a great deal of subjective bias in people's assessment of a patentable development, these numbers do not necessarily reflect the true distribution of inventive output across ownership categories. The number of patents actually granted may be a more objective indicator of the quality of inventive output. However, we were unable to collect data of reliable quality on the number of products and processes actually patented by firms.

There appears to be no relationship between the number of R & D personnel in a firm and the number of patentable products/processes it had developed. Similarly, the number of patentable products/processes developed by a firm did not vary appreciably across industries.

Until recently, the trend among our sample firms was not to bother with patenting formalities. One reason why the firms had hitherto not considered patenting an important activity is related to rigid industrial licensing laws in India. Industrial licenses restrict the type, size, number, and range of products that large Indian companies can manufacture. Thus, even if a firm was to develop a new product or process, the chances that a competitor would imitate and manufacture it would be rather small, since the competitor would have to go through a long and complicated bureaucratic process to obtain a government license to manufacture the product. Of course, small firms in the unregistered sector, who are not subject to industrial licensing rules, could imitate and manufacture the product, but their scale of operations would be too small for them to be a major threat to the larger firms.

Also, recall that our sample firms had ranked development of new products and innovations generally low on their list of R & D priorities. As such, the typical product and process used by these firms is unlikely to be innovative and patentable in the first place.

To assess the relevance of firms' R & D efforts to their operations, we obtained information on what percentage of the patentable developments referred to above had been incorporated by firms into their product lines. The indigenously owned private companies had incorporated between 50 and 100 per cent of their new developments in their product lines, with the average being 78 per cent (Table 4.23). The SOEs had incorporated between 35 and 100 per cent of their developments, with the average being 66 per cent, while the subsidiaries had incorporated all their significant R & D outputs into their product lines, at least in the heavy electricals industry -- the only industry for which data were available for subsidiaries.

Table 4.23

Range of percentages of patentable developments
actually incorporated into product lines, by industry
and ownership category

Industry	SOEs	Indigenous private firms	Subsidiaries
Pharmaceuticals	35–100	100	n.a.
Pumps & compressors	100	60–65	n.a.
Heavy electricals	90–95	50–100	100

Notes: n.a. = not available.

Source: Interview data.

Focus of adaptive work

We attempted to examine, in somewhat greater detail, the kind of adaptive work that was undertaken by the sample firms on their imported technologies. Across ownership categories, there is remarkable consistency in the responses. The most important type of adaptive work was "adjustment for different quality of raw materials", followed by "adapting the product to local demand conditions". "Scaling the technology down" was the third most important factor, followed by "adaptation to the work habits of the local work force". "Increasing labour intensity" was given the lowest ranking -- most firms regarded this as a totally irrelevant factor.

When the data are broken down by industry, the pattern changes. "Adjusting for quality of raw materials" is the most important aspect of adaptive work in the pharmaceuticals and heavy electricals industries, but it is ranked second in the pumps and compressors industry. In heavy electricals, both "adjustment to suit local demand conditions" and "scaling the technology down" rank as important as "adjustment for different quality of raw materials". "Scaling down technology" ranks relatively low in the pharmaceuticals and pumps and compressors industries. "Adaptation to the work habits of the local

125

work force" ranks about midway in all three industries. "Increasing labour intensity" is again seen as a uniformly irrelevant consideration in adaptive work in all industries.

The overall importance given to adaptation of imported technology to local raw materials availability is understandable, given the strict import controls on intermediate goods in India. Materials optimisation, therefore, becomes quite important for most firms. The relevance of adapting the product to local demand conditions stems from the differing consumption needs in India. For example, in the pharmaceuticals industry, formulations have to take into account certain biological and climatological factors that influence drug efficacy in different areas of the world. In industries such as heavy electricals and pumps and compressors, user needs with respect to tolerance levels, robustness, climatological factors, quality of maintenance, and repair sources are all important determinants of different demand conditions.

One would presume that scaling down the technology would have been an important part of adaptive work, given the generally small scale of production of most products in India. Of course, exports can expand the limited size of the domestic market and hence the scale of production, but few of the sample firms had significant exports. The low ranking for this activity may be reflecting a number of factors. For example, a few respondents mentioned that technology is usually purchased in a scaled-down form already. Second, as a respondent in a multinational subsidiary suggested, some firms may go in for technology of an earlier generation, which is usually on a lower scale of operations anyway.

The Indian work force was uniformly regarded by the sample firms as being accomplished and of high quality in terms of its capacity to adapt to the needs of a given technology. Most of the companies also had well-established training facilities to train labour to operate imported new technologies. As a result, adaptation of imported technologies to suit the work habits of the local work force was not cited as an important aspect of adaptive work by most respondents.

Use of outside technologists and service support

Of the 16 firms interviewed, 10 had used or continue to use the services of scientists and technologists from outside the firm to assist in R & D work. While three out of the five SOEs and seven out of the eight indigenously owned private companies use outside assistance, only one out of four subsidiaries do so. In almost all the cases, however, the use of outside assistance was mentioned to be of a supportive nature rather than full time.

Of the 10 firms who had used outside support, eight

had used government laboratories, six had used educational institutions (typically, the Indian Institutes of Technology), and five had used local private consultants. Only one company had used another company (a supplier) as a source of R & D support.

All 16 firms in the sample reported using engineers and scientists within the company for adaptation, modification, and trouble-shooting work. Only two companies (one in the state sector and one in the indigenous private sector) had used a foreign consultant. Firms thus appear to be virtually self-sufficient in terms of the personnel required for adaptation and modification of technology.

Interestingly, in relation to servicing contracts, only five out of the 16 sample firms had entered into service contracts with their foreign suppliers. Out of the five, one firm had entered into contracts only for machine tool imports and two others, only during the warranty period. Across-the-board service contracts were entered into only by two firms -- a subsidiary in the pumps and compressors industry and a SOE in the pharmaceuticals industry. The primary reasons why the sample firms did not bother with service contracts were (i) they regarded their own engineers as being adequately trained and competent to service foreign equipment, and (ii) they regarded service contracts offered by the suppliers as being too expensive.

Summary

The secondary data reveal both greater R & D effort as well as more patenting (at least in the chemical sector) in SOEs than in similarly placed POEs. The primary interview data also show that, among all the sample firms, SOEs have the largest number of R & D employees per firm as well as the largest ratio of R & D employees to total employees. (Note that the latter comparison may not necessarily be valid beyond our sample.)

The level of R & D effort is likely to be greater in SOEs than in POEs for a relatively simple reason: the average SOE tends to be larger in size than the average POE in a given industry. While we have held size constant in our comparisons by using indicators like the ratio of R & D expenditure to total value added and the ratio of R & D employees to total employees, it is likely that even the relative size of the R & D and technology adaptation effort is correlated positively with firm size. A survey of Indian firms engaged in foreign technology purchases found this to be the case, and concluded that "... large firms employ technical staff to supply a good deal of their requirements of technology, and go out to buy technology when either their staff or their R & D facilities cannot generate it, while small firms have to rely more heavily on purchases of technology ... The import content of technology thus decreases with the size of the firm".[16] The positive correlation between firm size and the share of R & D expenditure in sales turnover is a common empirical finding in the developed countries as well.[17]

Although the level of the R & D and technology adaptation effort is greater in SOEs than in POEs, the interview data suggest that the nature of this effort is very similar across SOEs and POEs. For example, managers in both types of firms who were interviewed regarded import substitution and process improvement as important goals of R & D. There was also remarkable consistency across the ownership categories in ranking the objectives of technology adaptation work.

V. TECHNOLOGY DIFFUSION

From a social point of view, the purpose of assimilating and indigenously producing foreign technology is to make it available to a larger number of domestic firms at lower cost. Firms that acquire technology from abroad, therefore, have to be judged also by their efforts at diffusing the know-how they acquire and assimilate to other firms in the industry.

Technology can be diffused from large enterprises to small firms in a number of ways. The large firm can sell the technology outright to the small firm or license it over a period of time. Another important avenue of diffusion is via a subcontracting relationship. Under such a relationship, the large firm engages small ancillary units to supply custom-made components and parts to it. In return, it provides the know-how, manufacturing specifications, and quality control specifications to the ancillary unit. In some cases, the large firm may have to assist the ancillary with other inputs like raw materials, credit, and financial assistance from financial institutions.

Technology Sale and Licensing Agreements: Data on the sale of technology to firms within and outside India are presented by ownership category and by industry in Tables 4.24 and 4.25. Approximately the same percentage of sample SOEs and indigenously owned private companies (about 60 per cent) reported transferring technologies through sale agreements within India. None of the sample subsidiaries had sold technologies to other firms in India. Surprisingly, as many as 40 per cent of the sample SOEs and 43 per cent of the sample indigenously owned private companies had sold technology to firms outside India, while only 25 per cent of the sample subsidiaries had done so.

Table 4.24

Percentage of firms in each ownership category selling
technology to other firms within and outside India

Technology sales	SOEs	Private firms	Subsidiaries
Within India	60	57	0
Outside India	40	43	25

Source: Interview data.

What is interesting to note is that most of the technology sales to firms within India, from both the SOEs and the indigenously owned private companies, had been to firms in the public or "joint" sector (i.e. ventures floated jointly by private and government sectors). Firms in the private sector typically entered into royalty agreements (and, in some cases, marketing tie-ups). However, most firms admitted that the income derived from their sales of technology was insignificant in relation to their total sales turnover. A senior executive of one indigenously owned private company even went so far as to say that his firm sold technology to other firms in India only when the technology had reached a "discard" stage in the production process in terms of cost and efficiency.

One of the subsidiaries in the heavy electricals industry had an opportunity to sell technology when it was forced to divest its holdings due to government foreign exchange regulations. The firm decided to set up an 'Indian' company, transferred its personnel wholesale to the new company, and then entered into a marketing agreement whereby the new company would sell its product to the subsidiary, and the subsidiary, in turn, would sell the product under its own brand name. Under the agreement, the subsidiary supplied the new company with technical know-how at a certain price.

Foreign sales of technology by the sample firms have largely been channelled via turnkey contracts to state-controlled projects in other countries. Most such contracts were won by the Indian firms through the international bidding process. Almost all such sales have been to other LDCs in Southeast Asia, the Middle East, and Africa. The relatively large number of sample firms engaged in technology exports agrees with the evidence presented by Lall on technology exports being an increasingly important activity in India.[18]

Industry trends (Table 4.25) indicate that the heavy electricals industry has had the largest extent of technology sales, followed by pharmaceuticals. Technology sales in the pumps and compressors industry have been limited. Further, technology sales in heavy electricals have largely been domestic sales, while technology sales in pharmaceuticals have been largely foreign sales.

Table 4.25

Percentage of firms in each industry selling
technology to other firms within and outside India

Technology sales	Pharma-ceuticals	Pumps and compressors	Heavy electricals
Within India	20	25	71
Outside India	60	0	43

Source: Interview data.

Subcontracting

Subcontractual relationships are more widely prevalent than technology sales in the Indian corporate sector. Subcontracting typically involves the manufacture of components and subassemblies by ancillary small-scale industrial units for large companies in the organised sector.

Of the 16 firms interviewed, 13 reported that they "often" or "always" subcontracted the manufacture of subassemblies and components to small-scale ancillary units. The three that "rarely" or "occasionally" did were all in the pharmaceuticals industry. This is understandable, because the scope for subcontracting subassemblies, parts, and components is limited in the pharmaceuticals industry because of the nature of manufacturing in that industry.

All 13 of the firms that used subcontracting reported that they 'always' or "often" provided their ancillary units with the technical know-how required to manufacture the part. There was no difference between industry and ownership categories on this point.

Subcontracting is determined as much by government regulations as by the independent decisions of large firms. A large number of products that can be classified as "low-technology" products are explicitly reserved by the GOI for the small-scale unorganised sector. Existing capacity in large-scale units for such products has been practically frozen since the last decade, and the only avenue for large firms to keep up their production is through the development of ancillary units.

Another reason given for using subcontracting lies in the problems, as perceived by large firms, of managing additional labour. As a way of saving the costs and difficulties associated with unionised labour, many large firms subcontract to smaller ancillary units that, being in the unorganised sector, typically have non-unionised labour.

Most of the firms in our sample go further than merely providing their ancillary units with technical know-how. All indigenously owned private companies and subsidiaries provided their ancillary units with detailed design and raw materials, as opposed to only 60 and 80 per cent, respectively, of the SOEs. Similarly, 60 and 66 per cent of the indigenously owned private companies and subsidiaries provided their ancillary units with credit, while none of the SOEs did so.

Industry-specific data show that the level of assistance to ancillary units is quite low in the pharmaceuticals industry but rather high in both the pumps and compressors and heavy electricals industries.

A couple of firms in the sample mentioned that they also provided services and equipment relating to inspection and quality control to their ancillary units. Finally, at least six sample firms had formalised vendor development programmes and schemes to encourage their staff to become entrepreneurs by setting up small-scale ancillary units.

How do firms effect transfer of know-how to ancillary units? In most cases, the relationship between firms and their ancillary units relies on mutual understanding and familiarity in dealing with each other over time. Only two of the firms had formalised contractual agreements with their ancillary suppliers, and one of them admitted that such agreements were difficult to enforce. The sample firms keep in close touch with their ancillary units by having their engineers and inspectors visit the units regularly for quality control and other checks.

With the exception of one firm, none appeared to be bothered by the possibilities of misuse of technical know-how by the ancillary units. Some respondents were aware of the fact that the know-how they supplied to ancillaries was sometimes resold to other small-scale firms, but they did not feel that this practice was pervasive enough to merit closer control or legal action. Also, some of the respondents felt that the resale of know-how per se, without the service and systems support that the large firms are capable of offering, would not be sustainable in the long run. The only firm that appeared to be bothered by this possibility took care of the problem by finely subdividing components and tasks among several ancillary units in such a manner that no single ancillary unit would gain from reselling the know-how for a particular component.

To summarise, with the exception of technical assistance provided by firms to their ancillary units via subcontracting, there is relatively little inter-firm transfer or diffusion of technology among our sample firms. The little technology transfer that does take place involves technologies that have reached a discard stage. Yet a surprisingly (relatively) large number of our sample firms export technology to other countries -- a finding that agrees with the evidence presented by Lall on the recent growth of technology exports from India.[19] These findings suggest that the technologies imported into and adapted in India find their way to third-country firms rather than to smaller firms within India. This has implications for policy which we discuss in Section VI.

Across ownership categories, technology sales to other firms in India are almost equally common among sample SOEs and indigenously owned private companies, but are totally absent among subsidiaries of multinational corporations. The extent of subcontracting does not vary across ownership categories, with virtually all of the sample firms engaging in substantial subcontracting. However, SOEs appear to provide slightly less support to ancillary units than do POEs.

VI. POLICY IMPLICATIONS

Our findings in this paper have several important implications for policy. First, our study suggests that the greater observed (capital and labour) inefficiency of SOEs in technology choice and/or technology operation is more likely to be the result of political interventions in their technology choice/operation decisions and differential relative prices of capital than the result of inherent motivational differences between SOE and POE managers. In fact, we found managers in both types of enterprises following very similar methods and criteria of selecting technologies. Incidentally, one reason for the similarity in management techniques is that increasingly the managers of SOEs are drawn from the same pool of candidates upon which POEs draw: graduates of business schools like the prestigious Indian Institutes of Management, and not ex-civil servants and bureaucrats.

What our findings suggest then is the need for greater autonomy for SOEs from their parent ministries in matters of both technology choice as well as operation. There have been numerous cases in India where parent ministries have imposed their choice of a particular foreign technology or a particular foreign collaborator on a SOE against the latter's best judgement. SOEs are also frequently subject to political pressures for employment creation, which means that they have to hire labour superfluous to the efficient operation of their chosen technologies. This sometimes introduces divergences in the technology choice and operation processes. For example, the SOE managers who were concerned with technology choice decisions listed labour absorptiveness of a technology to be an almost irrelevant criterion for technology selection (as did POE managers). Yet political pressure could persuade a personnel or plant manager in charge of operations to hire workers superfluous to the efficient operation of the same capital-intensive technology.

The greater capital-intensity of SOEs vis-à-vis POEs may also be due in part to the favourable prices they often face for capital. Soft government loans for capital purchases and foreign tied-aid project funds are examples of policies which distort the price of capital to SOEs and encourage inefficient technology choice and/or inefficient operation of technology.

A second implication for policy emerges from our observation that management in both SOEs and POEs generally gave great importance to the 'newness' and 'modernnesss' of the technology being imported and to the international reputation of the seller. On the other hand, cost considerations were cited as being relatively unimportant in the choice of a technology. Further, the employment-generating potential of a technology was regarded by most firms as a largely irrelevant consideration in technology choice. The latter finding is somewhat disturbing, especially in a labour-surplus country like India, but it probably reflects the distortion in government policies. Tax benefits and loan policies in India favour capital-intensive technology imports. Very few, if any, financial institutions give loans for training workers and enhancing their productivity. Respondents also felt that labour laws in India are often anti-employer rather than pro-employee; this results in employers deliberately going in for capital-intensive and labour-saving technologies.

A third implication for policy arises out of the complementarities observed between technology imports and technology production in the industry-level econometric analysis presented in Section IV. Out of a total of five exogenous variables included (viz. the level of international inventive activity, presence of foreign firms, presence of SOEs, fixed capital stock, and output), three in the light industry and chemical sectors and all five in the engineering sectors had the same-signed effects on both technology imports and domestic patenting. In other words, factors which result in larger technology imports by firms also appear to result in more technology adaptation and R & D being done by these firms. This suggests that Indian firms view technology imports not as a substitute for their own research effort but as complementary to it. Firms that have research and adaptation capabilities tend to import separate bits of technology, such as patents and pre-investment services, and put these bits together using their own technical staff. At the same time, firms that have had substantial experience with imported technology are likely to know more about these technologies and be in a better position to carry out adaptation and R & D work. The NCAER survey, referred to earlier, observed this process of learning in its sample of firms: "... firms learnt about technology by importing it, and their later imports included more advanced technology".[20]

If there are obvious complementarities between technology imports and technology adaptation/R & D, and the objectives of policy are to encourage more research and adaptation in India, the Government should be more flexible about technology imports than it has been in the past. There are currently ad hoc restrictions on the quantity and nature of technology imports, with the Government employing an elaborate system of screening foreign technical collaboration proposals. The NCAER study recommended abolishing such controls and replacing them perhaps with a new system of corporate taxes.

Finally, our results with respect to diffusion raise a fourth implication for policy. We observed a very low level of technology transfer (to other firms in India) from all our sample firms, but particularly from the sample subsidiaries. In 1971, the NCAER study had come up with a similar finding: it had come across only one case of intercorporate licensing within the country.

Sublicensing of imported technology is extremely important for an LDC because it brings down the average costs of technology imports (assuming these are paid in a lump-sum) by spreading them over a larger output. Sublicensing of technology can be encouraged by a more rational royalty and tax structure which distinguishes between royalties paid by an Indian licensee to a foreign firm and royalties paid by an Indian sublicensee to the original Indian licensee. There is currently no law governing the transfers of technology among Indian firms. The NCAER study mentions that the Ministry of Industry insists on scaling down royalty rates payable to Indian companies just as it would with royalty rates payable to foreign companies.

In recent years the Government has been offering tax concessions on royalty income earned by an Indian company from technology licensing within the country: a rebate of 40 per cent is given on such income (NCAER, 1971). Also, royalty income (as well as dividend income) from abroad received by an Indian company engaged in technology exports (and foreign investment) are free of tax. The differential treatment of royalty income from within the country and from abroad may help explain the rapid growth of technology exports by Indian firms in recent years -- a finding discussed by Lall.[21]

The case for strengthening the rebate on royalties paid within India can be best made by quoting the NCAER study:

"One of the strongest forces behind international transfer of technology is tariff and quota restrictions on the transfer of goods. This factor is missing in the case of a country's internal trade. Within the country there is free trade, and there is no discrimination in favour of trade in technology. Hence rather pronounced fiscal incentives might be necessary to encourage the latter. We would suggest that the special 25 per cent rate of tax on inter-corporate dividends be extended to technological payments within the country as well".[22]

APPENDIX A

Data sources for regression analysis data

1. Data on amounts of production labour, nonproduction labour, and fuel consumed; value of gross output; amount of fixed capital stock; wage rates for production and nonproduction labour; and the number of firms in each industry were obtained from various issues of Annual Survey of Industries.
2. Data on technology imports and on foreign equity shares in various industries were obtained from the Reserve Bank of India (1968) and the Reserve Bank of India (1974).
3. Data on the fuel price index were obtained from India, Planning Commission, Statistics and Surveys Division: Basic Statistics Relating to the Indian Economy 1950-51 to 1970-71, New Delhi, 1972.
4. Data on the share of the public sector in the output of each industry were obtained from the Commerce Yearbook of the Public Sector, Bombay, Commerce Publications, 1974.
5. Data on the number of patents granted in the United States were obtained, tabulated by industry, directly from the U.S. Patent Office.
6. Data on patenting by nationals in India were hand-tabulated from actual patent applications on file at the New Delhi office of the Indian Patent Office.

NOTES AND REFERENCES

*   Comments by Jeffrey James and Susumu Watanabe are gratefully acknowledged.

1. P. Evans (1977): "Multinationals, state-owned corporations and the transformation of imperialism: A Brazilian case study, in Economic Development and Cultural Change, Chicago, Vol. 26, Nov.

2. Commerce Research Bureau (1980): Basic statistics relating to the Indian economy, Bombay, Commerce Publications.

3. Government of India (GOI) (1979): Annual Report on the Working and Administration of the Company Act 1977-78, Department of Company Affairs, Ministry of Law, Justice and Company Affairs, New Delhi.

4. Government of India (GOI) (1980b): Annual Report 1978-79, Department of Company Affairs, Ministry of Law, Justice and Company Affairs, New Delhi.

5. Government of India (GOI) (1980a): Annual Report 1978-79, Department of Industry, New Delhi.

6. UNCTAD (1977): Case studies in the transfer of technology: The pharmaceutical industry in India, paper prepared by the Jawaharlal Nehru University and the Indian Council of Scientific and Industrial Research, Number TD/B/C.6/20.

7. R. Vernon (1977): State-owned enterprises in the international economic system: A prospectus, Harvard Business School, Boston (mimeo), pp. 8-9.

8. Harvey Leibenstein (1976): Beyond economic man: A new foundation for microeconomics, Cambridge, Massachusetts, Harvard University Press.

9. B. Vermeulen and R. Sethi (1982): "Labour-management conflict resolution in state-owned enterprises: A comparison of public- and private-sector practices in India." In L. P. Jones, ed.: Public enterprise in less-developed countries. New York, Cambridge University Press.

10. L.P. Jones and E.S. Mason (1982): "Role of economic factors in determining the size and structure of the public-enterprise sector in less-developed countries with mixed economies", in L. P. Jones (ed.) op. cit., p. 30.

11. M. Kidron (1965): Foreign investment in India, London, Oxford University Press, p. 263.

12. V.N. Balasubramanyam (1973): International transfer of technology to India, New York, Praeger, p. 16.

13. M.A. Amsalem (1983): Technology choice in developing countries: The textile and pulp and paper industry, Cambridge, Massachusetts, MIT Press.

14. C. Vaitsos (1974): Intercountry income distribution and transnational enterprises, Oxford, Clarendon Press.

15. M. Kamien and N. Schwartz (1975): "Market structure and innovation: A survey", in Journal of Economic Literature, Nashville, Tennessee, Vol. 13, Mar.
16. National Council of Applied Economic Research (NCAER) (1971): Foreign technology and investment: A study of their role in India's industrialisation, New Delhi, pp. 17-18.
17. Kamien and Schwartz, op. cit.
18. S. Lall (1982): Developing countries as exporters of technology: A first look at the Indian experience, London, Macmillan.
19. Ibid.
20. National Council of Applied Economic Research, op. cit.
21. Lall, op. cit.
22. National Council of Applied Economic Research, op. cit., p. 80.

Chapter 5

Technological Behaviour of Argentine Public Enterprises: The Case of Yacimientos Petrolíferos Fiscales

Jorge Lucángeli

I. INTRODUCTION

The principal aim of this paper is to analyse the economic and technological performance of the industrial activities of the state-owned enterprise – Yacimientos Petrolíferos Fiscales (YPF) – responsible for the overall oil cycle in Argentina.[1] This cycle consists basically of three stages or activities: (a) the extraction stage, whose main functions are oil exploration, drilling and production; (b) industrialisation, which consists of the raw material's transformation into by-products, and is carried out in the refineries and (c) the sale or marketing of the goods obtained and/or imported. A complementary activity that should be mentioned is transport, of both oil and by-products.

Interest in studying this enterprise does not arise exclusively from the successive changes that have occurred in the petroleum industry in recent years. Certain features of the oil by-products industry make it a very attractive candidate for analysis. These include: (i) the fact that in Argentina, as in most Latin American countries, the oil industry is to a large extent monopolised by or centralised in a large-scale state enterprise; (ii) the importance of fuel prices as a cost factor in all other manufacturing and service activities; (iii) the high growth rate in the demand for by-products; (iv) the high productivity per employee shown by this branch of industry in all countries; and (v) the concentration of the world supply of technology. To the foregoing should be added that it is not only the largest public enterprise but the leading enterprise among all firms in Argentina.

Our field of analysis is to be restricted to the industrialisation stage; that is, to YPF's refining activities. For the purpose of our study it was necessary to limit the areas of the enterprise. After exploration, drilling and the production of oil, refining is the most important activity in the state-owned enterprise and offers the advantage that it is possible to investigate the different performances of public and private enterprise, since some private firms are also involved in this activity. If the amount of petroleum processed annually is taken as an indicator of market share, the state-owned enterprise processed between 57 and 75 per cent of total crude oil in the past three decades. The other firms that hold leading positions are subsidiaries of two of the largest companies in the world petroleum business: Esso and Shell. Between the two of them they have absorbed amounts fluctuating between 22 and 40 per cent of processed petroleum (domestic and imported), in fairly similar proportions over time. The remaining amount, which has always been less than 10 per cent (and has tended towards values of around 3 per cent over the last decade), has been processed by five or six companies.[2]

Two kinds of behaviour can be distinguished in the analysis: short-term, when companies make adjustments and modifications to the output-mix and/or the amount of crude oil processed, maintaining a fixed capital equipment endowment and acting on plant flexibility. In the long-term analysis we attempt to explain the companies' decision to incorporate new equipment, taking into account the cost of capital goods and their relation to the value of crude oil and the companies' expectations with regard to the future development of the economy and the relative prices in the sector.

II. SHORT-RUN BEHAVIOUR MODEL

In order to investigate short-run behaviour we need to define a technical indicator that will enable us to label the refineries' different output-mix options. This indicator - the "conversion ratio" - measures the proportion of each of the five main distillates - petrol, diesel fuel, kerosene, distilled fuel oil and residual fuel oil - that each company obtains year by year from a total amount of processed crude oil. In the model this is the dependent variable and is linked mainly to the relative retained value of the distillates and to the firms' refining capacity utilisation rate. (The former independent variable is the amount retained for the refinery after various taxes are deducted from the retail price of distillates.)

In this initial formulation, the central hypothesis of this case-study asserts that the private companies - Esso and Shell - have evidenced a different behaviour from the state-owned enterprise - Yacimientos Petrolíferos Fiscales. During the entire period under study (namely, the past 30 years) the oil refining firms were faced with regulations that affected their conduct: the prices of both distillates and crude oil were fixed by the Energy Secretariat and this body was also responsible for the crude oil quota allocation - for both local and imported oil - to the companies in the sector.

Given the two restrictions noted, the enterprises could act neither as price nor quantity fixers, since in both cases, these were parameters. From the foregoing, it follows that the only thing the firms could do to maximise profits under these restrictions was to take measures in relation to the output-mix they were to produce. Given a quantity of crude oil and a particular ratio between the retained values of the distillates, the companies were in a position to adjust the mix of distillates, if their objective was to maximise profits.

Whereas the private companies were able to follow the course described above, the same did not occur in the case of the state-owned enterprise, since the latter had to act under an additional restriction: that of supplying excess distillate demand. These deficits resulted from two types of factors: (i) distillates' prices did not reflect their relative scarcities. It was the case rather that prices of distillates were kept artificially low through subsidies; (ii) as the private companies adjusted their output-mix to the relative retained values, the markets for the less profitable distillates ran short of supplies and the gap had to be filled by YPF at the request of the Energy Secretariat. The state-owned enterprise was thus forced to maximise production of the distillates whose demand was not met.

At this point, the case-study's hypothesis regarding the different behaviour of the state-owned enterprise and the private companies can be explained in greater detail. Whereas in the case of Shell and Esso, the relative retained values and the amount of crude oil available had a greater effect on the choice of output-mix, in the case of the state-owned enterprise the output-mix was determined by the excess demand for those distillates. Therefore, whereas the private companies tended to maximise profits, YPF was unable to follow a similar course, leading to a non-optimum economic outcome in most cases.

In the short-run, one characteristic of the technology of the refining industry acquires great importance. The oil refining process allows a certain amount of flexibility with regard to the choice of output-mix. That is, a particular quantity of crude oil can give variable proportions of distillates, within certain limits. Given a fixed capital equipment, flexibility appears mainly in two ways: (i) in topping as well as in the secondary processes, different by-product fractions can be obtained from the same volume of processed crude oil. This means that it is possible to process a greater proportion of light and intermediate distillates at the cost of the heavy distillates and vice versa. (ii) in the over-design that generally occurs in topping. As the crude oil must pass through this unit in the first stage, it is usually over-sized in comparison with the secondary process capacity, so that it does not become a refinery bottleneck. Once the secondary process capacity is filled, more oil can be processed by passing the excess crude oil through the topping process. The result is a lower conversion ratio (in terms of light distillates), since topping produces a high proportion of residual fuel oil or reduced crude oil.

In short, the refinery can alter its output-mix - given a certain amount of crude oil - by varying the distillate fractions in the primary and the conversion ratio, since greater usage of topping capacity means reducing the proportion of light and intermediate distillates.

With regard to the conversion ratio, the opportunity cost of keeping certain secondary processes partially out of action will determine its minimum limit. It can be said - in general - that a more complex refinery allows a greater degree of flexibility, due to the possibilities offered by the secondary processing equipment and the greater variety of distillates that can be obtained.[3]

This short-run behaviour model combines both the latter technological variable - refinery flexibility - and the two previously mentioned economic variables: the setting of the retained values and the quota allocation of oil for processing by the companies. In the case of an entrepreneur wishing to maximise profits, the refinery - once the prices of the distillates and the amount of crude oil available are known - will choose the distillate mix that maximises revenue, since the total cost of production does not alter significantly with the different output-mix alternatives.

The various options the enterprise has can be seen in Figure 5.1. In order to simplify the argument, only two by-products have been taken into account: petrol and residual fuel oil, to show the trade-off between the two distillates in refining. The transformation curve assumes different production combinations of the two by-products at the same total cost. Each curve represents a particular percentage utilisation of refinery capacity and is a function of the allocation of crude oil. Right-hand shifts of the curve mean a higher level of capacity usage, taking advantage of topping flexibility. The maximum is

Figure 5.1

Transformation curves, relative retained value and
short-run optimisation of the output-mix

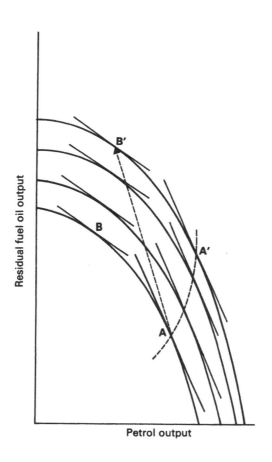

determined by the full topping capacity utilisation.

As can be seen in the figure, a higher level of capacity utilisation assumes a greater increase in the amount of residual fuel oil obtained than petrol. This reduction in the refinery's conversion ratio is due to the fact that the capacity of the secondary processes is considered to be filled for each of the transformation curves.

Once the crude oil quota has been allocated - which involves putting themselves on a particular transformation curve - the companies must choose the point on the curve at which they are going to stand, that is, what combination of residual fuel oil and petrol to produce. If the objective is to maximise profits, they will choose the point at which the retained values ratio line is tangent, since this ensures maximum revenue at those relative retained values.[4]

In that case, movements along the same transformation curve - "a substitution effect" - are the result of changes in relative prices. For example, a rise in the price of residual fuel oil in comparison with petrol produces a movement towards a combination of distillates that favours the production of residual fuel oil, such as the move from A to B or from A' to B'. A shift towards other transformation curves - keeping a constant ratio between the relative retained values - can be called a "quantity effect" and is the result of different rates of capacity utilisation. These shifts can be seen through the move from A to A' or B to B'. In both cases similar price ratios are assumed, and given the trade-off between capacity and the conversion ratio, they show that a higher proportion of residual fuel oil is obtained from an increase in the crude oil quota.

A third type of movement is the result of a combination of the two previously mentioned effects, as in the case of the move from A to B'. Both a greater availability of crude oil and a change in the relative retained values in favour of residual fuel oil would lead firms to sharply reverse the combination of distillates obtained. In the latter case, the final result would be a drastic change in the output-mix in favour of residual fuel oil.

The movements described have been observed in the firms' behaviour during the period under study. From the mid-fifties the proportion of petrol processed by the private companies began to decline and the proportion of residual fuel oil increased simultaneously. At the same time, YPF kept the two values relatively stable.

The modifications in the private companies' output-mix were the result of alterations both in the relative retained values and in the availability of crude oil. In fact, the retained value of petrol became cheaper in relation to that of residual fuel oil as from 1956 and continued to decline until it reached its lowest point in 1962. For their part, between 1955 and 1960 the private companies increased processing by about 90 per cent, due to the reversal in the crude oil allocation policy implemented by the Energy Secretariat. During the same period, the quota granted to YPF increased by only 25 per cent.

The private companies' response was based on a change in the composition of their distillates mix, with residual fuel oil starting to have considerable weight (See Figure 5.2.). In terms of the model set out above, both the movement of relative retained values and the rate of refinery capacity utilisation produced the shift towards a different output-mix composition; that is, a movement from A to B' which represents a combination of the substitution and quantity effects.[5]

YPF's behaviour during the fifties was very different. It did not replace petrol with residual fuel oil, but instead tended to increase the production of intermediate distillates. Between 1955 and 1960, total demand for intermediate distillates (kerosene, diesel fuel and distilled fuel oil) increased by about 50 per cent, whereas demand for residual fuel oil increased by less than 10 per cent. Sales of YPF medium distillates rose by 43 per cent even though the volume of processed crude oil increased by 25 per cent.

At the beginning of the sixties the proportion of residual fuel oil processed by the private companies reached its peak. From then on the distillate mix obtained by these companies began to change once again. Both the stagnation in demand for residual fuel oil and the improvement in the retained values ratio in favour of petrol and its rapid rise in demand led the firms mentioned to change their output-mix. Throughout this decade these companies adjusted their petrol conversion ratio according to the movement in relative retained values. During the same period, YPF continued shifting its distillate mix towards the processing of intermediate distillates, as can be seen in Figure 5.3.

At the beginning of the seventies, there was a change in the market equilibrium achieved. In this case it was not the result of price movements, but was attributable instead to changes in the crude oil quota distributed to the companies. From 1971 onwards there was a marked drop in the volume of oil processed by the private companies, in contrast to the great increase in processing by YPF. The crude oil allocation policy implemented by the Energy Secretariat favoured oil deliveries to the state-owned enterprise (see Table 5.3).

In the light of this development, the private

Figure 5.2

Relative output of petrol and residual fuel oil processed by Esso and Shell in Argentina, 1950–1980

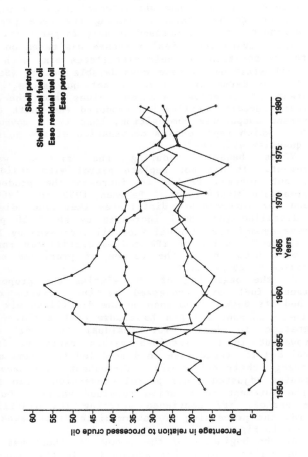

Source : Table 5, in Lucangeli (1986).

Figure 5.3

Relative output of main distillates processed by
YPF 1950–1980

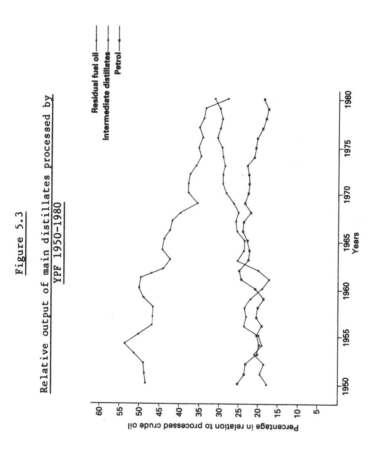

Source: Table 5, in Lucangeli (1986).

companies reacted by shifting their conversion level towards the production of light distillates. A reduced processing capacity utilisation rate led the private refineries to attempt to maximise the value of their output-mix. During those years Shell and Esso achieved their highest conversion ratio for petrol and their lowest for residual fuel oil since the mid-fifties. That is, faced with limited supplies of crude oil and a retained values ratio favourable to light distillates, the private companies showed a "backwards" flexibility in order to optimise profitability. During the last decade, in the case of YPF there were no significant modifications in the output-mix it processed, except for a slight increase in the proportion of the intermediate distillates in the manner discussed previously.

The analysis so far allows us to assume that the shifts observed in the petrol and residual fuel oil conversion level of the private companies were the result of changes both in retained values and of variations in the refineries' capacity usage level.

For the purpose of checking this hypothesis, a function was calculated in which the petrol conversion ratio (PCR) - the indicator of the refineries' output-mix - was considered dependent on the relative retained values of petrol (RVP) in relation to residual fuel oil (RVRFO) and of the inverse of the amount of crude oil available for processing, expressed by the refining capacity utilisation rate (RCUR).

$$PCR = F\left(\frac{R\ V\ P}{RVRFO}\ ;\ \frac{1}{RCUR}\right)$$

This function was estimated for the 1950-1973 period via annual observations for each of the three firms.[6] The petrol/residual fuel oil relative retained values used were the annual averages, and the refining capacity utilisation rate was calculated by extrapolation from the peaks observed in the annual volume of crude oil processed per firm.

We carried out the least squares regression of the logarithms of the values of the variables and the following results were obtained for the function:

$$Ln\ PCR = a + b\ Ln\ \frac{RVP}{RVRFO} + c\ Ln\ RCUR$$

FIRM	n	a	b	c	R^2	DW
Esso	24	5.40 (1.19)	0.59 (0.09)	-0.75 (0.24)	0.71	1.119
Shell	24	5.28 (1.49)	0.89 (0.09)	-1.04 (0.29)	0.85	1.265
YPF	24	4.99 (1.35)	0.03 (0.06)	-0.11 (0.30)	0.02	0.703

(Standard errors in brackets)

As can be seen, the R^2 values for the private companies are quite satisfactory and the values of the parameters calculated are significant (5 per cent). The private companies altered their petrol conversion ratio according to the relative retained values and inversely in relation to capacity utilisation rate. This means that, given the restrictions on their conduct, they behaved in line with the model we have developed in attempting to maximise profits.[7]

Aiming to obtain a high correlation coefficient for YPF would assume that we considered that the company had adopted the same guidelines in its economic and technical behaviour as the private companies. Maximising profits has not been the target of its conduct; it has had instead to meet other kinds of objectives, such as the supply of distillates processed in insufficient quantities by the other companies, provision to other state bodies or companies, the supply of fuels to remote places, etc. Owing to all of the foregoing arguments, the elements in the short-run behaviour model are not applicable.

In the results for YPF, it was not possible to find any association between capacity utilisation rate and output of the different distillates, which would indicate that the larger supplies of crude oil did not have a decisive effect on the combination of products in the short-run. But the regression analysis also shows that the state-owned enterprise did not react to variations in the relative retained values either. It remains to be clarified whether the state-owned enterprise has taken any other parameter into account in order to vary its output-mix in the short-run.[8]

The changes observed in YPF's distillates mix are not reactions to alterations in the main exogenous variables.

It is precisely this behaviour that allowed a certain stability in the distillates market. Covering the deficits left by the private companies involved modifying its output-mix inversely and to a lesser extent, given its higher processing volume than that of its competitors. The very fact that it is the market leader means that, had it altered its output-mix in line with a profit maximisation criterion, it would have introduced a very strong destabilising element into the distillates market.[9]

In short, the refineries' short-run behaviour depended on both technological and economic factors. The private companies used the plants' technical flexibility for short-run optimisation. Given that they acted as fixers of the distillates mix, this flexibility enabled them to adopt the output-mix that would ensure them better profitability levels.[10]

In this context, the overdesign function has a precise economic significance. Topping overdesign is what has enabled them to achieve plant flexibility and consequently to be able to adapt in the short-run to variations in certain parameters. In this respect, planned overdesign is a function of the firm's expectation with regard to distillate prices and the chances of obtaining sufficient volumes of crude oil to ensure full capacity utilisation.[11] The state-owned enterprise's greater technical complexity has enabled it to undertake compensatory supply functions. However, this conduct has almost always put it in a suboptimal economic position since the public firm in fact undertook production of the less profitable distillates.

III. LONG-TERM BEHAVIOUR

The short-run analysis was related to the refineries' technological flexibility, the shifts in the relative retained values and the availability of crude oil. In this section an analysis is made of an issue closely associated with the degree of complexity of the plants; that is, the incorporation of new equipment. This long-term analysis will focus precisely on the determining factors in the companies' investment decisions, particularly on the equipment that makes it possible to obtain a higher conversion ratio of light and intermediate distillates.

This has been the trend followed by the international technological frontier: the development of more complex processes to produce a higher proportion of light and medium distillates from the distillation residuals or from heavier crude oils. The study centres its attention on a particular type of equipment, catalytic cracking, since its development has been the most important phenomenon in refining technology in the last 30 years.

The attempts to find processes making it possible to increase petrol output with heavy fractions cracking goes back to the early years of this century. Catalytic cracking, the successor to thermal cracking, was the most spectacular development of the 1940-55 period and was the process that made it possible to differentiate between pre- and post-war technology. This process accepts a wide range of loads (as long as they do not contain asphalt) and high octane petrol and heavy diesel fuel are obtained. Around 1960, catalytic cracking was the most widely used process in refineries in the United States. If we measure the installed capacity per process as a percentage of crude oil processing capacity, this process represented 45 per cent, the most important at that time. Around 1951 it had already ousted thermal cracking as the most important secondary process.[12]

Our intention is to analyse the behaviour of the local refineries in the light of a steady increase in demand for light distillates along with the advance of the technological frontier which made continual progress in the development of more complex and technologically efficient "petrol" processes. Due to the fact that catalytic cracking has been the "petrol" process par excellence, the analysis will hinge on this process. Just as topping constitutes the basic equipment for achieving short-run refinery flexibility, so catalytic cracking proves to be the fundamental process for obtaining higher proportions of top quality petrol.

Between 1955 and 1962, the oil refining firms introduced catalytic cracking equipment. YPF was the leader, since it incorporated this process into the La Plata refinery in 1955. In 1962, YPF brought more of this type of equipment into operation, this time in the Luján de Cuyo refinery. In the same year Esso incorporated such equipment into the Campana refinery and the following year Shell inaugurated its own in the Dock Sud refinery. Whereas Esso and Shell updated at the same time, YPF updated several years before. This pattern of adoption is investigated below.

From the standpoint of an entrepreneur seeking to maximise profits, the best moment for updating is the point from which the present value of the new process's incorporation plan is greater than the present value of the modified equipment. In this scheme, the variables affecting the decision are projected revenues and costs, investment expenditure on new equipment or on the modernisation of the equipment in use and the maturation periods of the two alternatives in relation to the company's planning period.[13] Some of these variables can be calculated with some degree of certainty by the companies: price of the new equipment, its output, updating costs for the equipment in use, development of demand. But another group of variables are not only outside the company's control, but are also subject to a high degree of uncertainty: the relative price of distillates and of the price of distillates in relation to crude oil, future development of the equipment's technologies and their costs and movements of the interest rate.

As is clear from Table 5.4, crude oil and distillate prices have behaved rather erratically. This phenomenon introduced a high level of uncertainty into the companies' investment decisions and they tended to shorten their planning periods. This means that firms opt for projects with very short pay-off periods. However, this high level of uncertainty affects the private firms and the state company differently. While price fluctuations cause uncertainty regarding income and future costs for the former, in the case of the state-owned enterprise they cause a high degree of uncertainty regarding future demand movements.

Our hypothesis regarding the oil companies' long-term behaviour maintains that again the private firms and the state-owned enterprise have behaved differently. This difference in behaviour arises - as was indicated in the short-run model - from the different objectives assigned to the two kinds of enterprise: while the private firms aimed at maximising their profits, the state-owned enterprise's aim was to satisfy excess demand. The dissimilar technological behaviour observed in the refining industry derives precisely from the different objectives established for the private firms and the state-owned enterprise. This dissimilar technological behaviour was reflected in the different rate of incorporation of new processes. YPF has always been ahead in introducing frontier processes, while the private firms behaved more conservatively and in no case was their technological decision - the introduction of novel secondary processes - ahead of those of the state-owned enterprise.

However, the set of variables to be taken into account in long-term behaviour is much more complex than in the case of the short-run model. Long-term decisions are affected not only by crude oil and distillate prices but also by equipment prices; in the particular case of the oil-refining industry, moreover, access to technological knowledge has also exercised its influence. Whereas the private firms, subsidiaries of multinational corporations, had access to technological processes developed and tested by their parent companies, the state-owned enterprise had to resort to international engineering firms who owned the patents of certain processes. This issue is particularly significant in long-term behaviour, since it brings in the subject of technological uncertainty. As well as the strictly economic uncertainty deriving from the marked instability in the variables relevant to company decision-making - in the case of both public and private companies - the state-owned enterprise had to face greater technological uncertainty arising from its position in the international technological knowledge market.

Esso and Shell behaved according to the scheme set out above. At the point chosen for incorporating new processes, the values acquired by the significant variables ensured a shorter pay back and a lower level of uncertainty, both in technological and economic terms. From 1960 onwards petrol became more expensive in relation to residual fuel oil and crude oil, together with a fall in prices of catalytic cracking equipment. By the time of incorporation, the home companies had already sufficiently developed and tested their cracking processes. Dr. Frondizi's developmentalist economic policy had produced an atmosphere favourable to investment, particularly foreign investment.[14] Finally, the development of the automobile industry required high octane petrol, for which it was necessary to have catalytic cracking processes. The private companies could not lose share in a market that showed signs of being very dynamic. The moment chosen by YPF for introducing catalytic cracking, on the contrary, could not be considered the best from the point of view of the private entrepreneur out to maximise profits. In what follows we will investigate the behaviour of the main variables involved in the decision to incorporate new processes.

Around 1930, A. J. Houndry obtained the first patent for a catalytic cracking process, for which the equipment was subsequently developed and commercialised by the Sun Oil Co. In 1937 the first commercial plant was opened. From that point until the end of the fifties, catalytic cracking showed a swift rate of technological progress. This technical change affected all cracking inputs, though particularly labour and capital requirements.[15] This was reflected in the price of catalytic cracking equipment. As can be seen in Table 5.1, between 1946 and 1960 the price of catalytic cracking process units - for the same processing capacity - had fallen by half.

Catalytic cracking constitutes a very special case, since no other process unit underwent such a reduction in price. Furthermore, J. L. Enos has shown with regard to catalytic cracking that, in the stage following the commercial launching of a process, the rate of technical progress is higher than that of the new process in relation to the improved previous one.[16]

However, despite all the foregoing, the achievement of

Table 5.1

Cost index for process units, catalytic cracking
(Base index 1946=100, in current US$)

Year	Index	Year	Index
1946	100	1968	50
1950	84	1970	49
1960	48	1972	52

Source: W. L. Nelson: "Cost of Catalytic Cracking Plants",
in The Oil and Gas Journal, April 15, 1974.

both higher petrol output and a higher octane number
involved - in the mid-fifties - higher operating costs.
    The last two types of refinery in Table 5.2 each
include catalytic cracking equipment, whereas the two
intermediate ones (4.5 and 5.1 level of complexity) have
thermal cracking. From the table it can be seen that a
higher octane number requires higher operating costs per
unit of crude oil processed, with fairly similar outputs.
On the other hand, obtaining higher output - with an
equivalent octane number - also involves higher operating
costs, whether it is a question of catalytic or thermal
cracking.[17]
    With regard to relative prices - petrol in relation to
crude oil - these reached a peak during the second half of
the fifties, then declined and picked up again around the
early sixties (see Table 5.4). Despite the high price
ratio of 1954/55, the private companies did not introduce
catalytic cracking equipment. One reason is that the
relative prices of distillates do not play, in the
long-term, the same predominant role as in the short-term.
Moreover, the value assumed for the remaining variables and
the private companies' expectations discouraged investment
during those years. To this should be added a significant
political phenomenon: the last years of the Peronist
Government were surrounded by an atmosphere of marked
instability, an atmosphere that had a considerable
influence on investors.
    YPF put catalytic cracking into operation in La Plata
in 1955, but it was a project that had first been studied
prior to 1950. The reason for its introduction is to be
found in the level of local production, since at that time
a certain amount was still imported to meet consumption

Table 5.2

Operating costs for different types of refinery, 1956
(US cents per barrel of crude oil processed)

	Level of complexity					
Type of refinery	3.4	3.9	4.5	5.1	5.4	6.2
Petrol output (in percentage of crude oil processed)	11.2	11.3	34.7	34.8	34.2	36.3
Octane number	60-70	84-93	69-81	77-87	82-91	91-98
Operating costs	54.1	59.6	87.5	96.3	89.3	102.6

Source: W. L. Nelson: "Octane number is major factor in cost of refinery operation", in The Oil and Gas Journal, September 30, 1963.

Note: It is assumed that oil of 20° API (1.6 per cent sulphur) is used.

requirements.[18] The cracking process was contracted with M. W. Kellogg Co. and was a "side by side" process, a similar idea to that of the Esso range. The first two units incorporating this process were built by Kellogg in Canada and the United States in 1951. This process was soon obsolete, however, as a result of the rapid progress in catalytic cracking technology.

As can be deduced from these arguments, there is a marked difference in attitude to the incorporation of catalytic cracking on the part of the state-owned enterprise and of the private companies. YPF incorporated the new process at a period when the new technique was still at the height of its development phase. The likelihood of rapid obsolesence of the process was very high but so was demand pressure. This attitude to technological progress indicates the state-owned enterprise's inclination to accept the risk of testing and experimenting with processes that are at the limits of the technological frontier.

The characteristics of the international technological market constitute one of the variables that determine the different attitude of the state-owned enterprise vis-à-vis

Table 5.3

Domestic and imported crude oil processed by three enterprises in Argentina, 1950–1980

	YPF			Esso			Shell		
	Total	Domestic	Imported	Total	Domestic	Imported	Total	Domestic	Imported
1950	4,568	2,676	1,892	1,042	106	936	882	488	394
51	4,463	2,860	1,603	1,204	127	1,077	928	555	373
52	5,058	3,007	2,051	1,296	90	1,206	983	485	498
53	5,734	3,680	2,054	1,298	85	1,213	1,014	482	532
54	6,030	3,899	2,131	1,417	55	1,362	1,073	430	643
55	6,309	4,115	2,194	1,495	69	1,426	1,318	452	866
56	6,127	4,160	1,967	1,772	64	1,708	1,324	457	867
57	7,331	4,719	2,612	2,344	57	2,287	1,913	441	1,472
58	7,874	4,882	2,992	2,576	55	2,521	2,182	447	1,735
59	7,524	6,085	1,439	2,530	37	2,493	2,225	449	1,776
1960	7,808	7,485	323	2,663	731	1,932	2,744	1,328	1,416
61	8,461	8,367	94	2,856	1,555	1,301	3,107	2,624	483
62	9,847	9,647	200	2,948	2,403	545	3,539	3,152	387
63	9,853	9,797	56	2,647	2,319	328	3,343	2,952	391
64	10,333	9,748	585	2,869	2,452	417	3,599	3,089	510
65	11,628	8,575	3,053	3,370	2,934	436	3,931	3,429	502
66	12,499	9,416	3,083	3,546	3,187	368	3,969	3,485	484

Year								
67	12,584	11,350	1,234	3,717	2,988	729	3,994	3,132	862
68	12,589	11,521	1,068	3,967	3,447	520	4,722	4,045	677
69	13,535	12,409	1,126	4,241	3,682	559	4,724	3,901	823
1970	14,406	13,704	702	4,541	4,095	446	4,871	4,358	513
71	18,144	16,735	1,409	3,320	2,866	454	4,364	3,825	539
72	19,012	17,826	1,186	3,199	2,973	226	3,781	3,544	237
73	19,851	17,335	2,516	3,078	2,715	363	3,585	3,158	427
74	19,784	17,563	2,221	3,005	2,504	501	3,316	2,792	524
75	18,878	17,377	1,501	2,755	2,334	421	2,733	2,195	538
76	19,470	17,103	2,367	2,995	2,588	407	3,086	2,459	627
77	20,365	17,902	2,463	3,606	3,168	438	3,414	2,895	519
78	20,485	18,486	1,999	3,590	3,304	286	3,223	2,997	226
1980	21,312	19,744	1,568	4,026	3,803	223	3,837	3,352	485

Source: Secretaría de Estado de Energía: Anuarios Estadísticos.

Table 5.4

Ratios between oil prices and retained values of distillates, 1950-1980

	Average price of crude oil ($ 1960/m³) (1)	Average retained value petrol ($ 1960/m³) (2)	Retained value residual fuel oil ($ 1960/m³) (3)	Retained value against crude oil price (4)=(2)÷(1)	(5)=(3)÷(1)
1950	–	55.0	11.6	–	0.79
51	10.25	40.9	8.1	3.99	0.63
52	9.21	31.4	5.8	3.41	0.72
53	7.36	28.7	5.3	3.90	1.22
54	5.98	29.8	7.3	4.98	1.36
55	5.23	28.6	7.1	5.47	0.99
56	13.13	32.5	13.0	2.48	0.81
57	14.87	31.5	12.1	2.12	0.98
58	9.38	24.1	9.2	2.57	0.92
59	17.72	33.4	16.3	1.88	
1960	13.66	34.9	16.3	2.55	1.19
61	12.44	33.2	15.1	2.67	1.21
62	12.16	29.4	14.6	2.42	1.20
63	10.58	27.8	12.5	2.63	1.18

64	8.40	22.2	9.9	2.64	1.18
65	11.20	26.1	9.7	2.33	0.87
66	11.58	37.3	10.6	3.22	0.92
67	11.03	31.5	10.1	2.86	0.92
68	12.55	36.6	11.4	2.92	0.91
68	11.96	35.1	10.9	2.93	0.91
1970	10.57	31.1	9.6	2.94	0.91
71	9.17	26.7	7.6	2.91	0.83
72	7.54	23.4	8.7	3.10	1.15
73	9.62	32.9	10.2	3.42	1.06
74	19.62	62.5	9.7	3.19	0.49
75	15.69	62.5	7.5	3.98	0.48
76	14.46	44.6	8.7	3.08	0.60
77	14.23	33.9	13.7	2.38	0.96
78	14.08	37.1	21.4	2.63	1.52
79	11.37	30.2	16.6	2.66	1.46
1980	11.48	30.0	16.1	2.61	1.40

Source: (1) 1951-1958: Instituto Nacional de Estadísticas y Censos.
1959-1980: Secretaría de Estado de Energía: Annuarios Estadísticos
(2) and (3) Table 4, Lucángeli (1986).

Note: (2) From 1960 average of regular and extra petrol.
(1), (2) and (3) deflated by non-farm domestic wholesale price index,
National Institute for Statistics and Census.

the private firms (subsidiaries of multinational oil corporations) in relation to technological progress. The supply of technology is divided between two sets of companies: (a) those engineering firms that belong to or are subsidiaries of international oil companies and (b) independent engineering companies. The latter group is extremely heterogeneous: some are involved in construction, others in detail engineering and a very few are engaged in the whole cycle (basic, detail and construction engineering).

Around 1950 Universal Oil Products (U.O.P.) and the M. W. Kellogg Company were the only two independent engineering companies that had their own catalytic cracking processes. Esso was continuing to experiment with its "Fluid Catalytic Cracking" process, and Shell had no processes of its own.

Unlike the private firms, YPF had to deal with the independent engineering companies, primarily in relation to the licence for the basic process engineering. However, the process supply contracts also included the detail engineering and the construction of the units.

The engineering enterprises of Kellogg, U.O.P. and Lummus have been almost the exclusive suppliers of new processes to YPF. The reason for this preference must be found in the fact that they are almost the only independent companies that market basic engineering. However, although YPF has continued to depend on these engineering companies in relation to basic engineering (its R & D Laboratory has not developed basic engineering), the successive incorporation of processes and refinery remodelling have involved greater participation by local engineering firms in relation to detail engineering and construction. There is no doubt that, in this sense, the "Buy Local" law had its influence. (This law provides that 70 per cent of the value of a project will go to local suppliers, of both materials and of engineering and consultancy services.)

As can be appreciated, the access to technological information enjoyed by the different firms varies a great deal. Although the technological knowledge market provides a smooth flow of information, the state-owned enterprise must go out and seek information and assess it, whereas the subsidiaries of the multinational - despite playing a more passive role - have more direct access to technological information, but with one proviso: their position is more dependent, since their sole supplier is their parent company.

This different position in the market for technological knowledge produces a different attitude in relation to technological change. YPF must evaluate the technology to be incorporated, but with a lower level of information than its competitors. The private firms have a higher level of information, deriving from their condition as subsidiaries of multinational corporations which, in turn, develop technological knowledge. In this sense, the state-owned enterprise is more exposed to technological risk.

Our statement does not derive only from a detailed observation of YPF's incorporation of the first catalytic cracking process. A similar attitude can be seen in the last significant remodelling carried out in the refineries between the late sixties and early seventies. At that time YPF - in its Luján de Cuyo refinery - incorporated a hydro-cracking plant. At the time of the contract, only limited experiments had been carried out.[19]

The state-owned enterprise and the private firms show two different patterns as reflected in the greater speed with which the state-owned enterprise has adopted the frontier processes in comparison with the private firms. The state-owned enterprise has always been ahead in this respect.

The difference in pattern originates from the fact that the behaviour of the two kinds of firms corresponds to different objectives: the state-owned enterprise has been assigned the implicit objective of satisfying surplus demand, while the private firms pursue the objective of maximising profits, as far as the regulations imposed by the regulatory agency will allow.

The state-owned enterprise is alert to two major signals: expectations with regard to distillate demand movements and changes in the international technological frontier. The private firms, on the contrary, without ignoring the previous variables, take more notice of expectations regarding the relative prices of distillates and of equipment, and are more alert to information received from their parent companies in relation to new processes.[20] Whereas the private firms have behaved more like "economic man" in their choice of technologies, the public manager has behaved along the lines of "engineering man".[21]

Here what we want to say is that in the case of the private firms, economic variables weighed more in the choice of new processes than in the case of the state-owned enterprise. In the latter case, priority was given to the choice of processes that would ensure that the established objective would be achieved. In the state-owned enterprise's technological decisions, that is, some economic variables are ignored, since the regulatory agency indicates that the state-owned enterprise should be alert to demand signals.

However, given the close connection between output-mix and technological processes in this industry (deriving from the inflexibility caused by process technologies), the demand profile has been the variable that has governed the choice of technological processes. In this sense, the state-owned enterprise's use of criteria similar to those outlined in Wells' "engineering man" concept in the choice of technologies appears to be the only possible option. The adoption of a more "economic" criterion would have led to the inability to supply surplus demand and consequently to achieve the objective assigned. Wells indicates that the managers' choice of technology is influenced by two different objective functions. In the case of the YPF managers, the objective function of "engineering man" prevails over that of "economic man". However, what should be stressed in relation to this aspect is that the objective function is not the managers' choice, but is imposed by the regulatory agency.

The refinery remodelling carried out around 1970 was a widespread phenomenon. Both the private companies and YPF were involved. Technological change in the refineries hinged on the incorporation of the petrol catalytic reforming process. Platinum reforming (thus known due to the use of that metal as catalyst) was one of the booms of refining technology, since it made it possible to obtain petrol with a higher octane number with lower lead requirements. This is one of the typical processes deriving from the octane race. At the time of its incorporation in Argentina it was sufficiently well tested and developed, since it was in widespread use in the United States in the mid-fifties. This is an important item of information for an understanding of the private companies' reaction.

Between 1969 and 1971, four refineries had brought their catalytic reforming equipment into operation: YPF (La Plata) and Esso in 1969; YPF (Luján de Cuyo) and Shell in 1971. YPF's Plaza Huincul refinery began to build a unit in 1972. In this case, the private and state-owned enterprise incorporated the new equipment at the same time. The state-owned enterprise was not ahead of the others.

Several factors combine to explain this new behaviour in relation to the introduction of the first catalytic cracking equipment. During the sixties, the automobile boom demanded that efforts be concentrated on obtaining increasing quantities of petrol. The automobile industry's growth rate slowed down as it approached "stock balance", but at the same time the automobile industry concentrated its efforts on greater engine compression. The answer was better quality petrol. And the private firms agreed with the state-owned enterprise, since the processes were sufficiently well tested, particularly by their parent companies.[22]

162

At the same time that catalytic reforming was incorporated, the refineries expanded their processing capacity. Shell and Esso each raised their capacity to around 20,000 m^3 per day, by incorporating new topping units. YPF achieved something similar in its main refineries. But at the end of the seventies, the refining industry had a similar technological profile and processing capacity to those it had at the beginning of the decade.

The freezing of investment in refining during the seventies derived from one central factor: the slow-down in the rate of demand expansion. Between 1970 and 1980, sales of oil distillates grew at an adjusted average annual rate of 0.9 per cent, in significant contrast with that of previous years (7.5 per cent). Several factors combined to dampen demand. Firstly, the world oil crisis had local repercussions despite the high level of oil self-sufficiency achieved. During Minister Gelbard's administration, the prices of local crude oil and certain distillates rose along with international prices and thus depressed demand. Secondly, the marked stagnation in the Argentine economy that has been in evidence since 1975 also played its part in slowing down the rate of sales expansion.[23] Finally, there is a phenomenon that has had a considerable influence on the stagnation in demand for distillates and it may mean a significant structural change. We are referring to the discovery of large reserves of natural gas.[24] This event has produced significant changes in the economic structure of the Argentine energy sector. Natural gas had ousted residual fuel oil as a fuel in the large industries and in thermo-electric power plants. These activities currently use only gas. Over a period of a very few years it was possible to redirect their energy requirements thanks to an effective policy on the part of the Energy Secretariat.[25] The demand for distillates has become restricted almost exclusively to the transport sector and to medium and small industrial establishments, sectors in which the change will require longer periods.

This swift change in the demand structure for energy inputs meant that towards the end of the seventies refining was producing increasing surpluses of residual fuel oil, the main victim of the natural gas substitution process, since the conversion ratio of refineries as a whole made it impossible to reduce production of this distillate.[26]

The state-owned enterprise once again assumed the responsibility of covering the market imbalances, although in this case the situation is unprecedented: instead of shortages of distillates, there is a surplus of one of them. The current relative shortages of oil makes it inefficient to export residual fuel oil, a by-product with scant commercial value. YPF has consequently undertaken a project to increase conversion in the La Plata and Luján de Cuyo refineries, with the aim of reducing production of residual fuel oil and increasing production of light and intermediate distillates. The aim is to reduce residual fuel oil production by around 4,000,000 tons/year and increase production of light and intermediate distillates by 3 million m^3.[27]

The project, initiated in 1980, covers the incorporation of similar processes in the two refineries: a catalytic cracking unit, a retarded coke unit and a light diesel hydrogen treating unit. When contracted, this project was the most important investment in Argentina: US$800 million, something like 1 per cent of G.D.P. and over 10 per cent of the total gross investment of the Argentine public sector.

IV. SOME CONCLUSIONS

The concern of this study has been to analyse the economic and technological performance of the oil refining activities of the state-owned enterprise, Yacimientos Petrolíferos Fiscales (YPF), and to compare this performance with privately owned firms that are engaged in these activities. The comparison was conducted in the context of two different time periods, namely, the short-run, when firms make adjustments and modifications to the output-mix and/or the amount of crude oil processed on the basis of fixed capital equipment, and the long-term, when decisions to incorporate new capital equipment are made.

The oil companies - both state and private - have been subject to a common regulatory framework imposed by the Energy Secretariat: the regulatory agency adjusts prices of crude oil and distillates and fixes the quotas of crude oil to be processed by each company. However, the state oil company has been faced with an additional restriction: to supply excess demand, a restriction absent in the case of the private firms. This target assigned to the state-owned enterprise has meant that its behaviour has taken on certain specific characteristics. If this basic point is not taken into account, it is impossible to understand the difference in conduct between the state company and the private ones.

In the short-run, the private companies acted - on the basis of the restrictions imposed by the regulatory framework - by selecting the vector of distillates that would maximise their profits. But the state company's distillate vector was in line not with the relative prices vector, but with the surplus distillates demand vector. The least "profitable" distillates were supplied by the state-owned enterprise. While the private firms' conduct was orientated by their search for profitability, the state-owned enterprise's behaviour had to be directed at the maximisation of output.

In the long-run, as well, differences were discerned between the technological behaviour of the private and publicly owned firms. In particular, it was seen that YPF was ahead of the private companies in incorporating catalytic cracking, although the technological risk involved in adopting the new and unproven process was relatively high.

The YPF manager's conduct in this regard is likely to have followed what Arrow and Lind's model suggests should be the behaviour of a public manager: they essentially ignore risks and choose investments with the highest expected returns.[28] The YPF managers' behaviour is nevertheless remarkable, despite its coinciding with the "theoretical should-be".

Undoubtedly, the absence of performance-linked incentives for public sector managers led, in the case of the technological behaviour, to encouraging managers to ignore risk. Public managers' careers and incomes are independent - within broad limits - of the firm's performance. Thus errors in technological choice would affect neither the position nor the income of the public managers. But this would not be the only factor that would explain the attitude of the YPF managers, since the absence of incentives is common to all state-owned enterprises and different attitudes to risk can be found.

The history of the industry and the state-owned enterprise both help to explain YPF's attitude to risk. A highly profitable and fast growing industry makes it possible not only to disguise faulty decisions but also requires a high investment rate, which enables it to have access to more recent processes. If to this phenomenon is added the fact that the international technological frontier has undergone rapid shifts during the last fifty years, the need to satisfy the demand for distillates forced the state enterprise into a continuous "catching up" process in relation to the technological frontier. We consider this aspect to be of considerable importance. If autonomous fluctuations in demand tend towards a similar profile to that of the developed countries, demand dynamics will lead to the incorporation of new frontier processes that will make it possible to satisfy that profile. Demand fluctuations, together with the objective assigned to the state-owned enterprise, pushed the YPF managers into a continuous process of positioning themselves on the international technological frontier.

NOTES AND REFERENCES

1. This is a condensed version of an ILO World Employment Programme Working Paper, number 164, 1986, of the same title.

2. The companies that have had a minority share in total oil processing are as follows: Astrasur, D.A.P.S.A., La Isaura S.A., Sol, Cóndor, Ragor and Lottero Papini. Their processing capacity ranges from 13,000 to 49,000 m^3 of oil per year. Some of them have now ceased operation.

3. The degree of complexity of a refinery indicates the number of times more complex it is than crude oil topping. That is, the number of additional operations (secondary processes) beyond the distillation carried out by a refinery. The complexity factor is measured usually as the ratio between the cost of the different operating processes and the cost of the topping and desalting equipment. In this respect see: W. L. Nelson: "How to compute refinery 'complexity'", The Oil and Gas Journal, Tulsa, Oklahoma, 19 June, 1961.

4. The model does not include the price of oil as an exogenous variable since the retained value of residual fuel oil - in most years - was higher than the price of crude oil. Consequently, it was always profitable for the refineries to process a larger volume of oil. The unknown factor was the choice of mix that would maximise their revenue.

5. It is interesting to examine the solutions adopted by both Shell and Esso to increase their processing capacity without introducing new equipment. Both companies (according to information provided by them) not only took full advantage of the topping elasticity, but also introduced certain modifications that enabled them to achieve a greater processing capacity. Shell changed a rigorous thermal cracking unit - from which it obtained mainly coke and petrol - into a topping unit. In this way it lowered its conversion level to gain crude oil processing capacity. In 1957 Esso expanded sixfold the capacity of the atmospheric distillation unit (topping unit) at its Galván plant by revamping it.

6. The regression analysis was done for the 1950-1973 period. In mid-1974, the Government of Mrs. María E. M. Perón nationalised the refined fuels sales outlets, marketing being YPF's responsibility. In this situation, the private companies refined on YPF's account. This situation lasted until 1977, but it took some years longer for refining to return to normal.

7. The high degree of elasticity of the conversion ratio

in relation to the refining capacity utilisation rate (parameter c) and its great significance mean that, during the period under analysis, the private refineries made full utilisation of secondary equipment. As explained in the behavioural model, the trade-off between processing capacity and the conversion ratio appears from the point where secondary processing capacity is filled. The fact that we could not obtain detailed information regarding the equipment prevented us from authenticating this conduct.

8. Estimating a function that includes variables that reflect demand movements revealed some interesting conclusions. To the previous function was added a variable indicative of the growth of the petrol market. The inclusion of this variable did not substantially improve the R^2 value for the private companies (and the estimated parameters are not significant); but it did for YPF. The R^2 increases to 0.23 and is the only significant parameter. In any case, the results for YPF are not conclusive.

9. If YPF had followed the conduct of the private companies between 1955 and 1959, that is, reduced the petrol conversion ratio, 15 per cent of the market for this distillate would have been lacking supplies. This result is obtained by assuming elasticity in YPF's conversion level in relation to the relative retained values, similar to Esso's, according to the function estimated for that company.

10. The plants' technological flexibility has enabled the private companies to get to "second" or "third best", since, given the imperfections of the context in which they have developed, it would have been impossible to reach optimum situations.

11. F. C. Sercovich points out that one of the variables that influence the tendency to deliberately overdesign (planned overdesign) is the client's uncertainty with regard to demand or to the supply of inputs and their prices. See F. C. Sercovich (1978): Ingeniería de diseño y cambio técnico endógeno, IDB/ECLA Programme of Research in Science and Technology, Buenos Aires, pp. 44-6.

12. W. L. Nelson (1960): "Processing in U.S.A. refineries", The Oil and Gas Journal, 24 Oct.

13. A. Canitrot (1977): Un esquema para evaluar la significación de las variable macroeconómicas en el análisis de decisión de incorporación de tecnologías, Buenos Aires, IDB/ECLA Programme of Research in Science and Technology.

14. Total fixed investment exceeded 24 per cent of G.D.P., whereas in the mid-fifties it had fluctuated around 17

or 18 per cent of product. Furthermore, domestic gross investment showed a significant change in composition towards the purchase of new machinery and equipment. See R. Mallon and J. V. Sourrouille (1973): La política económica en una sociedad conflictiva. El caso argentino. (Economic policy in a society of conflict. The Argentine case). Amorrorty editores, 1st edition, Buenos Aires.

15. Between 1914 and 1956 the average growth rate for processing labour productivity was 12.0; raw material 3.7; power consumed 6.5 and capital 6.8. Both cracking processes (thermal and catalytic) are included. These are estimates made by J. L. Enos (1962): Petroleum Progress and Profits: A history of process innovation, Cambridge, Massachusetts, The M.I.T. Press, pp. 254-8.

16. That is, the rate of technical progress in the minor innovations introduced into the processes is higher than is implied by comparing a major innovation with the improved previous process. J. L. Enos (1958): "A Measure of the Rate of Technological Progress in the Petroleum Refining Industry", in Journal of Industrial Economics, Oxford, England, June.

17. Compare the refineries with complexity levels 3.9, 5.1 and 5.4 in which the octane number of the petrol obtained is similar. Both the one that uses thermal cracking (5.1) and the one that incorporates catalytic cracking (5.4) - which give similar outputs - have a much higher cost than the first one which includes no cracking process.

18. Towards the end of the forties, petrol imports amounted to around 15 per cent of total sales.

19. For a full discussion of this case see Lucángeli, op. cit.

20. It was quite clear from our interviews with managers from the private firms that decisions to incorporate new processes and also the provision of basic and detail engineering depended on decisions from the parent companies.

21. L. T. Wells, Jr. (1975): "Economic man and engineering man: Choice of technology in a low wage country", in C.P. Timmer et al.: The choice of technology in developing countries - Some cautionary tales, Harvard, Studies in International Affairs, number 32, Harvard University, pp. 71-86.

22. There is another factor that cannot be ignored. The decisions to incorporate new equipment were taken during the government of the Revolución Argentina, when Dr. Krieguer Vasena was Minister of Economic Affairs. During his administration a very favourable environment for private investment was created and the

Argentine economy seemed to be entering into a period of permanent stability. The rate of inflation for 1969 was 7 per cent, the lowest in 30 years.

23. Between 1974 and 1980 the gross domestic product increased at an average annual rate of 1 per cent. The G.D.P. per capita declined, since the population growth rate was around 1.7 per cent. The gross industrial product for 1980 was 5 per cent lower than in 1974. See J. V. Sourrouille and J. Lucángeli (1983): Política económica y procesos de desarrollo. La experiencia Argentina entre 1976 y 1981, Estudios e Informes de la CEPAL No. 27, Santiago de Chile, United Nations, pp. 95-121.

24. Towards the end of the seventies significant gas reserves were discovered in the Neuquén basin, which meant that the total proven reserves had increased threefold between 1974 and 1980; this ensures a horizon of about fifty years of consumption. However, there was no change in the proven oil reserves between 1970 and 1980. Oil reserves currently are equivalent to 12 years' consumption at present levels (see Subsecretaría de Combustibles: Anuario de Combustibles, Buenos Aires, 1981.

25. Apparent gas consumption increased at an adjusted average annual rate of 5.8 per cent between 1970 and 1980. See ibid.

26. This phenomenon has been reflected in the sector's trade balance. At the moment Argentina is a net exporter of oil and distillates, although this position has been achieved by export of its residual fuel oil surpluses, which represent around 60 per cent of the value of distillates exports.

27. YPF's residual fuel oil production will be reduced to a third of its present level. The conversion ratio will improve markedly, since the residual fuel oil represents only 13 per cent of distillate production. In the case of Luján de Cuyo in particular, the reconversion programme will mean it stops producing residual fuel oil.

28. K.J. Arrow and R.C. Lind (1970): "Uncertainty and the Evaluation of Public Investment Decisions", in American Economic Review, Nashville, Tennessee, Vol. IX, No. 3, June. Another possible explanation of YPF's behaviour is that this enterprise was expected to meet excess demand for particular types of petroleum products (which were unprofitable), in the face of a relatively "soft" budget constraint. Under these conditions, YPF's best strategy would be to expand capacity as much as possible, given the probable demand configuration and to build in as much flexibility in the plant as possible.

Chapter 6

Public Enterprises and the Transfer of Technology in the Ammonia Industry

Brian Levy

I. INTRODUCTION

Public enterprises are sometimes regarded as panaceas for economic development. Many obstacles to development result, it can be argued, from disparities between social costs and benefits and the calculations of private returns on which profit-seeking firms base their behaviour; it follows that public enterprises, basing their decisions on social returns, might undertake investments for which net social returns, though not necessarily private profits, are positive.

This perspective appears excessively optimistic in the light of recent research on how public enterprises actually behave.[1] The principal purpose of the present study, however, is not to review these research findings but rather to explore critically the grounds for one specific type of optimism, namely that public enterprises might significantly loosen the constraints on development that result from a dependence on technology imported from industrialised countries. The focus here is primarily on the divergence between the perceived and actual costs and benefits of the indigenous development of technology in developing countries, rather than on the specific patterns of behaviour of public enterprises. As a case study of the transfer of technology in a single industry, ammonia, this study is more in the nature of a cautionary tale than an attempt at overall generalisation. But, in common with much other research on public enterprises, its central implication is a warning against easy optimism that public enterprises can overcome some apparent obstacles to development.

The case of ammonia

The ammonia industry has a number of advantages as a case study of the role of public enterprises in the transfer of technology to developing countries. For one thing, ammonia and the various nitrogen compounds it helps to form account for about one half of world fertiliser consumption;[2] so a study of the industry has relevance for agricultural as well as industrial development. More importantly, public enterprises control over 70 per cent of ammonia production in developing countries, making ammonia (along with steel) one of the few industries that is dominated by public enterprises throughout the developing world.[3] This paper contrasts the strategies for the acquisition of ammonia technology in four countries – India, Republic of Korea, Mexico and Brazil. As Table 6.1 shows, the production of nitrogen fertilisers has grown rapidly since 1965 in all four countries. This expansion has been largely entrusted to public enterprises: the state-owned company Pemex in Mexico and subsidiaries of state-owned Petrobras in Brazil are the sole producers of ammonia in these two countries; enterprises that are entirely state-owned dominate the ammonia industry in India and account for more than half of the Republic of Korea's ammonia production; joint ventures with multinational firms produce the remainder in the Republic of Korea and about 15 per cent of total Indian production; and private local firms account for a further 10 per cent of Indian ammonia.

Unlike the broad similarities in ownership patterns, strategies for the transfer of ammonia technology have differed widely among the four countries. India's fertiliser programme has long placed a high priority on developing local skills to design, manage and fabricate the equipment needed to build an ammonia plant. Table 6.2 reveals a gradual increase over time in the role of local firms, especially in the share of equipment that they supply. It also reveals, however, that the trend to indigenisation has been highly erratic. Underlying these lurches from plant to plant in the extent of indigenous involvement lies a continual conflict within India over the extent to which indigenisation should be pursued.

The state-owned Fertiliser Corporation of India was the strongest proponent of indigenisation. From its inception, the FCI placed heavy emphasis on the development of indigenous technology, especially technology that was adapted to feedstocks available in India keeping to a minimum its long-term ties with foreign suppliers of technology.[4] The task of developing these technologies was entrusted to the corporation's Planning and Development division. By the late 1960s the FCI's strategy seemed to have paid off; its P and D division was assigned both

Table 6.1

Production of nitrogen fertilisers in India, Mexico,
Brazil and the Republic of Korea
(in thousands of tonnes)

Country	1965	1970	1975	1978
India	233	838	1,509	2,000
Mexico	155	330	607	611
Brazil	14	22	161	232
Republic of Korea	75	386	541	699

Source: Food and Agricultural Organisation, Fertiliser
Yearbook (United Nations, FAO: Rome, various
years).

engineering and management responsibilities for ten new
ammonia plants, three using coal as feedstock. By 1974 the
staff of the P and D division exceeded 3,000 including over
300 scientists, and more than 60 engineers.[5]

The FCI's pre-eminence proved to be short-lived.
Without field research, the reasons for its demise must
perforce remain uncertain, although the high costs of
indigenisation (on which more will follow later) doubtless
played a major role. What is certain is that already in
1972 India's planners began to look for foreign technical
and managerial assistance for their new plants. Finally,
in 1977, after years of continual criticism levelled at the
FCI, it was split into five separate companies; the P and D
division was reconstructed as an independent company which
was to compete with other engineering contractors on an
equal footing.[6]

After the eclipse of the FCI, India's planners relied
heavily on importing the skills needed to set up an ammonia
plant. Foreign skills were used extensively in at least
four new ammonia plants built between 1972 and 1979; there
was, to be sure, some local participation, but the
development of local skills no longer had as high a
priority.[7] By the end of the decade, however, policy
began to shift again with a renewed emphasis on the
development of indigenous capabilities. But unlike the
earlier strategy of going it alone as rapidly and as

Table 6.2

Relative shares of foreign and local suppliers of equipment
and engineering in selected Indian ammonia plants

Plant	Year on Stream	Equipment		Engineering	
		Foreign	Local	Foreign	Local
Trombay	1965	97.7%	2.3%	–	–
Gorakhpur	1969	98.1	1.9	–	–
Namrup	1969	78.9	21.1	–	–
Nangal	1978	68.5	31.5	66.0	34.0
Sindri	1978	68.6	31.4	49.1	50.9
Talcher	1978	43.4	56.6	52.5	47.5
Ramargundam	1978	48.5	51.5	55.6	44.4
Phulpur	1980	64.3	35.7	86.5	13.5
Hazira	1980	68.7	31.3	50.2	49.8

Sources: D.N. Daruvalla, "Design and Development of Fertiliser Plants in Developing Countries with Special Reference to India", in UNIDO, Fertiliser Production Technology and Use, (New York: United Nations, 1968) Table 3, P. 40; Usha Menon, "World Bank and Transfer of Technology", Economic and Political Weekly, August 23, 1980 p. 1438; and selected appraisal and completion reports written by Industrial Projects Division, World Bank.

extensively as possible, the emphasis now was on learning in close collaboration with foreign firms, an approach closely akin to that adopted in Brazil.[8]

Brazil, like India, has placed a high priority on increasing local skills and participation; but (at least until the most recent shift in Indian strategy) it had gone about this very differently. One key difference was in timing. While efforts at indigenisation in India were well underway by the mid-1960s, Brazilian efforts in ammonia have begun only recently. Firstly, as we shall see, by the time Brazil began to expand production, international competition among technology vendors to build ammonia plants had intensified, adding to the opportunities to secure favourable contract terms. Secondly, by the late 1970s, Brazil already had extensive experience in other areas of the petrochemical industry. So local engineers were well placed to take advantage of opportunities for indigenisation.

Another difference between the Indian and Brazilian approaches was in the strategy of acquiring basic technological know-how. As already noted, India, at least until the most recent agreements, sought to go it alone as rapidly and extensively as possible and gave short shrift to collaborative learning from foreign vendors of technology. Brazil, by contrast, has sought to secure long-term access to the best-practice technology of overseas vendors: Brazil selected the U.S. firm M. W. Kellogg (which, as will be seen, dominated the supply of ammonia technology worldwide throughout the 1970s) as the major foreign contractor for three of its four most recent ammonia projects; the transactional advantages of building and maintaining a long-term relationship was a key incentive in inducing Kellogg to participate in a collaborative effort to transfer technology. Finally – and this is another important difference from the Indian approach – Brazil has insulated efforts to transfer technology from the construction of new ammonia plants. The five-year agreement to collaborate on the transfer of technology that it signed with Kellogg in 1977 is a separate effort from Kellogg's contracts for the ammonia projects themselves.

The Mexican strategy[9] has been similar to Brazil's in the way in which it focused its collaboration on a single overseas firm: Kellogg has won the contracts for all eight ammonia plants built for state-owned PEMEX since 1970. The strategy has been different in its weaker emphasis on indigenisation. Mexico has, to be sure, made some efforts to provide opportunities for learning and participation by local engineers and equipment fabricators. But, at least in the ammonia industry, these efforts do not appear to have the same high priority as in

Brazil or India.

Like Mexico, the Republic of Korea also has not placed much emphasis on extending the use of indigenous resources in new ammonia plants; all equipment and engineering for most of the nitrogen plants undertaken in the 1970s came from abroad.[10] This does not imply, however, that the Republic of Korea also lacked indigenous capabilities in some of the less specialised activities needed to establish an ammonia plant. Indeed, as summary Table 6.3 shows, the Republic of Korea has extensive capabilities in plant construction and management, as well as in the provision of general purpose equipment and machinery.

In order to evaluate the divergent strategies of the four countries, we must examine more closely what goals underlie efforts to develop ammonia technology and what the costs of such efforts might be.

II. THE GOALS OF INDIGENOUS DEVELOPMENT OF AMMONIA TECHNOLOGY

In general, there are three distinct sets of reasons why countries might pursue the indigenous development of technology - as an effort to develop technologies closely aligned to local economic conditions, in an attempt to shift the balance of bargaining power away from foreigners, and as part of a distinctive strategy of development. This section will examine in turn the relevance of each of these reasons to efforts to develop indigenous technology in the ammonia industry.

Appropriate technology

The starting point for proponents of appropriate technology is that technologies developed in industrialised countries do not fit the requirements of developing nations. The ratio of investment to labour utilisation is too high, the minimum efficient scale is too large, and the level of skills required for operation and repair too great given the abundant supply of labour, lack of experience with large-scale organisation and shortages of technical skills in developing countries. A strategy of indigenous development of technology could lead to:
  "the introduction of a more appropriate technology (that) would reduce the large disparities in control over resources, labour productivity and income distribution between different parts of the country ... The major problems resulting from the distribution pattern - particularly those of imbalance in employment opportunities, the appearance of open

175

Table 6.3

Sources of supply of ammonia technology for Brazil, India, Mexico and the Republic of Korea

	Brazil Local	Brazil Foreign	India Local	India Foreign	Mexico Local	Mexico Foreign	Republic of Korea Local	Republic of Korea Foreign
Pre-project Planning	X		X		X		X	X
Project Management	X	X	X	X	X	X	X	X
Engineering								
(i) Basic		X	X	X		X		X
(ii) Detail	X		X		X	X		X
Procurement	X	X	X	X	X	X		X
Equipment								
(i) Complex	X	X	X	X		X		X
(ii) General	X		X	X	X		X	
Catalysts		X	X	X		X		X
Construction	X		X		X		X	
Start-up	X	X	X	X	X	X	X	X
Technical Services	X	?	X	?	X	?	X	?

unemployment as a chronic problem, and maldistribution of income – disappear if appropriate technology, especially if accessible to all, were introduced. If the technology were efficient, the absolute level of incomes should also rise ..."[11]

Notwithstanding these apparent advantages, in the countries studied here there have been no efforts to adapt ammonia technology to local conditions: the Brazilians have been quite explicit in their desire to absorb the state-of-the-art technology from abroad; as for India, even though until recently the strategy there was to go it alone as extensively as possible, from the first the goal was to master technology already in use abroad rather than to come up with alternative designs.

It is possible (although without field research the hypothesis cannot be tested) that bureaucratic slippage and a consequent failure to translate government goals into enterprise action (assuming, of course, that the development of appropriate technology is a goal of government), together with a desire on the part of engineering-oriented management to work at the technological frontier as defined in industrialised countries, account for a lack of interest in redesigning ammonia technology for local conditions. But a far more likely explanation has to do with the nature of ammonia technology itself: ammonia falls in a class of process industries for which the unit costs of production decline substantially as scale and the ratio of capital to labour rise. Scherer summarises the engineering logic that underlies this relationship:

"The output of a processing unit tends within certain physical limits to be roughly proportional to the volume of the unit, other things being equal, while the amount of materials and fabrication effort (and hence investment cost) required to construct the unit is more apt to be proportional to the surface area of the unit's reaction chambers, storage tanks, connecting pipes and the like. Since the area of a sphere or cylinder of constant proportions varies as the two-thirds power of volume, the cost of constructing process industry plants can be expected to rise as the two-thirds power of their output capacity, at least up to the point where they become so large that extra structural reinforcement and special fabrication techniques are required ... Energy usage also tends to rise less than proportionately with increases in processing vessel size ... Moreover the crew required to operate a large processing unit or machine is often little or no larger than what is needed for a unit of smaller capacity, so labour-costs per unit of output fall

sharply with scale-up."[12]
Advances in ammonia technology in the 1950s and the
development of a new plant design in the 1960s led to
continual increases in plant capacity and declines in
production costs. The cost per tonne of ammonia produced
in a plant with a capacity of 1,000 tonnes per day based on
the new design was 20 per cent below the cost in a plant of
330 tonnes per day; one half of these savings came via
economies of scale and the other half from the improved
technology of the new design.[13]

Bargaining power

A second reason to pursue the indigenous development
of technology may be a desire to shift the balance of
bargaining power away from foreigners. For developing
countries two distinct types of costs of foreign control of
technology are relevant here - the need to accept the
presence of multinational firms if production is to get
underway locally, and the need to pay to foreigners a high
proportion of the rents accruing from use of the technology
in order to induce them to make it available for local
production.[14] To what extent does the desire to reduce
these costs account for efforts to develop an indigenous
capability in ammonia technology?

Foreign investment is extensive in most industries in
which technology is continually advancing and is under the
close control of only a few companies.[15] The ammonia
industry is different. Even though the industry is
characterised by both close control and continually
advancing technology, there has been very little direct
foreign investment in either developing or industrialised
countries. The reason is not simply a desire by
governments to maintain national control in this basic
sector of industry (desire, to be realised, requires the
backing of bargaining power), but rather the unusual
international organisation of the industry: since the end
of the Second World War, the firms that control ammonia
technology have, by and large, been different from the
firms that produce ammonia. This is not the place to
explore the reasons for the separation of control over
technology from production;[16] it is the consequences that
are of special relevance here. The separation of control
over technology from control over production undermined the
incentive of firms active in the industry to invest abroad;
arms-length deals between national firms (usually
state-owned[17]) from developing (and sometimes industrialised) countries and vendors of technology became the medium
through which ammonia technology was diffused across
national boundaries. In the ammonia industry, at any rate,

it did not follow that if the balance of bargaining power lay entirely in the hands of technology vendors then developing countries would have to accede to foreign investment for production to get underway.

Even though unequal bargaining power in the ammonia industry did not have foreign investment as its consequence, vendors of technology were in a position to capture a high proportion of the rents from ammonia production for themselves. It does not follow, however, that the most efficient response to this imbalance is to try and develop an indigenous technological capability.

For one thing, the expected benefits of an increased share of rents must be weighed against the costs of developing technology at home; only if the present value of these benefits exceeds the costs of development (on which more later) would investment in technology lead to increased revenue for a developing country. Moreover, an increased domestic capability is not the only way through which a shift in bargaining power can occur: it could also result from an increase in the number of vendors and an ensuing rise in the degree of competition among them.

Competition among vendors of ammonia technology has increased substantially since the mid-1960s. In the mid-1960s M.W. Kellogg developed the radically new design for ammonia plants that was referred to earlier. With this new design Kellogg quickly began to dominate the world market for ammonia plants: one half of the additional ammonia capacity built worldwide between 1966 and 1978 was based on the new design; most of these plants were built by Kellogg itself or by one of the few other companies that Kellogg licensed to supply the design.[18] Yet, over time, Kellogg's technological lead has been whittled away by competing technologies, developed first by European firms and then, in time, by other American companies.[19]

One consequence has almost certainly been a decline in the profitability of supplying ammonia plants abroad. Although direct evidence is hard to come by, the increase in competition among suppliers - to cite one example, in 1980 about a dozen companies sought to submit proposals for a new ammonia complex in Indonesia[20] - makes such an outcome highly likely. A second consequence has been a growing willingness on the part of the vendors of ammonia technology to unbundle the supply of their services, thereby enabling developing countries to begin to develop their own technical capabilities. As long as only a few companies controlled the technology of ammonia plants, they could refuse to supply their special skills unless they were also hired to undertake other activities in plant construction for which they had no special advantage. But as competition grew, and as developing countries sought to increase the role of domestic firms in ammonia plant construction, technology vendors increasingly became willing to co-ordinate their activities with local firms from developing countries and undertake only those activities for which local firms lacked the skills. Indeed, as the example of Brazil illustrates, in return for the establishment of a long-term plant supply agreement with a developing country, they sometimes were willing to collaborate in the transfer of their most specialised technical skills.

For now, though, our task is not so much to outline the mechanisms through which technology transfer can be effected as it is to explain why some developing countries are so eager to take advantage of new opportunities to develop ammonia technology at home. As already noted, this desire appears unrelated to efforts to develop appropriate technology. Nor is it a response to a lack of bargaining power: even when foreign bargaining power was at its zenith, local ownership remained the norm, and as the number of ammonia plants has increased, the balance of bargaining power (and thus most likely the distribution of rents) has shifted decisively in favour of developing countries.

Indigenous technology as development strategy

The desire for indigenous technological development appears to be part of a strategy of economic development that is oriented towards the development of heavy industries, including the expansion of engineering firms and the fabrication of sophisticated industrial equipment. The greater is the extent of the indigenous provision of the engineering and construction skills and equipment needed for an ammonia plant, the larger are the number of opportunities for learning by doing (not to mention production and profits) available to local vendors.

The heavy emphasis in India on going it alone as rapidly and as extensively as possible in the provision of skills and equipment for ammonia plants is consistent with the country's strategy of industrialisation - a strategy which has been oriented towards rapid growth of these skill-intensive industries. Illustrative of this emphasis, between 1956 and 1976 engineering exports from India grew at an average rate of 25 per cent per annum; by 1976 they comprised 19 per cent of total exports of manufactures.[21] The Indian strategy stands in sharp contrast to that adopted by the Republic of Korea. The Republic of Korea has, until recently, placed little emphasis on developing sophisticated engineering and fabrication capabilities. The emphasis instead has been on production in light, labour-intensive sectors. The extraordinary

180

growth rates and increases in employment that followed from this strategy have been thoroughly documented else-where.[22] The cost of the strategy has been that local engineering and fabricating firms lost the opportunity to gain valuable experience as ammonia capacity expanded in the Republic of Korea.

But this is not the place for a comparative analysis of labour-intensive, export oriented and heavy industry, import substituting strategies of industrialisation. Ammonia plants are not built solely for the employment they provide and for the externalities they generate. Their primary function is to supply nitrogen fertiliser to farmers at the lowest possible cost. What is the effect on the cost of ammonia production of efforts to rely heavily on indigenous technology in the erection of new plants? It is to this question that we now turn.

III. THE COST OF INDIGENISATION

The total costs of indigenisation are not only the direct costs of investment in the development of indigenous skills in engineering and equipment fabrication. Efforts at indigenisation often lead to delays in the start-up of new ammonia plants and can also contribute to low subsequent rates of capacity utilisation once these plants are in operation. As will be seen, the costs of delays and of low capacity utilisation could well be way in excess of the direct costs of investment in new skills.

Although it has not been possible to undertake the in-depth field research needed to measure accurately the overall costs of indigenisation, some impressionistic evidence is available, especially for India, on the effects of indigenisation on delays and subsequent rates of capacity utilisation. As the next section shows, these effects appear to be substantial, but estimates of their magnitude are not sufficiently precise to estimate accurately their implications for the cost of ammonia. Instead, I use available evidence on the investment and production costs of ammonia in general to calculate the net present value of an ammonia operation across varying levels of capacity utilisation and delays in start-up; this net present value declines sharply as delays lengthen and capacity utilisation falls, confirming that indigenisation can add substantially to the cost of producing ammonia.

Delays and production shortfalls: Some evidence

Indigenisation is obviously not the only reason why delays in start-up or shortfalls in production might occur. Some problems can afflict all firms, public or private; others might be especially likely to affect public enterprises, irrespective of whether they are pursuing a strategy of indigenisation. Typical examples of the first group of problems include the late delivery of equipment from abroad, power breakdowns forcing a plant to shut down, and government bureaucracies that restrict the availability of some input needed for production. To cite just one instance, a branch of the Banco de Brasil, following its standard procedures, insisted on gaining the approval of individual manufacturers before giving permission to import, thereby delaying one ammonia project by nine months.

India provides a number of examples of burdens that weighed especially heavily on public enterprises, at least in the 1960s. The FCI apparently had to apply afresh for foreign exchange for each large overseas purchase that it made, and to clear each of these purchases with prospective local suppliers; in at least two instances, the need for such clearance led to delays of almost ten months; foreign contractors, by contrast, had ready access to foreign exchange, sometimes from grants of aid, sometimes released in a lump sum by the Indian government. More generally, the ministries and committees which had been assigned as overseers subjected the FCI to endless queries, criticisms and delays in clearance to proceed even with routine activities.

Notwithstanding the proliferation of alternative explanations, there is convincing (if still only anecdotal and partial) evidence that efforts at indigenisation have a major independent impact on delays and capacity utilisation. Evidence on the length of delays is available for eight plants in which the FCI's P and D division played a major role in design and construction.[23] All eight plants experienced long delays in completion. One was only completed three and a half years after its scheduled date; two more were each delayed for 27 months; a fourth was delayed for two years, and a fifth for 15 months; two other plants had still not produced significant quantities of ammonia by 1980, even though work on them had begun in 1971.

Delays in the delivery of overseas equipment bedevilled almost all the plants. Although at first sight such delays might appear to have little to do with indigenisation, they occurred in part because international fabricators of engineering equipment did not place much importance on cultivating a reputation of reliability with the FCI. Inefficient service to a major international contractor carried the risk of losing substantial business, not only for ammonia plants but also the other petrochemical and heavy engineering projects undertaken by technology vendors. By contrast, the FCI seemed unlikely ever to become a major customer. Problems at home usually were a result of the lack of experience of indigenous fabricators with the sophisticated equipment used in ammonia plants. Long delays in the delivery of equipment produced locally forced the postponement of start-up in at least three plants.

Turning to low capacity utilisation, here again much of the difficulty lay in problems with equipment. Crucial components sometimes failed to perform as efficiently as expected, keeping capacity utilisation low. Often the failures were in equipment fabricated locally, though imports also gave their share of difficulties; and faulty design led to low utilisation of capacity in at least two plants.

Table 6.4 presents data on the capacity utilisation of ammonia plants in India. The table reveals a striking discrepancy between the performance of plants that are wholly government-owned on the one hand and those that are joint ventures with private firms (and farmers co-operatives) or wholly privately owned on the other. What is more relevant for present purposes, however, is the difference in the average level of capacity utilisation within the public sector between plants that were erected largely by foreign contractors and those for which there was substantial local sourcing: in 1980-81 the average levels of capacity utilisation for the former group of plants was 19 per cent higher than the latter; and the projected gap for the following year[24] is in excess of 15 per cent. It is also noteworthy that once the independent impact of indigenisation is excluded, the production gap between the remaining public sector plants and plants in the private (though not joint) sector falls to only seven per cent. Evidence on capacity utilisation in Mexico offers an additional indication that indigenisation, rather than public ownership per se, is the primary explanation for low levels of performance of publicly owned plants. As noted earlier, ammonia production in Mexico is wholly state-controlled; at the same time there have been only limited efforts at indigenisation. As Table 6.5 shows, at no time between 1970 and 1980 did ammonia production in Mexico fall below 80 per cent of rated capacity.

In all, the anecdotal evidence suggests that efforts at indigenisation can lead to substantial delays and reductions in levels of capacity utilisation. What remains to be shown is the effect of delays and low levels of production on the cost of producing ammonia. It is to this issue that we now turn.

The net present value of an ammonia plant

Ammonia plants typically require high initial invest-

Table 6.4

The capacity utilisation of Indian ammonia plants,
grouped by owner and source of technology

Owner-Type	Capacity (tonnes)	PRODUCTION Actual 1980-81	Projected 1981-82
A. Public Sector			
Foreign Contractors Dominate[b]	1112	546.3 (49.1%)[a]	746.9 (67.2%)
Substantial Local Sourcing[c]	1323	398.3 (30.1)	766.1 (51.9)
Total Public Sector	2435	944.6 (30.1)	1513.0 (51.9)
B. Joint Sector[d]	1314	867.4 (68.3)	1083.9 (82.5)
C. Private Sector	644	360.7 (56.0)	500.6 (77.7)

Source: Data on capacity and production from Ministry of Petroleum Chemicals and Fertilisers, Department of Chemicals and Fertilisers, Annual Report 1981-82, pp. 28-9.

Notes: a Production as percentage of capacity.
        b Plants included are Neyveli, Rourkela, Gorakhpur, Nangal 1, Bhatinda, Panipat, Namrup I, Udyogomandal and Trombay 1.
        c Plants included are Sindri, Ramagundam, Talcher, Nangal 2, Durgapur, Barauni, Cochin 1 and Cochin 2.
        d Firms included are Madras Fertilisers, Gujarat State Fertilisers, Shiram Chemical and Fertilisers, Southern Petrochemical Industries and Indian Farmers Fertiliser Co-operative.

Table 6.5

Mexican ammonia production as percentage of rated capacity

Year	Capacity Utilisation
1970	80.9%
1971	82.0
1972	90.0
1973	94.5
1974	93.6
1975	93.1
1976	100.5
1977	109.6
1978	90.2
1979	94.4
1980	107.5

Source: PEMEX, internal documents.

ments which yield a return via flows of revenue over the long term.   If interest rates (and thus the opportunity cost of capital) are positive, then from the perspective of a prospective investor a dollar of this revenue flow earned at one point in time is not equal to a dollar earned at another point in time.   This distinction is especially relevant for this study, since the two parameters on which we focus - construction delays and variations in capacity utilisation - affect the time path and the magnitude of the flow of revenues and costs of ammonia production; so some common benchmark is needed if we are to compare the cost implications of variations in these parameters.   A measure of the net present value of the flow of revenues and costs of an ammonia plant provides the appropriate benchmark.

In general, the present value of a revenue producing project can be characterised as follows:

$$NPV = \int_a^{a+b} P_t Q_t e^{-rt}dt - \int_a^{a+b} C(Q_t)e^{-rt}dt \quad -C \int_a^{a+b} e^{-rt}dt -I_0 \quad (1)$$

$$\qquad\qquad (2) \qquad\qquad\qquad (3) \qquad\qquad\qquad (4) \qquad\quad (5)$$

a = year of start-up
b = plant lifetime
P_t = output price in time t
Q_t = output in time t
r = annual compounded rate of discount
$C(Q_t)$ = variable costs
C = fixed annual overhead costs
I_0 = initial investment cost.

Term (2) measures the present value of the estimated stream of revenues over the plant's lifetime, term (3) the present value of the lifetime stream of variable costs, term (4) the present value of annual overhead costs, and (5) the initial cost of investment. The NPV is greater than zero (and thus the project may be deemed profitable), if

$$(2) \;>\; (3) + (4) + (5).$$

Of course, in so far as the erection of an ammonia plant generates positive externalities, an NPV less than zero calculated on the basis of market prices would not necessarily imply that a given project is socially inefficient. Table 6.6 presents estimates of the value of the above parameters for a 1650 ton per day ammonia-urea plant.[25]
If we assume that the level of capacity utilisation – $Q_t/1650$ – does not vary over the plant's lifetime, then (1) can be rewritten as:

$$NPV = \left\{ Q\left[P - C(Q)\right] - C \right\} \int_a^{a+b} e^{-rt}dt - I_0 \quad,$$

from which it is a simple matter to calculate the net present value of an ammonia plant for selected levels of capacity utilisation (and thus Q) and length of delays from initial investment to start-up (measured by a). Table 6.7 shows the results of these calculations, assuming an annual compounded rate of discount (r) of 10 per cent.
The results in Table 6.7 reveal that the costs of delays and reduced capacity utilisation are high: a one-year increase in the time from initial investment to the start-up of production reduces NPV by about \$40 million; and for any given lead time, NPV falls by \$50-\$60

Table 6.6

Parameter estimates for a natural gas-based
ammonia-urea plant, 1980

Parameter	Value	Comments
I_o	$300 million	Depending on the extent of existing infrastructure, this measure can range from $200-$400 million
P	$263 per ton	Average urea price between 1964 and 1980
C(Q)	$121 per ton	$105 per ton feedstock costs
C	$15.4 million per annum	Maintenance, insurance and labour costs
b	30 years	An arbitrary assumption

Source: William F. Sheldrick, Fertiliser Unit, World Bank, Investment and Production Costs for Fertilisers, paper presented at FAO Commission on Fertilisers, Sixth Session, 1980.

million for every decline of 10 percent in the rate of capacity utilisation. The impressionistic evidence in the previous section suggests that a one year delay and a 10 per cent loss of capacity are plausible (and perhaps even low) estimates of the consequences of India's efforts to develop indigenous ammonia technology. On the basis of the calculations in this section, the cost of these consequences amounted to the equivalent of an increase in $100 million in the initial investment in the plant, one-third of the initial capital requirement. If we add the direct additions to cost of reliance on domestic expertise (for which no estimates are available) then the burden imposed by a strategy of indigenisation becomes even higher.

To what extent are estimates of the costs of delays and low utilisation of capacity sensitive to assumptions as to the rate of discount? As Table 6.8 shows, a reduction in the assumed rate of discount to 5 per cent per annum increases substantially the NPV for each lead time and capacity level. But this reduction does not affect much the magnitude of the declines in NPV that result from increases in delays and reductions in capacity utilisation. Now a one year rise in lead time reduces NPV by only $35 million; but a 10 per cent decline in production reduces NPV by fully $110 million. In general, other things being equal, as interest rates fall the NPV of any project that requires substantial initial investments increases; and it becomes marginally less costly to delay a project;[26] but since future revenues no longer are discounted as heavily, the costs of a reduced production potential rise substantially.

Table 6.7

The net present value of an ammonia plant for varying lead times and levels of capacity utilisation
(r = 0.1)

Capacity Utilisation	LEAD TIME			
	2 years	2.5 years	3 years	4 years
90%	121.5	101.0	81.4	45.1
80	61.4	43.8	27.0	−4.1
70	1.2	−13.4	−27.4	−53.4
60	−58.9	−70.7	−81.9	−102.6
50	−119.1	−127.9	−136.3	−151.9

IV. INDIGENISATION: AN OVERALL EVALUATION

The benefits of indigenous development of ammonia technology turn out to be fewer than they might appear at first sight. Two potential nonpecuniary benefits are entirely absent. The engineering economies embedded in an ammonia plant undermine the incentive to experiment with small scale, less investment-intensive techniques of production; and the international organisation of the industry makes foreign investment unlikely even in the absence of indigenous technological know-how. The value of the two remaining potential benefits appear to be either highly uncertain or very limited. Indigenisation appears to be part of a strategy of development that emphasises the growth of heavy industry, and efforts to develop indigenous ammonia technology may well generate some important linkages; but there is no obvious way of knowing what value should be imputed to them. Also uncertain is the extent to which indigenisation adds to the bargaining power of developing countries relative to foreign vendors of technology: in the 1960s there may have been some gains, but by the 1970s, once competition among vendors had intensified, the gains appear highly limited at best.

Table 6.8

The net present value of an ammonia plant for varying lead times and levels of capacity utilisation
(r = 0.05)

Capacity Utilisation	LEAD TIME			
	2 years	2.5 years	3 years	4 years
90%	461.8	443.0	424.6	389.3
80	353.1	337.0	321.2	290.9
70	244.4	231.0	217.8	192.6
60	135.7	125.0	114.4	94.2
50	27.0	18.9	11.0	-4.1

In evaluating the social efficiency of efforts at indigenisation in the ammonia industry, benefits must, of course, be compared with costs. On the cost side the uncertainties are fewer. To be sure, no estimates are available of the direct costs of investment in indigenisation, but the orders of magnitude of the indirect costs can be readily calculated: if efforts at indigenisation cause a delay of one year in start-up and a subsequent loss of capacity of 10 per cent, the indirect costs alone are in excess of $100 million. It is hard to imagine how a value of $100 million could be ascribed to the benefits listed above.

This is not to imply that all attempts to develop indigenous technology are misguided. For one thing, although at the time this paper was written no evidence was available as to the outcome of its efforts, the example of Brazil points to the possibility that if competition among

technology vendors is extensive there may be less costly
ways to pursue indigenisation than going it alone as
rapidly and extensively as possible - although, of course,
the rate of growth of skill-intensive sectors of industry
is likely to be slower. More importantly, in many sectors
the costs of indigenisation are not likely to be as high,
nor the benefits as low as they are in ammonia. The scope
for adaptation - and thus the potential to reap the
benefits of appropriate technology - may often be higher
outside the continual process industries; and in many
sectors the ratio of initial investment requirements to
variable costs is lower than it is in ammonia, with
corresponding reductions in the cost of delays and
production below capacity. But nor should the cautionary
value of the experience with technology transfer in the
ammonia industry be underestimated. Ammonia is not likely
to be the only industry for which the hidden costs of
indigenisation are high, while many of the purported
benefits turn out to be chimerical.

NOTES AND REFERENCES

1. For a review of this research, see Brian Levy (1983): "New Directions in Public Enterprise Analysis", Harvard Institute for International Development, _Development Discussion Paper_.

2. UNIDO (1980): _Fertiliser Manual_, Development and Transfer of Technology Series, Number 13, United Nations, New York, p. 9.

3. Estimated from data provided by the Tennessee Valley Authority. For an overview of ownership trends in the fertiliser industry, see John T. Shields and E.A. Harre (1978): "Capacity and Ownership Trends", in _Fertilizer Progress_, Washington, DC, Volume 9, Number 3, May-June, pp. 11-34.

4. According to at least one observer, the lure of foreign aid from a wide variety of sources at a time of scarce foreign exchange all but forced the FCI to alter continually its choice of vendor for specific technical components, thereby undermining further whatever opportunities for technological learning might otherwise have been present.

5. "Another 'Bechtel Deal'?", in _Economic and Political Weekly_, Bombay, 28 October, 1972, p. 2177; "Goodbye to self-reliance in fertiliser technology?", in _Commerce_, September 20, 1975, p. 480.

6. "Destruction of Fertiliser Corporation", in _Economic and Political Weekly_, 23 July, 1977, pp. 1168-9; "Mess in Fertilisers", in _Economic and Political Weekly_, 10 May, 1980, pp. 839-40.

7. "Growth at all costs", in _Economic and Political Weekly_, November 18, 1972, pp. 2264-5; and "NFL comes of age", in _Commerce_, Bombay, Special Feature, 29 March, 1980.

8. "Scuttling India's know-how in fertilisers", in _Economic and Political Weekly_, April 21, 1979, pp. 725-6; "World Bank cancels $250 million loan for Indian fertiliser complex", in _European Chemical News_, Sutton, Surrey, 12 January, 1981.

9. Information from interviews with PEMEX and Kellogg.

10. Kelloggram, _KOCO and Kellogg_ (M.W. Kellogg: Houston, 1972), pp. 5-6; Unico International Corporation: _Seventh fertiliser project in the Republic of Korea: Evaluation study_ (Tokyo, 1973), p. VI-I; Toyo Engineering: _Feasibility Report on a urea plant expansion in Chung-Ju Fertiliser Complex_ (Tokyo, 1974), p. 5-2.

11. Frances Stewart (1977): _Technology and underdevelopment_, Boulder, Colorado, Westview Press, p. 108.

12. F.M. Scherer (1980): _Industrial market structure and_

economic performance (2nd edition), Boston, Houghton Mifflin, pp. 82-3.

13. "Capacity surge, story of ammonia", in Oil and Gas Journal, Tulsa Oklahoma, 18 March, 1968, pp. 78-84.

14. For a more detailed discussion, see Peter Evans (1979): Dependent development, Princeton, Princeton University Press, especially Chapter 4.

15. For discussions of this relationship, see Richard E. Caves (1982): Multinational enterprise and economic analysis, Cambridge, England, Cambridge University Press; P.J. Buckley and Marc Casson (1986): The Future of the Multinational Enterprise, New York, Holmes and Meier; and Raymond Vernon (1977): Storm over the multinationals, Cambridge, Massachusetts, Harvard University Press.

16. These have to do with the unusual history of the industry, in particular political interventions which led to the break-up and loss of market power of the highest companies, together with the special character of the transactions costs of turnkey deals which reduce the cost disadvantages of arms-length over internal transactions.

17. Once again, I would argue that the reasons for state ownership have to do with market imperfections in the market for capital. Given the lack of development of capital markets in developing countries, private local firms typically cannot raise by themselves the capital needed to set up an ammonia plant.

18. Pullman Incorporated: 1978 Annual Report, p. 11.

19. These firms include Imperial Chemicals Industries (ICI), Uhde, Haldor Topsoe, W.R. Grace, Fluor, Braun and Bechtel.

20. See "Contractors shortlisted for ASEAN project", in European Chemical News, January 28, 1980, p. 27; "Toyo to build first ASEAN ammonia-urea complex" in European Chemical News, November 3, 1980.

21. Sanjaya Lall (1979): Developing countries as exporters of technology and capital goods: The Indian experience, Oxford University, Institute of Economics and Statistics, unpublished draft, June, p. 13.

22. For example, Kwang Suk Kim and Michael Roemer (1977): Studies in the modernisation of the Republic of Korea, 1945-75: Growth and structural transformation, Cambridge, Harvard University Press.

23. The discussion on delays and capacity utilisation in India draws on "Goodbye to self-reliance in fertiliser technology?" in Commerce, September 20, 1975, pp. 478-81; "Another 'Bechtel Deal'?", in Economic and Political Weekly, October 28, 1972, pp. 2177-8; "Slaughter of Fertiliser Corporation", in Economic and Political Weekly, April 5, 1975, pp. 571-2;

"Ramagundam coal-based fertiliser plant", in Commerce, August 23, 1975, pp. 328-9; and World Bank project reports.

24. Which presumably does not include losses in production for exogenous and unexpected reasons; in 1980-81 it is possible that these fell disproportionately in the group with lowest capacity utilisation.

25. Urea is the most common form in which nitrogen fertilisers are used.

26. Although no savings as a result of bureaucratic thoroughness are likely to come anywhere close to the $15 to $20 million that even a six month delay would cost.

Chapter 7

The Technological Behaviour of State-Owned Enterprises in Brazil

Alfonso Carlos Correa Fleury

I. INTRODUCTION

Brazil has made extensive use of state-owned enterprises during its rapid industrial development. According to one estimate the share of these enterprises in annual gross investment outside of agriculture has fluctuated between 25 and 30 per cent.[1] It follows from this degree of prominence of state-owned enterprises in the industrialisation of Brazil that the technological behaviour of these enterprises – construed broadly to include dynamic, learning aspects as well as choices made at a point of time – is important to an understanding of the process as a whole. This paper is concerned to discover the determinants of technological behaviour in two state-owned enterprises that have made an especially significant contribution to industrial development in the post-war period, both of which currently number among the largest enterprises in their respective fields in the world. For the purpose of this task numerous case studies from the experience of the two firms are examined in detail. The first part of the paper is devoted to the analysis of the setting up of two nitrogenated fertiliser factories by Petrobrás and the second part to the evolution of the various types of aircraft that comprise Embraer's technological strategy. The final section synthesises and compares the results of the two case-studies.

194

II. TECHNOLOGICAL CHOICE IN THE FERTILISER INDUSTRY

Government intervention in the fertiliser industry

The National Fertiliser and Agricultural Lime Programme (PNFCA)

The world economic crisis of 1973-74 had a considerable effect on Brazil's economic development policies. The Second National Development Plan (II PND) was designed to lay down new guidelines in tune with this experience of world crisis.

It was in the context of the new stage of import substitution that the Government introduced the National Fertiliser and Agricultural Lime Programme (PNFCA), which was intended to stimulate intensive industrialisation of existing mineral resources, thereby reducing or even eliminating, if possible, the predominant dependence on external supplies.

The PNFCA was drafted by a working group created as a result of the decision made by the Economic Development Council (CDE) on 23 July 1974, to prepare the National Fertiliser Programme, one of the Special Plans for Basic Feedstocks mentioned in the II PND.

The working group which prepared the PNFCA had its offices in the Ministry of Industry and Commerce, and it did not include any representatives of private enterprise. Indeed, the only representative of the productive sector was Petrobrás, which through its subsidiary Petroquisa controlled Nitrofértil (producing ammonia and urea in Bahia) and the recently incorporated Ultrafértil.

The Programme was based on supply and demand analyses which considered the country in terms of three regions - Northeast, Centre and South.

A comparison of projections of demand for fertilisers for 1980 with estimates of supply in the PNFCA for the same period produced predictions of probable deficits which would have to be eliminated. In order to neutralise these forecast deficits by expanding the supply of nutrients, the PNFCA estimated a required volume of funding of around US$1.3 billion. The strategy proposed was as follows:

A. "A schematic plan for supplying Brazilian agriculture with fertilisers must consider, as fundamental aspects, the location of natural resources and known raw materials which can be **economically exploited**, the regional areas where consumers are concentrated, and the fertilisers to be consumed.

In terms of known natural resources offering satisfactory conditions for exploitation, **technically and economically speaking**, Brazil does not have an abundance of natural gas, natural phosphorus, sulphur or sylvinite: the whole market cannot therefore be supplied according to the best standards of economic viability for the fertiliser industry so as to ensure self-reliance in market supplies.

The procurement plan to be adopted must therefore consider the following:

- known resources in the country and their availability: natural gas and petroleum fractions for nitrogenated products; apatite for phosphated products; pyrite and shale as sources of sulphur;
- supplementing known sources by importing raw materials (or products) directly to consumer regions, thus avoiding internal handling;
- diversifying supplies of nutrients for **economic and security reasons**, including imported raw materials or products; and
- concentration or regionalisation, aimed at **improving production scales whenever feasible**" (my emphasis).[2]

The PNFCA analysed the specific issue of nitrogenated fertilisers in the Centre region to draw the following conclusions:

B.   "The deficit forecast for 1980 can only be reduced in regional terms by the implementation of **at least two large-scale projects** for the production of nitrogenated fertilisers, in Paulínia and Araucária, both based on fuel supplied by large local refineries. These units will have a **production capacity compatible with present levels and proven technical standards**, as well as having a large-scale urea plant within the same industrial complex to convert most of the ammonia produced into fertiliser. Furthermore, considering the convenience of standardising designs to reduce investment, units shall be so dimensioned as to produce around 1000 tonnes/day of ammonia and 1500 tonnes/day of urea, corresponding to a significant increase in the supply of nitrogenated fertiliser".[3]

For the Northeast region, the PNFCA concluded that supplies "are guaranteed by the units already operating or under construction in Bahia, and it is possible to forecast that surpluses of ammonia and urea will be available for transfer to other regions for a number of years and beyond the end of the present decade".[4] In the following paragraph, however, it is recommended that: "A further project to produce ammonia and nitrogenous fertiliser from natural gas must be firmly investigated for implementation during the current decade, depending on prospection work being conducted by Petrobrás and which may indicate sufficient reserves of natural gas, especially in Alagoas".[5]

In short, the solution for nitrogenated fertilisers adopted by the PNFCA was based on the implementation of three major projects, which had already been decided on in terms of location and size. However, later developments led to changes in this plan - of the three plants mentioned, two were in fact installed as proposed (the nitrogenated fertiliser plants in Araucária, state of Paraná, and Laranjeiras, state of Sergipe), while the unit intended for Paulínia was later transferred to Rio de Janeiro and eventually cancelled.

Criteria for technological choice in the PNFCA

It is important to undertake an analysis, however brief, of the explicit and implicit content of the section quoted above from the PNFCA, in order to understand the criteria for technological choice and operational performance utilised by the group which prepared the document, and thereby offered to the institutions and people in charge of its implementation.

In section A above, the criteria for eligibility of the various alternatives first appear. These alternatives are to satisfy technical and economic criteria, with constraints regarding location in terms of the supply of raw materials and regional demand for fertilisers. Some consideration is given to security matters, and finally the convenience of "improving production scales whenever possible" is made explicit. Thus the official message of the Programme is clear: decision-making criteria must highlight the technical and economic factors, if not actually consider them exclusively; the main goal at which to aim is cost minimisation. But the PNFCA goes even further by specifying some of the decisions at the level of making the Programme operational.

Section B represents the result of applying these methods (though this is not made explicit in the text) to solving the problems of nitrogenated fertiliser production in the Central region. The solutions presented make it easier to understand the parameters which the Working Group hoped to achieve.

The first point to observe is the importance given to the large-scale projects. Second, the "present levels of production capacity and technical standards" which oriented the Working Group undoubtedly refer to the international scene. The capacities indicated for the projects (1000 tpd of ammonia and 1500 tpd of urea) corresponded to the most up-to-date processes then available, which were highly capital intensive. Levy[6] remarks that "ammonia falls into a class of process industries for which unit production costs decline substantially as scale and the capital-labour ratio rise... Advances in ammonia technology in the 1950s and the development of a new plant

197

design in the 1960s led to continual increases in plant capacity and decreases in production costs. The cost per tonne of ammonia produced by a plant with a capacity of 1000 tpd based on the new design was 20 per cent below the cost for a plant producing 330 tpd; one half of these savings came via economies of scale, and the other half from the improved technology of the new design."

Thus the logic behind the preparation of the Programme proves to be perfectly consistent, at the level of both criteria and choices. As to criteria, those that prevail are:

- the idea of large-scale projects;
- highly capital-intensive technologies;
- the most advanced technologies on the world market; and
- minimised production costs as a result.

As could be foreseen, these criteria, some explicitly expressed in the PNFCA and others left implicit, underlay the decision-making processes within the state-owned enterprises which became responsible for carrying out the PNFCA in practice.

Petrobrás and the PNFCA

Organisation and choice in Petrobrás

In order to co-ordinate and supervise the implementation of the PNFCA, the Executive Fertiliser Committee was set up in December 1973 under the jurisdiction of the Ministry of Industry and Commerce. Petrobrás was made responsible for the large-scale projects provided for in the Programme.

The reasons for the choice of Petrobrás are apparently bound up with the history of the enterprise and with its growth strategy. The scope of the present study does not permit a review of the whole history of the organisation, but it is worth underlining the main features of its technological strategy.

Petrobrás was founded in 1953 in a strongly nationalistic atmosphere. Evans[7] observes that "as a result of pressure from a broad coalition of nationalist forces that included everyone, from the Communists to the student movement to the military, Petrobrás was given a monopoly of refining and exploration of oil". The enterprise was set up with very well-defined functions on the operational level: its basic activity was to refine petroleum as efficiently as possible. It is true that nationalist ideology was by no means left aside - Petrobrás has always had considerable influence on the development of Brazilian industry, mainly as regards capital goods. The performance of this task, however, has usually clashed with, and often been subordinated to, the achievement of the original aim. In other words, from an overall standpoint it has been unusual for Petrobrás to fail to give priority to operational efficiency over other kinds of requirement. There are several examples where Petrobrás has preferred larger investments in technology and plant purchased from abroad in order to minimise delays in start-up and to maximise operational efficiency.

Already at the time of its creation, then, Petrobrás had a high degree of autonomy, and since then this has if anything increased. According to Abranches and Dain,[8] Petrobrás has always had financial autonomy and its field of operation has been given high priority in the country's development policies.

Its incursion into petrochemicals began with the Cubatão Fertiliser Company (Fafer) in 1958. In 1962 Petrobrás began operating a synthetic rubber factory (formerly Fabor, now Petroflex) in Rio de Janeiro, and this was its second petrochemicals plant. In 1963 the organisation decided to create the Bahia Petrochemicals Complex (now Nitrofértil), which began by producing ammonia and urea in 1971. From the creation of isolated units, Petrobrás proceeded to develop so-called "petrochemical poles", which are integrated groups of plants chain-processing raw materials into finished products. In 1968 the need to co-ordinate the creation of these poles led to the setting up of Petroquisa, "to act as a holding company with the main aim of promoting and developing the petrochemicals industry in Brazil" (Petroquisa currently has five wholly owned subsidiaries and 23 affiliates). In 1974, Petroquisa was, among other things, concluding the construction of the first petrochemicals pole (in São Paulo state), starting work on the second (in Bahia), and beginning the design stage for the third (in Rio Grande do Sul). The scale of these poles is gigantic: the second one, for example, had taken five years to finish when inaugurated in 1978, costing US$3.1 billion. Thus, Petroquisa's attentions were focused mainly on the poles.

Under these conditions, the first "gift" received by Petroquisa (i.e. Ultrafértil) was not entirely compatible with the enterprises's scale of priorities. But since Ultrafértil was a going concern, no significant rearrangements were needed. When the PNFCA's large-scale projects had to be implemented, however, it can be said that there was some resistance on the part of the organisation's technical personnel. This resistance was due not only to the scarcity of human resources and infrastructure, but also to the fact that although nitrogenated fertilisers (ammonia and urea) are part of the petroleum derivatives used by the petrochemicals industry, phosphated and potassic fertilisers are not. If it was to assume responsibility for designing and building plants to produce potassic and phosphated fertilisers, Petroquisa would thus have to develop activities outside its own specialised attributions.

The organisational solution for the preparation of the projects stipulated by the PNFCA was to set up a working group (task force) within the Engineering Department of Petrobrás which was to be placed in charge of the work. The Working Group did in fact make some decisions (such as the choice of technology for Fafen, the Paraná Nitrogenated Fertiliser Factory - see details below), but its decision-making autonomy was small. As a result, the pace of project development was slow, and the top management of Petrobrás proposed an alternative solution, consisting of the creation of a new subsidiary to be called Petrofértil.

Thus, Petrofértil was "set up on 24 March 1976 with the aim of bringing together under a single command the activities of Petrobrás in the fertiliser industry in compliance with instructions from the Federal Government, as expressed in the National Fertiliser and Agricultural Lime Programme". In order to achieve these aims, Petrofértil not only developed its own projects but also took over control of other organisations, as well as associating with private groups or other state-owned enterprises to set up fertiliser plants jointly.

The following chart shows the present structure of the Petrofértil system:

WHOLLY OWNED ORGANISATIONS	
Name	Previous owner
Ultrafértil	Ultra group, Petroquisa
Nitrofértil	Petroquisa
I.C.C.	Sidesc (Siderúrgica de Santa Catarina)

AFFILIATED ORGANISATIONS	
Arafértil	BNDE, Itaú group, Santista group
Goiasfértil	BNDE, Metago Metais de Goias S.A.
Fosfértil	BNDE, Companhia Vale do Rio Doce
Companhia Rio Grandense de Nitrogenados	BNDE, Rio Grande do Sul state administration

OWN PROJECTS	
Fafen (Paraná)	Nitrogenated fertiliser factory, Araucária
Fafen (Sergipe)	Nitrogenated fertiliser factory, Laranjeiras

Choice of technology for Fafen-Paraná

The first project tackled by the working group placed in charge of implementing the large-scale projects specified by the PNFCA was the Paraná Nitrogenated Fertiliser Factory (Fafen-PR). As already mentioned, the PNFCA stated that "a plant is to be built in Araucária, Paraná, with a production capacity of 1000 tpd of ammonia and 1500 tpd of urea, using asphalt waste from the Paraná refinery".

Practically all the critical decisions had therefore already been made, as to location, scale and feedstock. The Working Group had the conventional feasibility studies performed. The Planning Department prepared a market analysis and an economic feasibility study, while the Finance Department drafted a financial feasibility report. It is true, however, that these studies were intended merely to comply with formal requirements and establish operational procedures, since no decision on the feasibility of the project was needed.

Petrobrás had some experience in nitrogenated fertilisers, but the basic design features defined in the PNFCA were relatively unusual. The use of asphalt waste was fairly well-known for gasification, but there was little experience of producing ammonia from this feedstock on the required scale.

An engineer employed as an adviser to Cenpes (the acronym of the organisation's Research Centre) was selected to help the Group temporarily in the task of choosing technology. There were three permanent members of the Working Group: one from the Engineering Department, one from the Industrial Department and one from the Legal Department. Other people took part from time to time, depending on the subject under discussion.

In the case of Fafen-PR, the Group's first task was to acquaint itself with everything there was to know about the process involved, which consisted of four stages. They found that for the first stage two types of technology were available, developed by Shell and Texaco, but there had been only one instance of the application of this technology to obtain ammonia, using the Shell technology. This was in the Federal Republic of Germany, by the firm Veba Chimie, and their plant was used virtually all the time as a model to which the whole decision-making process was referred. Since there were two options for the first stage, then, the Group could have undertaken a stage-by-stage analysis and contracted for each one separately. But it was noticed that Veba Chimie had opted for a scheme which had given its designers, Lurgi, a design for the whole complex. Having analysed all four stages of the process, the Group concluded that Lurgi had control over three: gasification (where it was licensed by Shell),

partial oxidation (with its own technology) and removal
(also with its own technology). For ammonia synthesis,
however, Lurgi did not have its own technology, and Veba
Chimie had used the Haldor-Topsoe process with a design
developed by UHDE.

At this point, the Group abandoned the idea of dealing
with the process stage by stage, and taking the Veba plant
as a model, decided to order the Brazilian plant to produce
ammonia under similar specifications. Lurgi was to design
the first three stages and UHDE the fourth. As the group
co-ordinator put it: "We thought it wiser not to split it
up but to negotiate it as a whole, designing a process as
similar as possible to Veba's. That way we had standards
for selecting processes and conditioning the choice of
equipment, and we had a higher level of security".

For the urea unit, UHDE had considerable experience
and even its own technology, but the Veba plant had been
built with Stammicarbon technology. Moreover, if, as the
PNFCA stipulated, there was to be process standardisation,
Mitsui technology would have to be chosen instead, as this
is the technology used in most Petrobrás urea plants.
Nevertheless, the Group found that the technology from
Japan and the Federal Republic of Germany would be
incompatible and decided to exclude the former. It then
requested UHDE to prepare proposals based on its own
technology and on Stammicarbon's. Having compared the two,
the Group decided on the latter, but this time the criteria
used were technical and economic.

The proposal then approved by Petrobrás was that Lurgi
and UHDE should form a consortium to do all the basic
engineering for the plant, and no call for tenders was
issued. The Brazilian engineering firm asked to prepare
the detailed design was chosen by Lurgi and UHDE based on a
list of four names selected by Petrobrás from the group of
companies certified by the organisation.

An estimate was submitted to the World Bank via the
Brazilian Banco Nacional de Desenvolvimento Econômico
(BNDE). The estimated cost of the project was US$330
million, of which Petrobrás was to pay half. Of the rest,
25 per cent would be provided by the BNDE and 25 per cent
by the World Bank, as co-ordinator of a pool of other
banks. This would account for US$75 million in the form of
suppliers' credit. The project was submitted to the
Industrial Development Council (CDI, a federal Brazilian
body) for approval of exemptions from duties on plant
imports and tax incentives.

The contract signed by Petrobrás with the two firms
from the Federal Republic of Germany did not entail
technology transfer. According to the group co-ordinator,
this was due "not only to the fact that Petrobrás was not
yet ready to absorb technology, but also that the project

was considered virtually unrepeatable". It also stipulated that the main plant was to be imported – this was evidently a condition required by the international creditors, especially as regards the provision of suppliers' credit.

Once the contract had been signed, the Working Group was demobilised, and the responsibility for choices passed on to the designers; only a few administrative controls were maintained by Petrobrás. The contract was signed late in 1975, before the creation of Petrofértil, and start-up set for 1978. However, the plant was only completed in the last quarter of 1981 owing to a number of organisational and institutional problems.

Technological strategies and organisation

Reformulating the strategy

While the process of technological choice described above was going on, Petrobrás was experiencing a change in its stand on the technology issue. At the time of its creation, its basic mission was to refine petroleum as efficiently as possible. In other words, its performance criterion was fundamentally related to production. Thus, concern about technology was focused on oil refining technology, and most of the organisation's resources were reserved for this purpose. This was the field of activity with which the Petrobrás Petroleum Research and Development Centre (Cenap) was set up to deal in 1955; in 1966 it was replaced by Cenpes, which also started work in refining. According to the categories suggested by Dahlman and Westphal,[9] Petrobrás invested most of its efforts in production engineering.

In a recent article, Leitão[10] remarks that the activities of Cenap/Cenpes until 1975 were almost exclusively addressed to preparing labour and operational troubleshooting: "The initiative taken in setting up this Centre was due to the enlightened vision of some managers with considerable breadth of experience, rather than being a response to possible demands by the operational bodies within the enterprise... At that time the main concern was with building new refineries in order to meet the growing demand, using imported technology which was already finished and had been commercially tested, and with running these refineries in accordance with the design specifications."

The procedures adopted by Petrobrás for the design of plants and the equipment to be used in them were as follows:
- the basic design work was always awarded to a foreign engineering firm;
- the detail design work was commissioned from Brazilian engineering firms duly certified by Petrobrás, which

were to absorb technology from the foreign firms as far as possible; and

- to comply with the goal of indigenising equipment, Petrobrás endeavoured to order as much as possible from Brazilian capital goods manufacturers, thus enabling them to develop technologically and obtain further capabilities (although this was not the highest priority and in practice this has often obliged such firms to work under licence from foreign manufacturers[11]).

Within this scheme, "for many years Cenpes continued to look for a **raison d'être**, to try to find a role to play in the organisation... Interaction with the operational bodies was pretty difficult, since their interests were different from those in which Cenpes could take part. There was no interest in optimising processes as this would entail changes in the units, with the risk that production would be affected. On the other hand, the central bodies were basically concerned with studies geared to defining the location of new refineries and with the negotiations for the purchase of foreign technology."[12]

Thus, the corporation was oriented towards production, and the political power within Petrobrás was in the hands of the production personnel. This configuration prevailed in the early 1970s, when the top management of the organisation consisted mainly of the people who had taken part in the 1950s in installing the first plants, which had been equipped with imported technology, and had been responsible for their operation. This aspect may well be one of the reasons why, according to some groups within the organisation, "Petrobrás took too long to wake up to the real importance of the technology issue". But this position began to change from the early 1970s onwards.

The decision to endeavour to master and assume control of the technological process has a long history. According to the people in charge of Cenpes, it was over the period 1973-75 that the top executives of Petrobrás became aware of the need for this change. In 1975 a meeting was held with the staff of Finep, the federal agency responsible for funding research projects, attached to the Planning Secretariat. This meeting, considered to mark the moment of decision, was held to discuss the reasons why Petrobrás had, since its creation, always contracted with foreign engineering firms to develop similar basic design work. Once they had become aware of the issue, the Petrobrás Board of Directors began to analyse other aspects. For example, the issue of exporting technology and services could only be satisfactorily solved if the country produced its own plant, since Brazilian designs could hardly be sold to other countries if they themselves included foreign equipment. And this led, again, to the idea that there was the need to indigenise technology and that basic design and engineering work should be performed in Brazil.

Leitão analyses the question from another angle. According to him, the critical point in this change of attitude was the changing demand profile for petroleum derivates after 1975, as a result of the events of 1973. Table 7.1 below reflects this change.[13]

Table 7.1

Profile of demand for petroleum derivatives in Brazil

Demand profile	Up to 1975	Period 1975-79	After 1979
Petrol	33 %	24 %	18 %
Diesel	22 %	27 %	31 %
Fuel oil	28 %	29 %	22 %
Others	17 %	20 %	29 %

It should be pointed out that by 1976 all Petrobrás's refining capacity had already been installed. This led to a thoroughgoing change in the operational philosophy of the enterprise, which began to need Cenpes to perform studies enabling it to change the production processes then used in the plants, so as to match the new profile of demand. In other words, the oil shock led to a clear, firm and welldefined demand for technological knowledge which legitimised the role of Cenpes (and the importance of technology) within the enterprise for the first time since its creation.

Once it had been decided that technology had to be mastered, it followed that mastery of basic engineering was the fundamental goal in the petrochemicals industry. Some thought was given to the possibility of private enterprise undertaking this effort, but the hypothesis was rejected. The arguments in favour of this decision were the low level of operational experience acquired until then by Brazilian engineering firms, and above all the small size of the domestic market, which, because it would mean the introduction of protectionist barriers to benefit one organisation alone, was thought to pose a severe problem.

It was thus decided to create a Superintendency for Basic Engineering as a division of Cenpes, and this

decision was implemented in 1976. The strategy for achieving a capability in basic engineering was based on the use of three instruments concomitantly:
- technology transfer;
- research; and
- "unpackaging".

The current situation is such that Petrobrás now claims that it has the capability to design:
- a complete refinery;
- everything related to the use of natural gas; and
- little in the field of petrochemicals and fertilisers.

As regards the latter (petrochemicals and fertilisers), the strategy is, in fact, to concentrate on a few specific points. This, it is argued, is because there is a high product density in the petrochemicals industry, which uses very complex processes and has few repeatable elements for installing new plants.

Investment in technological development in this field shall be made with a view to:
- strategic interests (related to government plans and programmes);
- installation cost (the higher the cost the greater the interest in developing the capability); and
- the possibility of transferring the knowledge obtained to other fields.

On the basis of this technological strategy, a new set of routines and procedures began to be established. The process of technological choice now proceeds in the manner outlined below.

Once top management has decided that an investment is to be made, the first body consulted is Cenpes, which is asked whether it has the required technology, and if not whether the process of acquiring it will involve absorption. If it is indeed a case of absorbing technology, Cenpes is responsible for this process. The Project Management Division of the Engineering Department is placed in charge of managing the administrative aspects of the project, from basic design to purchasing and construction. Whether the basic design is awarded to Cenpes or to a foreign engineering firm, the detail engineering is done by Brazilians in all cases (Brazilian firms must of course be suitably qualified and registered). Once the detail engineering has been completed, the Brazilian firm responsible issues orders for supplies of material, which are sent to the Materials Department. The latter then proceeds with procurement, takes the final decisions regarding suppliers and plant, and is responsible for inspection and supervision.

An example of a choice made in accordance with these criteria is the case of Copesul's Materials Centre (Cemat), as described by Sercovitch.[14] The option in this case was for absorbing and consolidating technology for hydrocarbon pyrolysis to obtain olefins and aromatics, since knowledge of this field could be transferred immediately to others (indeed it was used as a basis for developing Copene's aromatics extraction plant) and would enable assistance to be given to operational bodies, especially within Copene and Copesul.[15]

The technology for the second Nitrogenated Fertiliser Factory, to be built in Sergipe (henceforth known as Fafen-SE), was chosen after Petrobrás had established its technological strategy and following the institutionalisation of Petrofértil.

Technological choice for Fafen-SE

This case of technological choice has already been described by Levy[16] and is similar to the case of Cemat mentioned above, which points to the stability of the organisation's administrative procedures. The process can be summarised as follows:

- based on the PNFCA specifications, Cenpes prepared a call for tenders, with the winning bids coming from Kellogg (ammonia) and Mitsui (urea), in the second half of 1976;

- the detail design work was awarded to Brazilian engineers Promon (with Kellogg) and Internacional (with Mitsui);

- the project entailed technology transfer: differentiated schemes were set up so that the technology transfer would not interfere with the deadlines for preparation of the basic and detailed design;

- the technology transfer process was co-ordinated by Cenpes, which sent 12 engineers for training by Kellogg over periods of about eight months: in addition to the specific documentation for the design of Fafen-SE, Kellogg also sent other manuals related to design procedures; on the engineers' return to Brazil, a large-scale exercise was developed to simulate the design of a plant similar to Fafen-SE, and all the doubts arising therefrom were discussed and solved with Kellogg specialists, who then supplemented the documentation already sent over; and

- the technology thus absorbed has since been used for a plant designed for Companhia Riograndense de Nitrogenados, a Petrofértil affiliate.

Start-up of Fafen-SE was originally planned for 1980. However, the flow of funds from the Federal Government was held up, as were deliveries of equipment from Brazilian suppliers, and this entailed postponement of the pre-operational stage to April 1982, and the start of commercial operations to July 1982.

Various important dimensions of this case are worthy of analysis. The first aspect is the question of the relations between Petrobrás and the state.

In the above description of the technological choices made for the Fafens, the most obvious assumption about Petrobrás's behaviour was that it complied strictly with the governmental plans and programmes. Yet, the way in which the PNFCA was drafted and the typically entrepreneurial arguments used in it would seem to point to the reverse: that is, the considerable power wielded by Petrobrás in terms of the support it could organise within the federal administration. Rather than a conflict between the aims of government and those of the state-owned enterprise in question, what can be observed in this case is the creation of a scenario at the level of the Federal Government aimed at legitimising the action of the state-owned enterprise, even though a partial rationale for this action was derived from the Government's own plans (the II PND). It would seem, indeed, that this case serves to corroborate the remark by Vernon quoted in James[17] to the effect that "some (state corporations) succeed in dominating the ministries that are supposed to oversee their activities or disregard such ministries altogether".

This situation, however, changed over time, and part of the delay in implementing the Fafens may be explained by the budget restrictions imposed by the Federal Government on state enterprises when the economic crisis Brazil has been undergoing for some time began to enter a more serious phase.

In sum, the case of Petrobrás shows that the degree of autonomy exercised by a state-owned enterprise, that is determined by the amount of state control and its effectiveness, varies with time as a consequence of the power relations governing this interaction. It can also be observed that any disputes which may occur have to do above all with available finances and do not necessarily involve different conceptions of the role of state-owned enterprises, particularly as regards the creation of jobs.

In terms of organisational behaviour, the technological choice for Fafen-PR, however, reveals a certain segmentation within Petrobrás as a whole, which does not seem to have been ready for increased involvement in fertilisers, possibly even including a great deal of unawareness at the middle management level. The decision made by top management was not duly attended to at the tactical level, and the first step towards implementing it seems somewhat improvised, as pointed out above in the description of the way in which the Working Group was set up.

The Group's behaviour seems to have been considerably affected by the knowledge that it was transitory, in addition to the fact that it was not made responsible for taking decisions and was working in a field in which its members were not specialists (let alone the fact that the organisation did not formally recognise such a specialisation). The unusual nature of the design specifications (introduced by the PNFCA) forced the Group to undertake a search, since the traditional supplier of technology (Kellogg) was not equipped to supply the type in question. This search process, however, was geared to finding plant of equivalent specifications to the system under discussion. It is true that a brief effort at analysis and itemisation seems to have ensued, but this apparently evolved only to a point where it led to arguments which could justify the decision which the Group was inclined to take. It seems evident here that the use of decision-making models based on technical and economic rationality to make a few isolated decisions in the midst of a process such as this does not necessarily confer rationality on the final decision. To employ the classical terminology, it can be inferred that the Group adopted the first "satisficing" solution that appeared.

Until then, there had been no concern with the transfer and absorption of design technology, so that the terms of the contract and the failure to assimilate the knowledge generated by the group at the time the decision was taken, were in line with usual procedures.

The change in technological strategy was the outcome of a change in the ideas of two groups within the enterprise: (i) top management, which began to deal in practice with the exportation of services and equipment in the field of petroleum refining; and (ii) the technical staff of the production area, who began to need the support of Cenpes in the process of adjusting the firm's production capacity to the new demand profile. This change was reflected in the setting up of an effective scheme for the mastery of technology. This change in strategy meant re-organising the enterprise, leading to the creation of new functions and departments (e.g. Basic Engineering) and the reformulation of procedures and routines.

III. TECHNOLOGICAL CHOICE IN THE AERONAUTICS INDUSTRY

The creation of the Brazilian aeronautics industry

There are two distinct versions of the reasons for Embraer's appearance. One recognises that the enterprise was the fruit of the persistence and idealism of certain people who had for some time been developing a Brazilian aeronautical project, which was presented to the authorities as a virtual **fait accompli**. The Government then decided to subsidise it, but avoided any closer involvement with the project.

The second version links the creation of Embraer with a governmental drive to create an arms industry based on the ideology of national security. From this angle, Embraer is said to be part of a complex network of institutions co-ordinated by the "military ministries" and especially close to the Aeronautics Ministry.

To retrace the history of Embraer, one has to go back to 1941 when the Ministry for Aeronautics was created, and then to 1950 when the Instituto Tecnológico da Aeronáutica (ITA), a training college for aeronautical engineers, and the Centro Tecnológico da Aeronáutica (CTA), a research centre, were actually established in São José dos Campos, about 50 miles from São Paulo.

The first group of aeronautical engineers graduated in 1954 and most of them went to work for the newly created Research and Development Institute (IPD) of the CTA (the actual date of creation was 1 January 1954). This group was to have considerable influence on the creation of Embraer 16 years later.

In 1962, the IPD group began to realise that the change then occurring in civil aviation represented a serious problem for the Brazilian setting. At that time transport aircraft were beginning to use jet propulsion, and in some cases turbo-propeller engines, while generally increasing in size and carrying capacity. These aircraft were far more complex to run and maintain than conventional planes, and required an operational infrastructure which did not exist at virtually any of Brazil's airports. Meanwhile, the DC-3s which were basic equipment in Brazilian civil aviation were reaching the end of their working lives.

Studies conducted by the IPD group showed that the number of Brazilian towns served by air was dropping noticeably and that even considering the international market, no aircraft currently being produced, met all the technical and economic requirements for operation under the existing conditions in Brazil. The group, therefore, prepared a report for the Aeronautics Ministry requesting aid for the development of a twin-engine metallic turboprop. The first prototype of this airplane, known as "Bandeirante" was flown in October, 1968. In August 1969, by the Decree-Law 770, the Brazilian Government created Embraer, which was sponsored by means of a special tax policy.

The core of the new corporation's personnel came from the IPD. As to its facilities, Embraer built a new factory adjoining the São José dos Campos airport.

Embraer's technological strategy

The institutional framework within the Aeronautics Ministry

Before proceeding to the discussion of Embraer's technological strategy, some remarks must be made about the institutional framework generated by the creation of the enterprise (Figure 7.1). The fact that Embraer is an "indirectly administered" institution gives it a very large degree of autonomy both at the strategic and tactical and at the operational level. This is not the case with the CTA, however, which is obliged to conduct its affairs in accordance with the guidelines, procedures and budgets laid down by the Ministry.

Since both institutions are linked through the Ministry, a direct functional relationship exists, through which the CTA supports and complements Embraer's activities. The following aspects are worthy of special mention:

a) an aeroplane is basically made up of three parts: the fuselage, the propulsion unit, and the avionics. Like most aeronautical firms around the world, Embraer designs and makes the fuselage, and assembles the aircraft using propulsion units and avionics from outside suppliers. The scope of the firm's activities is thus limited to technology for the design and production of fuselages;

b) Embraer does not do any R & D; this is performed by the CTA, through the IPD, so that the enterprise acts as a virtually captive market. IPD, for example, now has a group developing the avionics for future use by Embraer;

c) Embraer receives support from Instituto de Fomento Industrial (IFI), which is an agency linked to CTA and whose job is to help the enterprise to choose and develop domestic suppliers. More precisely, IFI's task for certain aircraft components is to identify Brazilian firms with the real or potential capability of producing such components in compliance with the quality standards required by the aeronautics industry. (Here it is useful to point out that there was a time when it was said in Brazilian technical and scientific circles that by setting up an aeronautics industry in the country the Government hoped to trigger off a qualitative advance in the production capacity of the domestic industrial base, which had not occurred when the auto industry was set up. From this point of view, IFI plays a very important role.) The main difficulty with which IFI has always been faced is to convince Brazilian entrepreneurs to invest in the manufacturing of a product of high quality but on a very small scale. One tactic used by IFI to

Figure 7.1

Organisational structure of Aeronautics Ministry

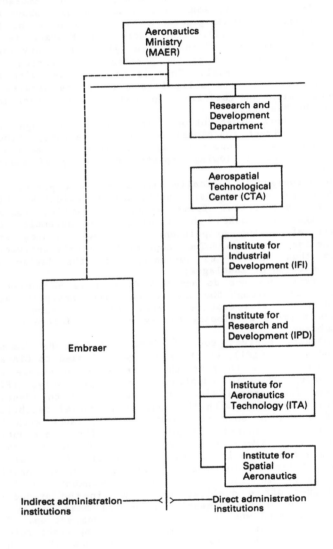

solve this problem has been to look abroad for aeronautics firms in need of similar products, whose demand, when added to that of Embraer, could justify the investment to be made by the Brazilian firm. IFI has been successful in such a course of action on some occasions. Internally, the agency is guided by a number of programmes, each of which is designed to deal with different parts of the aeroplane (fuselage, engine and electronics) and one of which involves wind-tunnel tests, in which case IFI performs services not only for Embraer but for any interested party; and

d)   finally, the ITA continues to train the aeronautical engineers required for the permanent expansion of Embraer.

This, then, is Embraer's support structure, which is not formally linked to it but plays an important role in its technological strategy.

General lines of Embraer's technological strategy

It is very important to note that Embraer began by manufacturing two aircraft of its own design, the Bandeirante and the Ipanema, and by assembling the military jet MB-326 from Aermacchi in Italy (the AT-26 Xavante) under licence. Since the technical personnel came from the field of design, there were a number of initial difficulties with production, especially for the Bandeirante. According to the Industrial Director, this led to holdups in deliveries of the early products, as various modifications had to be made to the design in order to adapt it to a production-line system.

This first stage, which lasted until 1974–75, can accurately be dubbed the period of "learning by doing", especially in terms of production technology. Nevertheless, to keep abreast of aeronautical production technology, some efforts were made, albeit in isolation, to absorb technology. For example, in the early 1970s a number of techniques were being developed for bonding rather than riveting the structural parts of the aircraft. Embraer managed to have a clause included in a contract between the Aeronautics Ministry and Northrop for the purchase of F-5 fighters, by which its engineers could be trained on their premises in order to assimilate modern aeronautical technologies. From then on, a technological strategy of the technological learning/mastery type began to be developed, originally through licensing arrangements and later on through joint ventures to carry out specific projects. For this strategy, Embraer always relied on the discreet but effective collaboration of the Aeronautics Ministry.

The strategy was made operational through massive investment in human resources, with a working programme based on "organisational learning", which meant that the enterprise learned to organise itself so as to handle the technological issue and on a scheme for formal treatment of technological information mostly developed after some experience of the certification process. These elements of the strategy are illustrated in the discussion that follows.

The case of lightweight aircraft

At about the time of Embraer's foundation, the general aviation market in Brazil began to grow at an exceptionally fast rate. In 1972, 258 small aircraft (single and twin engine) were imported; in 1973, this figure rose to 528, and estimates for 1974 were that it would again rise to 700. But the number of lightweight planes in fact imported in 1974 was as high as 726, worth a total of US$600 million. Of these, 400 were manufactured by Cessna, which thus captured roughly 60 per cent of the market.

In the same year, however, the Federal Government intensified its drive to achieve an equilibrium in the balance of payments, since the oil crisis had made its appearance on the scene. To deal with the matter of imported lightweight aircraft, a drastic scheme of duties was adopted to attempt to reduce the current account deficit. At this point, a number of contacts were made between the Planning Secretariat, the Aeronautics Ministry and Embraer to discuss the feasibility of having these lightweight aircraft manufactured by Embraer under licence.

Brazil then sent a mission to the major American manufacturers of lightweight aircraft to discuss proposals for a licensing agreement to make American planes in Brazil. Talks involved Cessna, Piper and Beech. The basic rule to be accepted in these negotiations was that technology transfer should be complete, in the sense of training and developing Embraer's technicians for design, production, management and marketing of lightweight aircraft. In return it was agreed to reserve the Brazilian market (then the USA's largest export market) for the aircraft made in Brazil, and the American firm was to be remunerated by a percentage of the sale of components which it was to send to Embraer.

At the beginning there was fierce competition between the three US companies, but Beech, which seems to have realised the true implications of the proposal, withdrew and refused to transfer its technology to the Brazilian firm. Embraer's preference was for Cessna, whose products not only dominated the Brazilian market but also had reputation and reliability. A further important aspect was that Cessna had already set up a broad network for distribution and technical assistance in this country. But soon after Beech had withdrawn, Cessna also pulled out of the deal.

214

The reasons for Cessna's withdrawal have never been totally explained, but two clauses were strongly opposed by the American firm: one authorising Embraer to make the modifications it deemed necessary in the aircraft, and another stipulating the remuneration system. As regards this latter point, Embraer did not wish to commit itself to a system of royalties, whereas Cessna insisted that this would be the appropriate way to reimburse it for the technology it was going to transfer. Cessna's questioning of the former clause apparently created hard feelings among the Embraer personnel, who resented the suspicion that the quality and reliability of the product would be jeopardised if changes were made. Thus Cessna pulled out, but as will be seen below, the problems did not disappear as a result.

The industrial co-operation contract then established with Piper consisted of three stages, all of which were actually carried out:[18]

- Stage I: Piper sent complete structures, such as fuselages, rudders and wings, to Embraer for assembly of all components and systems;
- Stage II: Piper sent sub-assembled components and the jigwork to Embraer which assembled the complete product;
- Stage III: this stage can be subdivided into three –
    1: involved the substitution of parts made in Brazil for parts made by Piper, including those mentioned above and up to 50 per cent of the acrylic and fibreglass parts;
    2: covered the substitution of all acrylic and fibreglass parts, and intensified the replacement of parts made by Piper; and
    3: production of the complete aircraft in Brazil with parts and components made locally except for those which had technological limitations or problems of production scale.

At the same time, Piper maintained a training scheme and free access to design and administrative aspects. As can be inferred, Piper's return decreased as the locally manufactured components were substituted for foreign parts. Nevertheless, Piper is still being remunerated for maintenance services. The Embraer-Piper Programme involved a licensing agreement, which in the medium and long term could have led to the development of new products, but did not since Embraer concentrated on other product lines.

As stated above, however, the dispute with Cessna had not yet finished. This firm attempted to recover the market by organising another project, together with its representatives in Brazil, to assemble its own planes in this country. According to Andrade and Piochi, "the

215

project as a whole was well organised and had support from the Government and entrepreneurs in the state of Rio Grande do Sul".[19] But the Aeronautics Ministry refused permission for further work on the project. This refusal led to a strong reaction from Cessna, which began to lobby the US Government, asking for retaliation by blocking Brazilian imports, especially footwear. The issue then worked its way up to government level, where it was absorbed as just one of the countless problems affecting trade relations between Brazil and the United States at the time, although it had some impact on the certification of the Bandeirante in 1977-78 (see below).

The case of the development of the Bandeirante-Xingu-Brasília family

The original Bandeirante was later modified several times. Damiani attributes these alterations to the "increased design capacity and improved productive organisation of Embraer, and its flexibility in meeting customers' needs".[20]

One source of pressure for change was related to the question of obtaining approval from international bodies for Embraer to export its product. This is an important point to explore, not only as an illustration of the technological learning issue but also as a way to explain some important aspects of Embraer's technological strategy.

When the Bandeirante design was being developed, the vision of the group responsible was especially addressed to the Brazilian market. The design was therefore based on international standards but did not comply fully with all of them. As its products evolved, Embraer achieved a high level of self-confidence, reinforced by its recent success in the Piper case. Starting with an initial projection of a plant with 1000 employees, the enterprise ended 1974 with close on 3,500 and a number of orders for Bandeirantes from Latin American countries (Chile and Uruguay).

Although the favourable terms eventually obtained through the negotiations with Piper were largely due to the protection of the Brazilian market, Embraer recognised what it had already known for a long time, namely, that the aircraft market is a worldwide business, and it then began to organise with a view to working with this in mind. (It is also worth noting that this move was made at the same time as Petrobrás began to turn its attentions to the international market.)

To operate on the international market, it was necessary not only to develop special marketing capabilities (some of which had indeed been absorbed from Piper) but fundamentally to comply with international standards as to design and production of the aircraft in order to obtain certification, without which Embraer could not market the Bandeirante in the developed countries. The most stringent of the certification agencies is the Federal Aviation Agency (FAA) in the USA, and recognition of any product by this body is enough to open up the world market.

Embraer thus began to modify the design of the Bandeirante and the dynamics of its production system in order to comply with the requirements of international certification, thus leading to far-reaching changes in the enterprise itself. As an example of such changes on the strategic level, the FAA requires that firms make their "organisational philosophy" explicit: this covers everything from conception of designs and manufacturing processes to the creation of a "quality awareness" involving all the firm's employees (Embraer was in fact one of the first Brazilian firms to introduce quality circles with great success in 1977). In the operational field, it requires the introduction of a number of techniques geared to product quality (quality assurance, traceability methods, etc.), in addition to systems standardisation, integration of production planning and control systems etc. But the main emphasis is on the treatment of technological information, requiring complete design manuals, production methods, and the registration and filing of production information for periods ranging from two to five years.

However, it was not only by implementing this scheme that Embraer won the recognition of the FAA. In December 1977, the Bandeirante was approved by the French authorities and soon after by the British. The United States FAA, however, did not recognise the plane until August 1978, after a long wrangle in which Embraer had to resort to the backing of the Brazilian Government.

The main point in dispute was not of a technical nature: it was politico-economic, and still an after-effect of the Piper-Embraer-Cessna affair. In a few words, the Americans' argument was that since the Brazilians had reserved the Brazilian market for lightweight aircraft of their own making, which was detrimental to the American industry, there was no sense in opening up the American market to Brazilian aircraft. The dispute was apparently settled when Embraer pointed out that, in fact, only the fuselage of the plane was Brazilian-made, the propulsion and avionics being almost entirely American. The closing of the American market to the Bandeirante would thus have meant a reduction in demand for the American manufacturers involved, in that the airlines interested in this type of plane would resort to a similar product, almost certainly of European make, and thus exclude the American components. In August 1978, therefore, the Bandeirante was approved by the FAA, and today there are more Bandeirantes in operation in the USA than in Brazil.

It is obvious that this whole process entailed several technological improvements to the Bandeirante. In his analysis of the plane as it stands today, Damiani remarks: "At this point it can be said that the stage has been reached where additional modifications to the aircraft will only produce marginal negative benefits. To make these positive, it will certainly be necessary to invest large amounts in redesigning the original plane and incorporating large-scale changes (such as pressurising the cabin) into the production line."[21]

Andrade and Piochi point out that the Bandeirante was designed within the limited technical possibilities available to the Brazilian industry in 1968-69: "It is built by industrial methods dating from the 1960s and makes no use of the most up-to-date aeronautical techniques in aerodynamic profiles, compound structures, new metal alloys and bonding systems... For this reason, in 1973 Embraer began studying a new 'family' of pressurised transportation aircraft which could take better advantage of recent technological advances."[22]

The first product in this new line was the Xingu, a twin-turboprop executive aircraft which has been coming off the production line since 1979. The conception of the Xingu reflects not only the strict commitment of the firm to technological learning, but also a growing maturity in its organisation, due to the clearly visible influence of the marketing strategy on the development of the product. It should be stressed that the choices implicit in the design of the Xingu suggest an effort to deal with a series of technical problems which were not solved by the Bandeirante design, while also creating a product which would be easy to sell on the market. The Xingu was intended to be not only for executives but to have sufficiently sophisticated avionics to make an excellent low-cost choice for training commercial jet pilots.

The second product in the new family is the Brasília, but before proceeding to discuss this case, it is important to give a brief description of Embraer's organisational structure and thereby illustrate how the process of technological choice occurred on this occasion.

The decision to develop a more sophisticated design was part of the organisation's overall strategy. The technological component of the strategy was the outcome of a whole organisational process, which was not highly formal and in which the different technical departments were involved and asked to give an opinion. The main impact on the process, however, came from the Project Planning Staff Group, which included the most experienced members of the firm, some of them renowned for more than 30 years of design work. This group could be called the firm's "think tank".

In the case of the Brasília, it is fundamental to note that it was designed virtually exclusively with a view to satisfying the requirements of the international airlines, which in brief consist of economy and reliability, incorporating the latest technological developments. As already mentioned, the question of reliability is dealt with through the certification process. One of the first decisions made about the Brasília, and one which caused considerable repercussions, concerned the choice of the technical standards which would be used as criteria for designing and manufacturing the plane. The preference was for the FAA's FAR-25, a standard which applies to aircraft carrying more than 25 passengers, and hence the large jet planes also have to meet it when requesting certification by the FAA.

The issue of economy and performance depends on the fuselage and propulsion system. Thus, another fundamental decision was the choice of engine, as from this flow a series of design specifications. The opposite procedure would be unthinkable (to develop the engine in terms of the type of plane), since the development cost of an engine is far greater than that of an aircraft.

Embraer pre-selected three engine manufacturers: Pratt and Whitney, General Electric, and Garret. A comparative technical analysis of a theoretical nature and lasting around three months led to the choice of the Pratt and Whitney PW-115, which was being developed at the time. The risk implicit in this decision was offset by the possibility of developing the aircraft design while the engine was being improved. Embraer had had a very successful experience in the case of the Bandeirante, when the Pratt and Whitney PT6A engine was chosen. This engine was also being developed at the time of the decision, but since it was at the beginning of its life cycle, Embraer was able to increase the working life of its own product. In terms of figures, the first Bandeirante could take off carrying a load of 5,600 kilogrammes (18 passengers), whereas the current version can do so with 5,900 kg (23 passengers) thanks to an increase in engine power from 680 SHP to 750 SHP.

In the case of the Brasília, the first prototype flight was also the first flight propelled by P&W 115 engines. This choice was also aimed especially to create a positive image for the enterprise and for the product amongst its customers. This was so not only for the propulsion system but also for other systems. Following the example of the Xingu, Embraer developed a relatively sophisticated avionics system for the Brasília.

In dealing with propulsion and avionics, however, Embraer is only a buyer, but it has to invest in the structural part in order to keep up to date. As already mentioned, in the early 1970s the fastest developing field in the world's industry was the bonding of metal elements, with the aim of simplifying construction methods. The oil crisis changed all that, however, and the focus then became the search for innovations which could make aircraft lighter without jeopardising reliability.

The main current developments are connected with carbon fibre, especially Kevlar. Some American and French fighter planes have their wings mounted by superimposing two parts which are entirely moulded in Kevlar. The moving parts of the wings of modern Boeing 757s and 767s are made of Kevlar. Thus, as would be expected, Embraer is striving to keep abreast of the development of this technique. Some parts of the Brasília are moulded in Kevlar, and for this purpose Embraer is investing not only in new facilities but in human resources – eight members of it staff are now developing special knowledge in this field in different parts of the world. From Embraer's standpoint, this effort is justified not only by the need for a lighter aircraft but also because the resulting product will incorporate the latest technological developments. Paradoxically, though, this process is more expensive than the traditional ones in terms of cost of labour, because it reduces the amount of labour but at the same time requires highly skilled workers.

Such then are the reasons, in outline form, for the basic choices involved in the development of the Brasília – standards, propulsion system, avionics and innovations in structure.

After technical specifications have been approved, the engineering work is usually conducted in three stages: the basic design, the detail design, and the planning of manufacturing methods and processes. Embraer's organisational structure fits into this scheme: Aeronautical Engineering does the basic design, Product Engineering the detail design, and Systems and Methods plans the methods. This solution may seem obvious, but in fact the firm gradually developed this configuration as a result of its experience. Early on, for example, there was a Systems and Methods department for each type of plane, until it became evident that new departments corresponding to new planes made the same mistakes the older ones had made before. It was therefore decided to consolidate the planning of methods into a single department, which today does all the work on production technology, thus facilitating the process of technological learning within the firm.

Embraer's structure is of the matrix type, which greatly favours communication and, above all, feedback into the groups in charge of basic and detail designs, thus ensuring that learning is efficient. The co-ordination of the whole structure is performed by a Modification Analysis Group co-ordinated by Production personnel, but in which people from Sales, Aeronautical Engineering, Product Engineering, and Systems and Methods take part. This group also co-ordinates and controls the whole process of documentation for design and production.

The dynamics of this structure are geared not only to facilitating the co-ordination and communication processes, but also to creating processes in which the crucial decisions are exhaustively discussed before they are actually made. This is necessary because even once the basic choices for the design have been made, those for the manufacturing process remain, and they are all highly interdependent. One such decision, which was being discussed at the time the research for this study was being done, concerned the jigwork for the production of the Brasília. The result of this decision will only be known two or three years later, and upon it depends the success or failure of the Brasília in terms of costs.

The case of military aircraft

Embraer's first involvement with military aircraft was limited to assembly operations. This was the case with the AT-26 Xavante, 182 of which were delivered by 1983. Military aircraft, however, are included in the technological learning strategy established for the firm as a whole.

In 1978 Embraer began to design a military training aircraft. The group in charge of the design included some engineers who had designed other training aircraft for other Brazilian firms.

In December 1978, the Aeronautics Ministry signed a contract with Embraer for the development of this aircraft, and ordered 118 in advance. The prototype was flown in August 1980, and since then the plane – known as the Tucano – has been internationally accepted owing to its technical characteristics, price and sophistication in terms of weaponry.

On the international market, Embraer won a tender issued by the Egyptian Government, for 110 Tucanos. Apparently, one of the reasons which led the Egyptians to choose Embraer was that it undertook to transfer technology by installing a plant to assemble 100 planes in Egypt.

Embraer is currently bidding to supply Tucanos to the British RAF. The tender, which has been under way for some time, involved the pre-selection of two firms, Embraer and a British competitor. During the final stage of negotiations, Embraer's last bid to strengthen its hand was an industrial co-operation agreement with Short Bros., a British company, which provided for the construction of the plane in the United Kingdom if Embraer is awarded the contract.

Finally, there are the jets. With the production of the AT-26 Xavante, Embraer has amassed a great deal of experience in the manufacturing of jet planes on a production line basis. This experience was reinforced by the contract between the Brazilian Government and Northrop for the F-5 fighters mentioned above, involving production by Embraer of vertical rudder units and bomb housings. To construct these components, Embraer's technicians had to master the technology of metal-to-metal bonding processes, machining using machine tools with numerical control, and the use of compound materials (Kevlar). It was this experience which legitimated Embraer's participation in the joint development of a new jet fighter with two Italian companies, Aermacchi and Aeritalia.

Embraer was asked to develop this scheme by the Aeronautics Ministry in the mid-1970s. A number of projects began to be discussed by technicians from the two institutions. However, in the development of military jets, it is not only the technical factors that matter - the cost is also very important, and it rises as the number of planes to be produced decreases. Thus, by 1978 an alternative scheme involving production of the plane in co-operation with the two Italian firms had been hit upon. Aermacchi had already developed the preliminary design of a jet fighter with similar features to those required by the Brazilian Aeronautics Ministry. Negotiations included members of both governments, and in March 1980 a co-operation agreement was signed to cover the design and manufacturing of the aircraft, which was called the AMX.

Embraer was to be responsible for designing the wings, as well as other structural details: horizontal stabilisers, external fuel tanks, engine air inlets etc. The team now developing these designs includes Italian specialists together with Embraer's technicians. When production begins, both countries will be able to make the whole plane.

Part of the technology absorbed for the AMX is being applied to the development of the Tucano and Brasília, especially the latter. The major impact will come from the machining of structural parts from a single metal blank using numerically controlled machinery. Although this process leads to higher costs, the parts produced by it are far more reliable.

Technological choice and employment

Embraer is a rapidly growing enterprise: while it employed 5,500 people by the end of 1981, in April 1984 it boasted 7,300. This increase in personnel can be justified by the expansion in the product line and by the demand for the new products, as well as the continued production of the older ones. The initial idea amongst the firm's staff was that the Brasília would start production at the same time as that of the Bandeirante stopped. But since orders for this latter plane have continued to be reasonably high, with an average of something like two planes a month coming off the line, the Bandeirante is still being produced.

With the Tucano coming on stream (seven a month) together with the Brasília (two a month), and with the AMX programmed to start production in mid-1985, Embraer is investing in facilities, human resources and equipment. On the latter item, some remarks are worth making on specific decisions. One of these is an order for about 50 NC-machine tools, to be delivered by the end of 1985. As is well-known, the use of this type of equipment is highly controversial, since one single machine of this type replaces several conventional ones.[23] In an aeronautical firm dealing on the foreign market, however, it is practically imperative to use them. The specification for their use was drawn up with the production processes for the AMX and Brasília in mind, and in accordance with international quality standards.

It is difficult to weigh up to what extent Embraer could change the characteristics of this choice and develop processes which could lead to products of the same quality but using a larger amount of labour. This would involve serious risks, with unpredictable consequences for Embraer's image as seen by the airlines. The enterprise therefore complies with the standards and rules dictated by the market.

Nevertheless, while there is no explicit effort to create jobs, there is a concern to avoid creating unemployment in an unjustifiable manner. While the present study was under way, for example, Embraer decided not to buy the equipment for tracing parts, offered for about US$600,000, since this machine would make redundant about 30 employees without any significant improvement in quality.

The technology-oriented state enterprise

Embraer may be taken to be a fairly typical technology-oriented enterprise, but for this to be the case a whole range of factors had to come into play. First, it must be recognised that the firm was set up and still operates in a highly privileged position. This is so in relation to the following factors:
-    the financial support scheme – tax incentives still guarantee a significant input of money;
-    the protected market whereby aircraft equivalent to

those made by Embraer cannot be imported, in addition
to the procurement policy of the Aeronautics Ministry
which guarantees demand;
- the creation and maintenance of an extensive
  supporting infrastructure in the form of the CTA,
  which is funded entirely by the Aeronautics Ministry
  and involves R & D, human resources and supplies; and
- the existence of a political support scheme, which
  enables Embraer to achieve strong bargaining positions
  not only on the international market but also at home.

These conditions have enabled Embraer to establish, in
Katz's[24] words, an evolutionary technological strategy,
with a long-range objective; through a process of learning,
the firm has endeavoured gradually to master the technology
involved and to become organisationally equipped to enter
new markets.

From the standpoint of internal organisation, one
noteworthy fact is the objectivity of the decision-making
processes regarding the technological strategy developed,
as if there were a continuous flow of interdependent
decisions in a synergistic manner. There are two main
factors to which this can be attributed.

First, it must be remembered that the idea of creating
Embraer had been fostered for nearly 15 years by a group of
technicians who later became the Board of Directors of the
enterprise. It seems safe to assume the existence of a
high degree of integration among these people in terms of
expectations, values and attitudes, and they, after all,
are the organisation's main decision-makers.

Second, the authority of the Board of Directors to
make decisions is recognised by the technical staff; in
other words, it is assumed to be legitimate, in recognition
not only of the administrative competence and skill in
political articulation of the individuals involved, but
also from the technical standpoint, for it was they who
developed the design for the Bandeirante, which is still
the "champion product" of the firm. The "political game"
component is therefore relatively limited in scope, and
this contributes to a marked reduction in behaviour
considered dysfunctional as regards attaining the corporate
objectives of the organisation. To the extent that the
objectives, strategies and tactics are evident to all, and
they in their turn understand their role in achieving such
objectives, the decision-making process takes place in a
rational manner.

It can be seen at the same time that Embraer is a
clear demonstration that there is no technological learning
without organisational learning. The contract with Piper,
which stipulated the transfer not only of technical
know-how but also of management and marketing, exemplifies
this concern. The absorption, processing and internal

dissemination of FAA's requirements, to the extent that a formal system for handling technological information was created and a highly organic structure was established and maintained (in the sense used by Burns and Stalker),[25] reflect the interdependence between the ability to handle technology and the need for adequate organisation.

IV. CONCLUSIONS

From this study of two significant cases of Brazilian state-owned enterprises it can be concluded that the establishment of a technological strategy aims simultaneously to fulfil three major determinations:
-   guidelines laid down by the state;
-   market relationships; and
-   power relationships within the enterprise.

The idea that the state's orientations influence the behaviour of state-owned enterprises, including their technological choices, is irrefutable. In the case of Brazil, indeed, this applies to all enterprises without exception, through incentives or other systems regulating transfer and purchase of technology, etc. However, as agencies for the implementation of government policies, state-owned enterprises suffer the impact of these determinations in a much more intense manner.

The cases in question pointed strongly to the rapid response to the appearance of government determinations. As examples, the following are relevant: (i) the sharp turn taken by Petrobrás and Embraer towards the international market after 1974; (ii) the decision by Petrobrás to enter the fertiliser industry, then defined as a strategic sector for the country's agricultural performance, by assuming the role of co-ordinator in such a way as to guarantee the programme's success; and (iii) the technological evolution of Embraer, and its likely role as articulator of an arms manufacturing system, another sector considered vital to national security.

These governmental determinations not only directed the field of action of the state-owned enterprises, but conditioned their choice of technology. In the case of nitrogenated fertilisers, for example, the technology was probably chosen with a view to the world market (in 1982 Petrobrás exported 300,000 tonnes of ammonia and urea, worth US\$30 million, to Argentina, Ecuador, the United States, Colombia and China).[26] It would therefore seem reasonable that the committee which prepared the PNFCA had the exportation of nitrogenated fertilisers in mind.

However, state-owned enterprises do not take a passive attitude to the guidelines of the state. In the cases examined here, they attempted to influence these guidelines from the moment of their inception and to negotiate the conditions under which they were to be implemented. The involvement of Petrobrás in the PNFCA drafting committee is a case in point. Similarly, Embraer's technological strategy seems to have been negotiated with the Aeronautics Ministry, which provided the firm with the necessary support in its search for technological mastery, above all for the development of military aircraft.

The state-owned enterprise's ability to influence and negotiate is linked in turn to its place with regard to the market. This is the second determination. The relationships of the state-owned enterprise to the domestic and international market are powerful factors which condition the establishment of its technological strategy. The two cases in point clearly illustrate this statement. The case of Embraer provides especially persuasive evidence.

From the moment Embraer began to concentrate on the international market, the guidelines and organisation of the firm began to change: the product features began to be defined in accordance with the requirements of the airlines operating in the developed countries, while the production process was designed to fit in with the standards of the international certification institutes. When the firm's operations were limited to the Brazilian market alone, it had been subject to a different set of determinations, which were less restrictive.

In the case of Petrobrás, the conditions prevailing on the national and international market imposed modifications in its technological strategy in the sense that it had to obtain a technical design capability.

It is by identifying these market conditions and by outlining a corporate strategy that the state-owned enterprise can strengthen its hand when negotiating with the state, so as to guarantee the necessary support for the effective performance of the task assigned to it. Perhaps the clearest example of this type of negotiation and influence is the maintenance of the "captive" relationship between Embraer and the Aeronautics Ministry.

The definition of these strategies, however, follows the orientation of the dominant group in the enterprise, which is responsible for influencing and negotiating with the state to obtain its support.

Petrobrás is a mostly production-oriented enterprise, whereas Embraer is a technology-oriented enterprise. These orientations evidently are derived from the field of action, although Levy reports the case of the Fertiliser Corporation of India, which for some time was technology-oriented.[27] In other words, it seems reasonable to suppose that whatever the field of action of an enterprise may be, the dominant group will endeavour to bring about an orientation which fits in with its own

226

capabilities and interests as well as bearing in mind its relations with the state, the market and the other groups within the enterprise.

Similarly, the technological strategy of the enterprise is established in such a way that the dominant group can maintain and expand its basis for domination within the enterprise. It is at this point that internal conflicts may arise, thus making the stage of operationalising the strategy more difficult. The case of technological choice by Fafen-PR illustrates this point well. In that of Embraer, however, no breakdowns in the decision-making process can be seen. This is connected with the very legitimacy of the dominant group's authority over the technical staff and with the latter's identification with the strategy proposed. In brief, the technological strategy is established by the dominant group, bearing in mind a set of commitments and interests, as well as the constraints determined by the state and the market.

NOTES AND REFERENCES

1. M. Gillis (1980): "The role of state enterprises in economic development", Development Discussion Paper No. 83, Harvard Institute for International Development.

2. Programa Nacional de Fertilizantes e Calcáreo Agrícola: Brasília, Ministério da Industria e Comércio, 1974, p. 20.

3. Ibid., p. 25.

4. Ibid., p. 23.

5. Ibid., p. 23.

6. B. Levy: "Public enterprises and the transfer of technology in the ammonia industry", Chapter 6, this volume, p. 177-8.

7. P. Evans (1977): "Multinationals, state-owned corporations and the transformation of imperialism: A Brazilian case study", in Economic Development and Cultural Change, Chicago, 26 (1), p. 48.

8. S. Abranches and S. Dain (1977): "A empresa estatal no Brasil: Padrões estruturais e estratégias de ação", FINEP, Relatório 01/78 do Grupo de Estudos sobre o Setor Público, restricted, Rio de Janeiro, p. 10.

9. C. Dahlman and L. Westphal: "Technological effort in industrial development - An interpretive survey of recent research", in F. Stewart and J. James (eds.): The economics of new technology in developing countries, London, Frances Pinter, 1982.

10. D.M. Leitao (1984): O processo de aprendizado tecnológico nos países em desenvolvimento, mimeographed paper, CENPES/PETROBRAS, Oct., p. 7.

11. F. Erber (1982): Technology issues in the capital goods sector: A case study of leading industrial machinery producers in Brazil, mimeographed paper TD/B/C.6/AC.7/6, Geneva, UNCTAD; A.C.C. Fleury (1983): "A questão da tecnologia e a organização da engenharia na empresa industrial Brasileíra" mimeographed thesis, Escola Politécnica da Universidade de São Paulo, 1983.

12. D.M. Leitão, op. cit., 1984, p. 8.

13. Ibid., p. 9.

14. F.C. Sercovitch (1980): "State-owned enterprises and dynamic comparative advantages in the world petrochemical industry", mimeo, Cambridge, Massachusetts, Harvard Institute for International Development, Discussion Paper No. 96.

15. Copesul stands for Companhia Petroquímica do Sul and Copene for Companhia Petroquímica do Nordeste. These are two of the three "petrochemical" poles in Brazil.

16. B. Levy, op. cit.

17. J. James: "Public enterprise, technology and employment in developing countries", Chapter 2, this volume.

18. J. Baranson (1980): "Tecnologia e as multíonais", São Paulo, Ed. Zahar.

19. R.P. Andrade and A.E. Piochi (1982): História da construcao aeronáutica no Brasil, São Paulo, Editora Distribuidora de Livros, p. 264.

20. J.H.S. Damiani (1983): "O EMB-11Q Bandeirante e o processo de inovação tecnológica", mimeo, São José dos Campos, Instituto Tecnológico da Aeronáutica.

21. Ibid., p. 17.

22. R.P. Andrade and A.E. Piochi (1982): op. cit., p. 277.

23. D. Noble (1978): "Social choice in machine design: The case of automatically controlled machine-tools", in A. Zimbalist (ed.): Case studies in the labor process, New York, Monthly Review Press; B. Coriat (1983): "Autómatos, robôs e a classe operária", Novos Estudos, São Paulo, CEBRAP, July, pp. 31-8.

24. J. Katz (1980): Domestic technology generation in LDCs: A review of research findings, mimeographed IDB/ECLA Research Program in Science and Technology, Working Paper, Buenos Aires.

25. T. Burns and G.M. Stalker (1961): The Management of Innovation, London, Tavistock Publications.

26. Petroleo e petroquímica, Rio de Janeiro, Aug. 1983, p. 4.

27. Levy, op. cit.

Index

Index

For Product Safety Concerns and Information please contact our EU
representative GPSR@taylorandfrancis.com Taylor & Francis Verlag GmbH,
Kaufingerstraße 24, 80331 München, Germany

Printed and bound by CPI Group (UK) Ltd, Croydon, CR0 4YY

08/05/2025

01864414-0003